Advance Praise for
Crises Then as Now

"In this eminently timely book, McLeod Rogers and company recuperate the insights of McLuhan, Tyrwhitt and Kepes into the environmental and social crises of their day (which have only been exacerbated by the passage of time), and draw out the lessons of the trio's highly productive intellectual collaboration for designing an alternative, more balanced future imbued with hope, rather than anxiety and despair. This book is essential reading for scholars interested in urban planning, re-understanding media, and the fusion of art and science."

—David Howes, author of *The Sensory Studies Manifesto: Tracking the Sensorial Revolution in the Arts and Human Sciences*

"This is a timely and necessary book. It considers the ways in which three crucial mid-20th century thinkers understood the epochal challenges of their time, and thought of ways to both articulate these challenges and think strategies to face them. As McLeod Rogers phrases it in her Introduction: "Identifying McLuhan, Kepes, and Tyrwhitt as early allies in recognizing the intersectional damage arising from 'human activity' gone rogue advances a conception of shared generational logics." It is further evidence of the continued relevance of these three figures who've passed in and out of style, but whose "interthinking" approach (as Kepes put it), opened broad avenues for crisis- and future-focused thought involving deep knowledge of technology, art, science and the "natural" environment. They did not have the concept of the "anthropocene" at their disposal, but they thought along its terms. Why is this history important? I will quote McLeod Rogers again: "While establishing a line of positive kinship between then and now does not improve material conditions—does not decrease strife, deterioration, and threat–it does provide a more nuanced and contextualized understanding of intellectual lineage and avoid generational blaming." I can think of no better scholars than McLeod Rogers, Ellen Shoskes and Charissa Terranova to have tackled this complex subject matter. Highly recommended!"

—Oliver A. I. Botar, Associate Director, Graduate Studies and Research, University of Manitoba

"*Crises Then as Now* expands our understanding of Marshall McLuhan by contextualizing his thinking in relation to two influential contemporaries and colleagues, Tyrwhitt and Kepes. Without sacrificing the distinctiveness of each protagonist, the reader is provided a venn diagram of the confluence of interest in the impact of technological developments on environments, ecologies, and humanity. This work draws a tread between theorist, planner, artist and, between then and now, to not merely identify the roots of the current planetary crisis, but to point to potential solutions."

—Susan Drucker, Lawrence Stessin Distinguished Professor of Journalism, Lawrence Herbert School of Communication, Hofstra University.

"*Crises Then as Now* discusses ideas and research practices of three major intellectuals of the previous century – McLuhan, Tyrwhitt, Kepes – through a diffractive and effective approach that highlights, in an original way, the interactive ontological and theoretical connections between their diverse modus operandi . In their works, "crisis" is a common thread, as these thinkers explored the consequences of human activity potentially going rogue at a time when "the bomb" was in the air and media were becoming the new nature; theirs was a fast changing, critical scenario that resonates now. Fortunately, this is a book that does not fuel fear but critical thinking, civic awareness and, therefore, hope. By rereading McLuhan through Tyrwhitt and Kepes, this book teaches us shared strategies for responding, even today, to stormy change. It is a fascinating book that encourages us to think creatively and together to face the new challenges posed by our complex realities."

—Elena Lamberti, author of *Marshall McLuhan's Mosaic. Probing the Origins of Media Studies* (U of T Press, 2012)

"A rare experience to find a book now that with great agility and eloquence engages McLuhan through art, city and urban planning and design, literature, media contemplations and scholarly musing. …Why rare? Because McLuhan disdained specialization and strived to perceive communication processes in a whole vision. Jaqueline McLeod Rogers achieves this kind of imperative vision in a beautifully written, collaborative work that emphasizes an original fractal approach to art, science, civics and poetics. What is its imperative? In a time of deepest media crises of information and anti-information, of traumatic emergences at crossroads, of technological cruxes, of crucial moments in our ways of perceiving, this book addresses the riddles we face while seeking hopeful patterns. The emergences and traumas speak of possible extinction. Jaqueline McLeod Rogers, co-creating with Ellen Shoshkes and Charissa N. Terranova, provides us with educating ideas and perceptions that bravely encounter where we are, and how McLuhan, Tyrwhitt and Kepes can become guides. This work goes past antithetical critique toward creative and recreative possibility."

—B.W. Powe, author of *Mysteria, Ladders Made of Water, The Charge in the Global Membrane, Where Seas and Fables Meet, Marshall McLuhan* and *Northrop Frye, Apocalypse and Alchemy*; Associate Professor, York University's Departments of English and Humanities.

Crises Then as Now

Lance Strate
General Editor

Vol. 15

Jaqueline McLeod Rogers,
with Ellen Shoshkes and Charissa N. Terranova

Crises Then as Now

Marshall McLuhan, with Urbanist Jaqueline
Tyrwhitt and Artist György Kepes

PETER LANG
New York - Berlin - Bruxelles - Chennai - Lausanne - Oxford

Library of Congress Cataloging-in-Publication Data

Names: McLeod Rogers, Jaqueline, author. | Shoshkes, Ellen, author. | Terranova, Charissa N., author.
Title: Crises then as now : Marshall McLuhan, with urbanist Jaqueline Tyrwhitt and artist György Kepes / Jaqueline McLeod Rogers ; with Ellen Shoshkes, and Charissa N. Terranova.
Description: New York : Peter Lang, 2025. | Series: Understanding media ecology; 15 | Includes bibliographical references and index.
Identifiers: LCCN 2024042280 (print) | LCCN 2024042281 (ebook) | ISBN 9781433197819 (paperback) | ISBN 9781433197826 (hardback) | ISBN 9781433197833 (ebook) | ISBN 9781433197840 (epub)
Subjects: LCSH: Mass media–Philosophy. | Mass media and culture. | Civilization, Modern–21st century–Philosophy. | McLuhan, Marshall, 1911-1980–Criticism and interpretation. | Tyrwhitt, Jaqueline–Criticism and interpretation. | Kepes, György, 1906-2001–Criticism and interpretation.
Classification: LCC P90 .R61325 2025 (print) | LCC P90 (ebook) | DDC 302.2301–dc23/eng/20240916
LC record available at https://lccn.loc.gov/2024042280
LC ebook record available at https://lccn.loc.gov/2024042281
DOI 10.3726/b22410

Bibliographic information published by the Deutsche Nationalbibliothek.
The German National Library lists this publication in the German National Bibliography; detailed bibliographic data is available on the Internet at http://dnb.d-nb.de.

Cover design by Peter Lang Group AG

ISSN 2374-7676 (print)
ISBN 9781433197819 (paperback)
ISBN 9781433197826 (hardback)
ISBN 9781433197833 (ebook)
ISBN 9781433197840 (epub)
DOI 10.3726/b22410

© 2025 Peter Lang Group AG, Lausanne
Published by Peter Lang Publishing Inc., New York, USA
info@peterlang.com - www.peterlang.com

All rights reserved.
All parts of this publication are protected by copyright.
Any utilization outside the strict limits of the copyright law, without the permission of the publisher, is forbidden and liable to prosecution.
This applies in particular to reproductions, translations, microfilming, and storage and processing in electronic retrieval systems.

This publication has been peer reviewed.

Table of Contents

Acknowledgements vii
Note to the Reader ix

Introduction: Meeting Crises, Then as Now 1
Chapter 1   McLuhan and Environmental Crises 25
Chapter 2   McLuhan's Collaboration with Jaqueline Tyrwhitt: Humanizing Visual and Acoustic Space 49
Chapter 3   Jaqueline Tyrwhitt's Relations with Marshall McLuhan and György Kepes
Ellen Shoshkes 71
Chapter 4   McLuhan and Kepes: Art, Science, and Civics "in a new kind of world city" (McLuhan to Kepes, August 1972, *Letters*, p. 453) 97
Chapter 5   Curating the Cybernetic: the Brief Collaboration of György Kepes and Marshall McLuhan 121
Charissa N. Terranova
Conclusion: Legacy for Emergency: World Ending and Making 143

Index 161
Index of Names 169

Acknowledgements

I want to thank The University of Winnipeg for funding this research. I have received generous grants that have enabled travel for archival research and assistance with index and manuscript preparation.

Within my Department, I enjoy the support and friendship of gifted colleagues, whose interests enrich and inform mine. I'd like to acknowledge Matt Flisfeder, for his energy and encouragement and for doing inspiring work on humanism (among other topics). I'd like to acknowledge Jason Hannan, for years of friendship and good conversation and for contributing to ethical culture. I am grateful to Andrew McGillivray for modelling creative scholarship and for his informative intercultural work. I want to acknowledge Helen Lepp Friesen who is inspiring as a collaborator and as a dedicated educator who models the dialogical skills she explores in her research. I have also benefitted from other colleagues in the university, and will name a few here: Adina Balint, Lloyd Kornelsen, Judith Harris, and Fiona Green. Thanks, too, to Ian Fraser who helped with finding library sources.

I also want to thank colleagues in the Media Ecology Association, a professional organization that has recognized my research with several awards. Within the organization, I'd like to thank Lance Strate, whose research is definitional. I have found Adriana Braga, Elaine Kahn, Julia Hildebrand and Susan Drucker inspiring affiliates, and benefitted from the urban studies of Gary Gumpert, Austin

Hestdalen, and Erik Garrett. I am also appreciative of the McLuhan-inspired work of Paolo Granata and B.W. Powe.

I have benefitted from scholarly exchanges about Sensory Studies research with David Howes at Concordia University. William Buxton's work on Harold Innis and Gary Genosko's on Harley Parker have also informed my approach. I would also like to thank colleagues in the Langer Circle for valuable research sharing.

I have benefited from consulting with Teri McLuhan, especially hearing her memories of Jaqueline Tyrwhitt. Meeting Kathryn Hutchon [Kawasaki] provided valuable insight into some the context surrounding production of *City as Classroom*.

Supportive of other McLuhan-based research projects, I'd like to acknowledge Katherine Reilly, along with Gillian Russell and Rachel Horst, all at Simon Fraser University; collaborative work with them has pushed me to identify links between McLuhan and climate crisis literature. I should also thank Pascale Chapdelaine and Tetanya [Tanya] Krupiy, with whom I have co-authored studies about McLuhan and law.

Of course, I want to extend appreciation to Charissa Terranova and Ellen Shoshkes, who have provided brilliant studies of Kepes and Tyrwhitt for this volume and who have been patient over the long course of its production.

Students have helped my McLuhan studies come to new life. I'd like to thank Maddy Nowosad for general research assistance and Scott Maier for the precision of his bibliographic work.

At Peter Lang, I have benefitted from the help of Elizabeth (Lizzie) Howard in making decisions to push publication forward.

My family members remain supportive of these big book projects: thanks to my husband Warren, and to wonderful daughters Hartley and Morgan.

Note to the Reader

In in-text citations in each chapter, only first-time references to primary sources will provide the year of publication.

All three figures often use the word "man" as a generic term rather than choosing the non-gendered "human" which is now preferred. In my own commentary I use the word "human"; when I quote from primary sources, I do not adjust the word "man" as it appeared in the original, for to do so would require excessive textual changes.

Introduction: Meeting Crises, Then as Now

This book focuses on Marshall McLuhan (1911–1980), public intellectual and media and communications scholar, reading him in connection to two distinguished contemporaries: urban planner and professor Jaqueline Tyrwhitt (1905–83) and artist and art theorist György Kepes (1906–2001). All were prolific and influential (from about 1950 to 1975) and, despite different disciplinary affiliations, shared an understanding of the dynamic and interdisciplinary nature of knowledge and the need for integrated science and humanities work. They were acquainted with each other on a personal level, familiar with each other's work, and professionally affiliated in a collaborative knowledge culture. Reading them together sharpens our appreciation of their intellectual environment. Aligning them in a "diffractive" approach enables identifying unexpected resonances without dismissing contextual and theoretical differences (Barad, *Meeting*, 2007, p. 30). Each addressed conflict and crises—arising from swift and sweeping technological change, legacy and ongoing military violence, increasingly visible social inequities, and evidence of environmental degradation. We may be bolstered by considering their determination to meet change and find hope amidst threat as they faced world crises that resemble ours today. Although crises is now accelerant on some fronts, finding transfer power in their concerns and programs—particularly their advocacy of structuring environments and experiences to foster citizen engagement and of amalgamating art and science knowledge and practice—provides context and intelligence for what we are facing.

McLuhan and contemporaries Tyrwhitt and Kepes addressed social and civic problems manifest in North America where all spent productive career years—problems contributing to global tensions. Communication theorist Michel A. Moos characterizes the mid-twentieth century as "chaotic", and the 60s—a decade of significant interaction amongst the three—as "exuberant and savage days of cultural and social revolution" (1997, p. xv). Moos suggests the atom bomb also contributed to the sense of fragility and turbulence—radiating "nuclear consciousness" through the collective awareness that destruction was siloed in-the-ready, that radar blanketed the hemispheres awaiting incoming warheads, and that "a nerve-like constellation of wires[encircled] the Earth" (p. 165). There were civil rights protests, public outrage against poverty, racism and police brutality, and anger over the war and mounting casualties in Vietnam. While actual events fanned the flames of unrest, so did the non-stop home delivery of media coverage of carnage and confrontation, shorn of gravitas by being collaged with commercials and comedies. Writing of the zeitgeist in 1965, Susan Sontag referred to an oppressive "Imagination of Disaster," fueled by "unremitting banality" in tension with "inconceivable terror" (para. 1). Whether exercised in memory or as futuristic foreboding, or experienced as actual events or mediated reproductions, trauma abounded in end-of-the world anxiety.

Along with fearing overt human-against-human acts of aggression and war, McLuhan, Tyrwhitt and Kepes were also aware that human-made industry and devices were damaging planetary ecologies. All three understood the impacts of media and innovation as intersectional, with each new development affecting human lives, creatures, and environments. While they often depoliticized technology by linking it to advances in science—deemphasizing its links to industry and capital[1]—they otherwise anticipated Guittari's summation in *The Three Ecologies* (2000) that human activities and products reshape—often deform—human subjectivity, social relations, and the environment.

While McLuhan did not have the term "Anthropocene" at hand, he anticipated what we have now learned to call the "Anthropocene"[2] in frequent references to the transformative effects of human industry on both human and planetary nature. In dialogue with Norman Mailer (1968), for example, he said, "The planet is no longer nature. It's no longer the external world. It's now the content of an artwork. Nature has ceased to exist." It would be inaccurate to hear this as sanguine observation or happy talk of the progress of human creativity. Instead, it expresses his sense of the urgent need for widespread public recognition of presenting and impending dangers and, with this, for a public undertaking of responsibility and involvement in collaborative and creative responses. He offered few details to pave a definitive path and no reassurance of resolution, but emphasized the urgency of making an effort, of waking up, believing, similar to Donna Haraway (2016), that doing nothing is the worst response; believing, similar to N. Katherine Hayles (2017), that more mindful practices of perception, cognition and consciousness offer "intelligent beings" a "deeper appreciation" of patterns and multilevel "total engagement" of intellect, senses and emotions (2017, 1: 49).

In *The Democratic Surround* (2013), Fred Turner makes the case that 60s radicalism did not spring out of nowhere but was an extension of Post World War II intellectual movements to denounce fascism and control and to support democratic ideals of freedom and individuality. Sixties "counterculture," while reacting against dominant cultural values, was also a culmination of "the deeply democratic vision. . . across the 1950s and into the 1960s" (2013, p. 11). Like Turner, I am revisiting historical intellectual connections: while he spoke the link from the 40s to the 60s, I am considering how key figures and ideas from the 60s and 70s inform our present. Identifying McLuhan, Kepes, and Tyrwhitt as early allies in recognizing the intersectional damage arising from "human activity" gone rogue advances a conception of shared generational logics. By this reading, the past was not entirely saturated by colonial vision and energy, gifting only burdens to be overcome; by this reading, some eyes and minds were open pre-twenty-first century to social and planetary ills. While establishing a line of positive kinship between then and now does not improve material conditions—does not decrease strife, deterioration, and threat—it does provide a more nuanced and contextualized understanding of intellectual lineage and avoid generational blaming.

There's no question that current crises is plural, complex, and entangled—for many, it is irreversible, still accelerant and, to some, unprecedented. For Latour, for example, we are entering a crisis like none before, for "there is quite simply no precedent for the current situation" in which humans have damaged earth systems (*Down*, 2018, p. 42), affecting human and non-human actors and networks. Others establish precedent by going to science and evidence of prior extinctions (Grusin, 2016; Baker & McPherson, 2014). Precedented or not, no path leads to safety. Isabelle Stengers agrees with Latour that there is no easy answer to the question "What is to be done?" (*Catastrophic*, 2015, p. 24), yet warns against inaction saying that "the catastrophic could well become cataclysmic should we carry on as if nothing were happening, other than making a few cosmetic adjustments" (*Another Science*, 2018, p. 21). For Stengers who understands history as entangled and diffractive, the value of looking at the past is to identify sources that provoked current maladies as well as those modelling correctives and opening channels of intra-action. Calling for "reclaiming efforts" to meet current struggles, Stengers says the past offers models of positive resistance, such as in what the "resistance movements on the ground learned to do during the Second World War in Europe" (*Another Science,* p. 132). Closer to "home" and closer in time, I'm suggesting looking at some of the resistance strategies developed and tried in the 60s and 70s to see if there is transfer power in their models for responding to storm.

Crisis and Radical Hope

In current eco-criticism, "extinction" is often used to refer to the end of colonial, industrial, and capitalist practices that have precipitated planetary crises, making space for "an alternative and pluriversal politics" (Richardson, 2024, p. 3). Sometimes, it refers to species extinction and the end of human life, as in John Durham Peters' ruminations towards the end of *The Marvelous Clouds* (2015, p. 385). While such speculations can reflect purposefully on scientific information about past extinctions (Connolly, 2018) or philosophically about replacing the concept of progress with possibility (Savransky, 2021), they can, as Richard Grusin (2018) notes, slide into fatalism and resignation: "Could it be possible, then, that our current preoccupation with questions of extinction, like our preoccupation with the Anthropocene in all of its varieties, represents not an engagement with the pressing concerns of the twenty-first century but rather the opposite? Could our theorization and speculation about anthropogenic mass extinction be a way of escaping, avoiding, or minimizing such concerns through the premediation of anthropogenic, climatological apocalypse?" ("Introduction," x).

Grusin's questions gain force when welcoming extinction is contrasted to what Johnathan Lear describes as exercising "radical hope" (2006). Charles Taylor tells us that "beyond biological survival," radical hope posits that "life may continue in a yet to be defined new form," attaining profundity commensurate with "lucidity" when one is "really responding to the situation and not just projecting wishes" (para. 33, 2007). McLuhan models this form of "radical hope." For him, the death of nature gave new urgency to questions of how best to monitor and deliver media, especially in urban landscapes needing to be rebuilt or restructured to stimulate sentience and enable new forms of citizen involvement. While his work predated "human non-human" vocabulary and theory, his relational and ecological outlook assumed a view now widely circulated that we "humans are suspended in many webs... that human animals are far from alone in weaving" (Tsing et al., 2019, p. 187). He also anticipated a view many currently hold that innovation has irreversible, intersectional impacts: he observed change occurring on a "total field" ("Electronic Age," 1962, p. 29), for changing any one thing meant changing everything. It is this insight, articulated by Postman (1992, p. 18) and more recently by Naomi Klein (2014), that forms the basis of McLuhan-inflected Media Ecology studies, which exchange cause and effect progression for a more complex reading of "the interaction, the relations that constitute the ground from which effects emerge" (Strate, 2017, p. 179). As a practitioner of "radical hope," McLuhan tempered his hope that collective lucidity would generate new civics and structures with the knowledge of an indeterminate future. For McLuhan, while change is inevitable, progress is not, and harms and imbalances inflicted on humans and the environment are not self-correcting and in some instances beyond correction.

Crisis is not like "moral panic." McLuhan used this term to refer to the irrational fear and fussiness expressed by those who see "a lamentable decline in values" and attempt a remedy by substituting their narrow "point of view for insight" ("Electronic Age," in Moos, p. 29). The crises he along with Tyrwhitt and Kepes hoped to avert was not the product of whipped up collective outrage against a singular easily-targeted offence. They approached crisis in line with its definition from its Greek origin, meaning "turning point" accompanied by both threat and opportunity. In their view, "opportunities" presented as openings for helpful human activity. They did not seek false reassurance by imagining a "good anthropocene" in which "everything happens for the best," or "Whatever is, is right," or that disruptions are treatable side effects subject to "bounceback" (Hamilton, 2015, p. 234, 237). McLuhan proposed as "a simple survival strategy" nothing less than that all of us "become aware of what is happening" (*Playboy*, 1969, p. 237).

This definition of "crisis" brings to mind another term from the Greek, the "pharmakon" that Stiegler connected to what he took to be the tendency of media to be either helpful or harmful, poisonous or healling. Communications theorist Marcel O'Gorman challenges such binary application and invites instead consideration of "the dynamic range of asymmetries that characterize contemporary technoculture" (2020, p. 235). What he has in mind by refusing binary categorization resembles McLuhan's mid-century thought similarly opposed to forms of binary thinking. The figure and ground concept helps us envision how, for him, any one thing or word carries its opposite within it. His "laws of media" capture simultaneity and relationality as definitive of media, for any innovation brings dormant qualities to light and pushes those that have been visible and operative into recessive positions. New media and the broader culture of new aurality carried within them possibilities for good and harm; characterizing them one way or the other could only be done provisionally given that change is constant.

A recent study examining Anthropocene impacts asks whether we can "acknowledge catastrophe while also imagining possibility" (Tsing et al., 2019, p. 192). Such a question was rooted in McLuhan's project, underpinning his assertion that being alert to warnings inherent in antienvironments can provide an "indispensable means of orientation to future problems" ("The Relation," 2011 (1966), p. 15). This book explores how a question like this drove the studies and practices of McLuhan, Tyrwhitt, and Kepes. Seeing a cadre of North American intellectuals, mid-century, as activists practising forms of radical hope allows that it was possible in that milieu to express creative resistance to structures of exploitation and expropriation rather than serving as its practitioners and apologists.[3]

Constellating McLuhan, Tyrwhitt, and Kepes

This book focuses on Marshall McLuhan as the primary figure of interest—a founding theorist in media studies.[4] It examines how our understanding of McLuhan is improved or extended by placing him within the context of mid-century culture, since so much of his work drew from and circled back into the intellectual climate of his times. We know McLuhan himself consulted and deliberately sought out experts in fields beyond his own. It is also true that McLuhan often conveyed his ideas in the form of fragmentary probes or developed them in metaphor and epigraph. This is another reason our understanding is improved by reading him through the more fully articulated narratives of other figures whom he admired and worked alongside. There are many. His texts are replete with references to contemporaries he found profound and engaging.

The choice to study this constellation of figures and not others rests on my experiences as reader and researcher. When I studied McLuhan's view of the city and technology in *McLuhan's Techno-Sensorium City* (2021), the influence of Kepes and Tyrwhitt on McLuhan and the correspondences between his thinking and theirs stood out. Reading him alongside Tyrwhitt explains his take on the benefits and limits of planning a fully technologized urban environment, as well as his hesitancy to take political positions or practical action. For example, he was more concerned about controlling non-stop, non-curated feeds of information and entertainment—to balance or harmonize inner and outer life—than with building equitable housing and planetary greening, forms of action he considered obsolescent and value-laden (*Techno-Sensorium*, p. 84). In a 1972 letter to Kepes, having attended an Ekistics global planning meeting with Kepes and Tyrwhitt among other luminaries, he dismissed discussions about improving living conditions as the work of "brick-and-mortar or hardware men who belong almost entirely in the 19th century" (Molinaro, *Letters*, 1987, p. 453). He worried their "rear-view mirror" solutions, however ethical and well-meaning, failed to account for the "totally new situation" (*Massage*, 1967, pp. 74–75). Reading him alongside Kepes expands his view of the artist as teacher and leader, providing counterbalance to oppressive forms of status quo regulations and expectations. He agreed with Kepes that technology controlled by art and humanistic values might address human and environmental needs.

My chapters linking McLuhan to Tyrwhitt and Kepes (Chapters 2 and 4) use a McLuhan- inflected lens to study how their work illuminates his. To enrich this approach and correct for my reading bias as McLuhan scholar, the chapters on Tyrwhitt (Chapter 3 by Shoshkes) and on Kepes (Chapter 5 by Terranova) present them as lead figures, some of whose interests intersected with McLuhan's and some proceeding independently. Let me provide a brief introduction to Tyrwhitt and Kepes, figures less familiar than McLuhan to many readers.

In her 2013 biography, *Jaqueline Tyrwhitt: A Transnational Life in Urban Planning and Design*, Ellen Shoshkes (who contributes Chapter 3 here) profiles "British town planner, editor, and educator" Jaqueline Tyrwhitt as central to shaping "the post-war modern movement," yet as someone who remains "insufficiently appreciated" because she worked largely in a "behind the scenes role" as catalyst and recording secretary at the high-profile intellectual summits she organized (pp. 3–4). Shoshkes identifies Tyrwhitt as prolific and impactful in contributing to the development of "ideas and networks" connecting Europe to North America and "East and West": "creating new programs to train planners in England, North America and Asia; shaping post-war CIAM discourse on urbanism and assisting CIAM president Jose Luis Sert establish a new professional field of urban design, based on this discourse at Harvard University (1956–1969); consulting to the United Nations (UN); collaborating with Sigfried Giedion on all his major publications in English from 1947 on; and helping Constantinos Doxiadis promote a holistic understanding of human settlements which he termed Ekistics, as a founding editor of the journal *Ekistics* and in the ten DELOS symposia Doxiadis hosted (1963–1972)" (p. 3). In her chapter in this book, Shoshkes documents the history of the personal and professional relationships linking Jaqueline Tyrwhitt with Marshall McLuhan and György Kepes, and situates these interactions within the context of Tyrwhitt's career as a planner, educator, and editor.

Studying Tyrwhitt's ties to the formation of Canadian media and communication studies in the 1950's and to McLuhan, Michael Darroch (2008) provides a who's who roster of her affiliations and contribution:

> Jaqueline Tyrwhitt's many affiliations across the arts and humanities included town planners and architectural historians such as Lewis Mumford, Constantinos Doxiadis, and Sigfried Giedion; Bauhaus figures such as Walter Gropius and László Moholy-Nagy; and anthropologist Edmund Carpenter, as well as culture and communications scholar Marshall McLuhan. It was McLuhan and Carpenter who, along with

> Tyrwhitt, political economist Tom Easterbrook, and psychologist D. Carl Williams, cofounded the Explorations Group and the Ford Foundation Seminar on Culture and Communication at the University of Toronto in 1953. (p. 148)

As Darroch shows, the intellectual friendship and connection between McLuhan and Tyrwhitt spanned at least 20 years, with Tyrwhitt quoting McLuhan on how "global consciousness" has become "the new human scale" in one of her final publications in 1972 (Darroch, p. 167; Bell & Tyrwhitt, p. 527).

Hungarian-born György Kepes studied art in Budapest before moving to Berlin in 1930 and then to London in 1936, following his mentor, fellow Hungarian Bauhaus figure, László Moholy-Nagy. In 1937, he accepted Moholy's invitation to head a workshop at the New Bauhaus school in Chicago (Blakinger, 2019, pp. 2, 6). In 1967, he founded the Center for Advanced Visual Studies (CAVS) at MIT and worked there until 1974 with the aim of creating art-and-science platforms for "confronting, combining, and comparing knowledge" and for "the circulation of ideas to find channels of communication that interconnect various disciplines" (Kepes, qtd. in Blakinger, p. 7). To understand how he defined and played the role of artist as technocrat, it helps to consult his personal and cultural history. Blakinger reports that war "decimated" the Kepes family: "although assimilated, Kepes's family was Jewish in origin and the Nazis began systematic deportations from Hungary after occupying the country in 1944" (p. 6). Relocated to America, Kepes directly experienced Cold War terror; positioned at MIT with the atomic bomb down the hall as "the quintessential symbol of mid-century science and technology" (p. 227), he framed the urgent question, "What is the purpose of art in a brave new world dominated by science and technology?" (p. 7).

Charissa N. Terranova, who discusses Kepes's and McLuhan's use of Cybernetic language and theory in Chapter 5, provides an in-depth chapter on Kepes's light images in *Art as Organism* (2016), explaining that in addition to exploring technology in art projects and installations, Kepes devised his multi-volume book project as a powerful "museum without walls"[5] to engage the public imagination and open "new territory within publishing that was not simply pop science but pop art-and-science" (p. 95). His volumes with "a bio-aesthetic mix of participants" create "a tour de force of the third culture that is science melded into art":

> [His volumes contain] essays by manifold scientists, many of whom he knew through his time in England, including Lancelot Law Whyte, James J. Gibson, J. Bronowski, C.F.A. Pantin, Norbert Wiener, Paul Weiss, Heinz von Foerster, Lawrence K. Frank, Conrad Waddington, and Ludwig von Bertalanffy. These essays appeared alongside writings by doyens of the art and design world, including Rudolph Arnheim, Will

Burtin, Sigfried Giedion, Marcel Breuer, Jean Arp, Saul Bass, John Cage, Naum Gabo, and Fernand Leger. (p. 69)

His sole-authored publication was the influential *Language of Vision* (1944). His edited volumes include *The New Landscape in Art and Science* (1956) and "the seven anthologies that make up Kepes's *Vision + Value* series (1965–66), with a seventh published later *Arts of Environment* (1972)" (Terranova, *Organism*, p. 79). If Shoshkes profiles Tyrwhitt as a powerhouse in brokering live engagements—conferences and meetings for intellectual dialogue and collaborations—Terranova presents Kepes's genius for agglomerating "enumerable images and marginal quotes from artists, ancient, medieval and renaissance poets and philosophers, and known and anonymous scientists" in books containing "essays by almost 130 different authors, some of whom published more than once, coming from the hard sciences, soft sciences, and humanities" (*Organism*, p. 79). McLuhan was one of the 130 contributors. Connecting McLuhan and Kepes, this book makes several references to McLuhan's chapter, "The Emperor's Old Clothes" that appeared in *The Man-Made Environment* (1966);[6] there are also references to Kepes' article "Art and Science," published in the first volume of the McLuhan-group *Explorations* journal (1953). Kepes presented the value of bringing art and science together so that the "verifiable statements about the external world" produced by science inform "images of our external world" created by art (p. 73).

McLuhan's Science and Art Against Crisis

McLuhan, too, wanted a co-mingled art and science—well before the concept was circulated for public debate by C.P. Snow in his 1959 Rede lectures tracing division between *The Two Cultures*. McLuhan's chapter for Kepes argued that science and technology have changed human subjectivity and environmental conditions, that humans need to be more aware of technology's impact on both how and what we perceive, and that only a science enriched with humanistic values will support conscious life and planetary health: "The making and shaping of consciousness from moment to moment is the supreme artistic challenge of all individuals. To qualify and to perfect this process on a world environmental scale is the inherent potential of each new technology" ("Old Clothes," 1966, p. 103). McLuhan frequently pursued the double-edged point that humanistic thinking should inform science research—moving it in ethical and responsible directions—and that science should shape art, both conceptually and materially—updating images of the environment for public education and engagement.

McLuhan also went to science to understand the process of selectivity in knowing and discovery, comprehending it as a system composed by researcher and beholder with "all axioms culturally determined" (Nevitt & McLuhan, 1994, p. 259). He captured this in an homage to mathematician and theorist Alfred North Whitehead who, he said, "explained how the great discovery of the nineteenth century was the discovery of the technique of discovery" (*Understanding Media*, 1964, p. 93). As part of his friendship with artist/curator Harley Parker, he explored the science of art—perspective and form, "movement, colour and light" in kinetic art, audience involvement modulated by the "controlled exploration of multisensory effects," including olfactory stimulus and "sounds and recorded voices, both thundering and quiet" (Genosko, 2017, pp. 161–2). He also conducted several studies with physicist Robert Logan (Marchand, 1989, p. 139) and explored quantum science toward the latter part of his career, counterbalancing his rich understanding of literary arts.

In laying the groundwork for the relational framework of *Laws of Media* (1989), Marshall and Eric McLuhan noted the role of quantum discoveries in overturning "linear, logical and sequential" ordering principles of visual or "Euclidian" space (pp. 44, 90). Paul Grosswiler describes McLuhan's method of probing rather than proving as related to quantum principles of "discontinuity and contradiction, as well as the unexpected" (1994, p. 9). In a chapter called "From Art to Science and Vice Versa," Barrington Nevitt (with Maurice McLuhan) notes that McLuhan was taken with Bohr's observation that "the opposite of a profound truth may well be another profound truth" (1994, p. 259) and that this science-based observation propelled McLuhan's unwillingness to defend his own statements, as in the noncommittal rejoinder attributed to him: "You don't like those ideas? I got others!" ("The Medium," [Lecture], 1977). Beyond laughs, he sought profundity in playing with the figure of Humpty Dumpty to explain what science did to Western sureties about time and space. Once this human-faced and clothed figure crashed, nothing—not power, nor money, nor war—could suture the shards ("Emperor's New Clothes," *Vanishing*, 1968, p. 245).

The "electric age" marked a watershed for McLuhan, and its apocryphal danger and transformative potential is the crux of his probes. Before electricity, we remained "grounded," living in and with nature, assisted by tools. Excesses of the mechanical age were easy targets of criticism because they were visible "extensions" of the human body—performing actions formerly executed by human actors, and with this, elevating leisure and consumerism, entrenched in exploitative practices.[7] Electricity, he countended, did not litter the planet with stuff and things, but worked unseen to spread a glut of information and endless connections and communications. Electricity extended the human nervous system, removing all barriers between self and outer world, which had harmonious potential (if this new form of consciousness was managed to discourage antagonsims) as well as lurking dangers (especially threatening without the exercise of well-intentioned and forward-looking interventions). Calling for exercising restraint (the primary domain of science and technology) and for envisioning balance (the primary domain of art), he ended his *Playboy* interview with apocalytic and utopian options, citing "the potential for realizing the Anti-Christ—Yeats' rough beast" or "a cosmic harmony that transcends time and space" (pp. 20,21).

Pre-electricity, we had a vestigial sense of natural law and order; with electricity, we live in a human-run artificial environment, with all boundaries obsolete. The effects of electric light and power are "totally radical, pervasive, and decentralized," for they "eliminate time and space factors" (*Understanding Media*, p. 21). Electricity—symbolized by the electric light or the light bulb—completed what McLuhan viewed as a longstanding transfer of creative power from God to humans. Once sole property of the Old Testament God, the ability to control the environment was first ceded to humans, McLuhan said, with the Incarnation, symbolizing the merger of human and divine power: "whereas the first Adam was an esthete, viewing and naming and enjoying creatures, a resident in a world he never made, the second Adam remade His first establishment and conferred on man totally new powers of creativity such as the first Adam had not known" (*War and Peace*, 1968, p. 59). This passage—unusual in textual McLuhan which commonly avoids bringing God into the argument—reveals how a Christian understanding of spirtiual mission inspired his urgent advocacy of collective responsibilty for controlling electronic technologies. Failure to take control, abdicating responsibility, could lead to apocalyptic outcomes, affecting human life and all earth.

Tyrhwitt and Kepes did not share McLuhan's Catholic-faith infused views of transformation—even impending apocalyse. But they did share his recognition that science and technologies were radically changing all we know and do, bringing challenges and opportunities; that the environment, not inert and separate from humanity but sharing organic and vital principles, needed to support and reflect humanistic values; that publics needed to flourish under such advances; that citizens needed to more science knowledge; and that the arts were epistemic agents and assets.

McLuhan's Mosaic/Tyrwhitt's Collective Brain/ Kepes's Haptic Unconscious: Thought Movement and Patterns

Readers familiar with McLuhan will know his view of knowledge-making as composite and collaborative. No one person generates entirely new thoughts for scholarship proceeds by drawing together a variety of sources to provide a reconfigured perspective. Elena Lamberti (2012) calls McLuhan's a "mosaic" approach that sets aside notions of linear progression to conceive of knowledge as an interactive "continuum to be investigated in all its complexity" (p. 7). This approach also explains the non-linear style of many of his arguments and the language/image combination he uses that gives "the written page a tactile and multi-sensorial dimension," a *"verbo-vocal-visual* interface" (p. 44).

Art historian Alexander Nagel finds ahistoricity in McLuhan's mosaic view of life and meaning, which he links to the cross-generational work of medieval mosaic production:

> the artist uses chunks of readymade material and patches them into a composition that is understood as an application of a program—a program typically not of the artist's invention. Once it is in place the mosaic has a very long life, not only because its materials—glass and stone—are more durable than pigment on canvas or panel, but because it is by nature structurally amenable to ongoing restoration. Many 'ancient' or 'medieval' mosaics are in fact the ongoing work of succeeding generations (2012, p. 159). [8]

According to Nagel, McLuhan saw the mosaic as more than a technique—as "a model for understanding communication in the present age" as non-sequential and -rational and as simultaneous and haptic (pp. 157–161). More recently, Alexander Kitnick (2021) has described McLuhan's theory as undoing boundaries between artifact and observer, cancelling distinctions between "inside and out" to establish a critical position that works alongside its object of study in "a condition similar to sonic experience in which information hits an individual at every angle" (p. 9).

McLuhan's view of knowledge-making as composite and collaborative assemblage can be understood in relation to his four laws of media, "reversal/obsolescence/retrieval/ enhancement" (*Laws*, 1992, pp. 93–128). The tetrads reveal his understanding of change and return, in "complementary" rather "reciprocal" figure and ground arrangements (*Formal Cause*, 2011, p. 45). Nothing is ever lost, for things obsolesced become part of shadowy ground, hovering unseen until eventually colliding with a new set of "actors" (human and non-human), forming a configuration altered by new context or environment. McLuhan's won method of textual composition enacts these laws, "retrieving" points from past sources, using these in refreshed or "enhanced" form to open new channels and "reverse" currents he considered finished or "obsolete." Obsolescence, thus, does not mean erasure. Mark Wigley—noting Buckminster Fuller's rival claim to being first in with the idea of technologies as extensions—paraphrases Fuller's characterization of McLuhan's remix approach: "McLuhan never had original ideas, nor claimed to. He simply remixed available material in an original way" (Wigley, 2001, p. 86). McLuhan's method, as Fuller observed, involved radical borrowing and paraphrasing of source materials, often inserting passages by others in his own text, without coherent exegesis (as in the copious excerpts from Joyce that offset the text in *War and Peace*, for example). This paratactic presentation aimed at engaging readers in connecting and deciphering meaning.

Texts about McLuhan typically look at the Mosaic approach as "his."[9] Yet reading McLuhan alongside Tyrwhitt and Kepes reveals they also understood knowing as collaborative exercise (albeit without "mosaic" terminology). We know Tyrwhitt depended on the absorptive and accretive power of the "collective brain" (qtd. in Shoshkes, *Transnational*, 2013, p. 186). Tyrwhitt's idea about collectivity and interconnectivity was also informed by Sigfried Giedion's concept of anonymous history, which acknowledged the world-making power of everyday objects and invisible practices as more influential than heroes and great books: so that gardening practices were as significant in forming culture as great books. Like a mosaic structure that reveals different patterns depending on the identity and position of the viewer, anonymous history can account for "something that hides itself in the present—it is a history written in order to reveal the powerful presence of the seemingly absent past" (Norwood, 2023, p. 11). Tyrwhitt had thorough knowledge of Giedion's method of seeing multiple elements of the past in the present. Anonymous history, like a knowledge mosaic, is additive rather than hierarchical and exclusive, including unexpected things in non-linear patchwork.

Kepes's work, often collaborative, extended his Bauhaus inheritance. Terranova suggests that the term "haptic unconscious" catches his approach to knowing as "not just something happening via the brain [but by] ... bodily grasping" and as referring to "the philosophy and training linking people to art forms of light in the twentieth century" (*Organism*, 2016, p. 2). She tells us, too, that Kepes's work has current-day iterations, feeding "theories of distributed consciousness, an ecology of the mind, and the embodiment of virtual technologies and the new media art in the present" (p. 245). This description of the "haptic unconscious" resonates with McLuhan's sensory mosaic, extended, environmental and shared—there is never one discrete and finished image or idea, but a multi-form experience that viewers or readers help shape with mind/body engagements.

"Mosaic"/"collective brain"/"haptic unconscious"—these terms are similar if not synonymous. Constellating them enriches our understanding of how these figures tied knowledge making to networking, both in theory and practice. In our Deleuzian-saturated critical moment, such relational approaches are now common. The art journal *October* (2022), for example, editorializes that an artist is shaped by multi-level "encounters," forged "across chronologies, generations, movements and secret categories"; influences are not "uni-directional or top down" but haunted and dynamic, so that "implicit conversations" inform our understanding of present circumstances and developments, differences and continuances (Maus, 2022, p. 133). Precedent for this relational/intersectional view of knowledge is clearly established in McLuhan, Tyrwhitt and Kepes, who in this were stirred by and stirring the intellectual currents of their day which as art theorists Stimson and Shollette tell us eventuated in a post-modern movement toward collectivisms (2006).

Mosaics and Diffractions: Mattering Now and Then

By examining the three figures from different angles and in different pairings and then suggesting connections between then and now, my approach is congenial with theirs. I am also following diffractive reading practices. In *Meeting the Universe Halfway* (2007), theoretical physicist Karen Barad explores diffractive reading as a method for mapping multiple entanglements that assumes patterns of influence and connection as always/already at work. If traditional western models characterize physical things as separate and in individual spaces, quantum experiments have revealed that any "two" things separate in space can still be the same thing. Nothing is stable or separate, and an observable change can cause myriad ripples, seen and unseen, here and somewhere there. Barad defines diffractive reading method as "a matter of reading insights through rather than against each other in an effort to make evident the always, already entangling of specific ideas and materiality." (Troubling Time/s, 2018, video, 21:33). Diffractive reading reveals inherent relations between objects of study that "are not intertwinings of separate entities, but rather irreducible relations of responsibility" (*Meeting the Universe*, 2007, p. 265). She argues it is our responsibility "to speak with ghosts … to take responsibility for that which we inherit (from the past and the future), for the entangled relationalities of inheritance that 'we' are, to acknowledge and be responsive to the noncontemporaneity of the present, to put oneself at risk, to risk oneself (which is never one or self), to open oneself up to indeterminacy in moving towards what is to come" (*Meeting the Universe*, p. 264).

Diffractive reading has been used as a feminist strategy to avoid positioning traditional phallocentric texts as master narratives from which to dissent or in which to intervene. If texts interact and inform each other, none is definitionally superior or dominant. While diffractive reading discourages privileging one text over another, it does not mean that anything goes. The researcher composing the cartography is positioned to see the relations amongst ideas, and to decide which to play up or underplay. Recently, for example, Iris van der Tuin sketched how we might merge an approach from Achille Mbembe's critical black theory on "unkinning" (letting go of racist and colonial relations and inheritance patterns) with Donna Haraway's encouragement to choose kin (making deliberate choices in building relations with human and non-human actors). Van der Tuin suggests that rather than seeing binary conflict in these approaches, diffraction reads their co-existence in current culture-making practices. ("On Research Worthy of the Present," 2019, p. 14).

Researchers choose their research materials, and meaningful and responsible studies, Barad says, are both critical and generative. Her attitude to her own mentor figure—quantum physicist Nils Bohr—involves neither idolizing him nor acting as "undutiful daughter": her purpose is "to read various insights through one another and to produce something new, new patterns of thinking-being, while at the same time being very attentive to what it is that Bohr is trying to say to us" (Dolphjin & van der Tuin, 2012, interview). To the extent that McLuhan is the central figure of this study, Barad's positioning in relation to the freighted and patriarchal figure of Bohr is germane. We can reject the colonial/patriarchal/masculinist and racist assumptions that contributed to McLuhan's thinking and world view, recognizing that these limitations haunt current efforts to appreciate his insights, while considering which of his insights retain explanatory power. Diffractive reading frees texts from canonical interpretations, provides provisional insights and as Iris van der Tuin theorizes "allows scholarly work to remain in motion" ("Without," 2014, p. 246).

Connecting scholarly work across disciplines and time frames and setting aside strict claims to authorial ownership to view knowledge as shared, mobile and dynamic is at the heart of our research story. This book puts McLuhan in conversation with Kepes and Tyrwhitt and, in tracing interactive connections, highlights some they knew of as well as some that with the passage of time are clearer to us. Alike, they supported the formation of broad intellectual coalitions and citizen engagement. They shared a view of art as a potential force for good, and thus for generating hope for human and earth futures. Each argued for new governance strategies, if with different foci—benevolent global oversight as practiced by a global intellectual coalition (Tyrwhitt); new forms of civic engagement (Kepes);

multilevel transformations to promote relationality and interactivity and to create de-territorialized and de-materialized conditions (McLuhan).

A diffractive approach also encourages observing how these figures connect to our day. Readers can consider how the mid-century sense of crises and response continues and shifts now. Then as now there was no shortage of actual trauma and threat: residual affects of World War II, Cold War tensions, Viet Nam and other wars, and violent domestic confrontations, supported by arsenals of military technologies and militaristic responses. The Bomb was a presence as was non-stop media information. In North America and globally, there was also raw economic and racial inequity, sparking widespread protest movements. Crises then was forerunner—forewarning—of crises now.

Crises Then as Now

This introduction presents the book's aims and methodological moves: reading McLuhan as primary figure alongside Kepes and Tyrwhitt and reading McLuhan through Kepes and Tyrwhitt, as Shoshkes and Terranova shift the lens to put the main focus on these figures and the under-recognized legacies of each. It also stakes the claim that the book explores: that crises then resonates now. The book considers—and asks readers to consider—how mid-century address of crises informs current responses, potentially reinvigorating our sense of purpose and hope.

Chapter 1 explores McLuhan on crisis and recovery, working with his references to Poe's Mariner. The Mariner's tale is a parable of the human encounter with unstoppable technological developments, these doing violence to our individual psyches, to habituated cultural practices, and to earth itself as a zone of artifice. Salvation requires scientific intuition and artistic creativity together. The Mariner can steer a safe course after paying attention to unfolding patterns, performing beyond what machinic or cybernetic interventions might accomplish. Chapter 1 goes on to connect how McLuhan saw loss of nature and governance as part of incoming "aurality" and how this sense of loss applies in our time.

Chapter 2 and 3 are "paired" around the McLuhan/Tyrwhitt interface. Chapter 2 gives my reading of McLuhan and Tyrwhitt, depicting her as a figure whose knowledge of European art and city theory he admired. Over time, there was a rift in their thinking and affiliations, as McLuhan drew toward imagining aural culture supplanting visual. I examine the different paths they took when confronting similar problems. McLuhan speculated on transformative effects and dissociated from coalitional efforts—however thoughtful—to improve human and environmental relations. In Chapter 3, Ellen Shoshkes, Tyrwhitt's biographer, shifts the focus to Tyrwhitt and assesses her as a figure of influence within design and planning culture and on both McLuhan and Kepes. She demonstrates Tyrwhitt's adept commitment to global planning and action for equity, and shows McLuhan's withdrawal form this work.

Chapters 4 and 5 pair McLuhan and Kepes. In Chapter 4, I outline what I take to be powerful similarities between the two, both of whom imagined art as central to civility and survival. Both engaged in programs to merge art and science/technology rather than having them operate as binary and bounded fields and both offered educational programs to engage public minds and bodies. A key difference is that Kepes was fascinated by vision and visual properties, whereas McLuhan gravitated to a model of poly-sensory knowing as corrective to Western overreliance on the eye. In Chapter 5, renowned Kepes scholar Charissa Terranova considers how McLuhan and Kepes were attracted to Cybernetic theory—especially how its language allowed them to share ideas of relationality and pattern. Her approach also exposes differences: she notes that Kepes had a more theoretically-infused understanding of bio-material transfer, informed by early twentieth century Bauhaus theory, whereas McLuhan's theory of extensions reads as comparatively thin. Her observations track confluent as well as different intellectual histories.

The conclusion takes up the options for meeting crisis. Variants of cybernetic hope continue to circulate in our time: in arguments that algorithms and AI support our learning and leisure; that technology will provide solutions to everything we make and break; indeed, that such a thing as "a solution" might put an end to what relational thinkers like Latour characterize as ongoing work. The conclusion also examines crisis and anxiety as inheritance. It considers options endorsed by all three figures as stays against crisis: attending to the unanimous call raised by McLuhan, Tyrwhitt, and Kepes to value the creative and ethical energy of art designed for public engagement and to suffuse, even redirect, crisis. It also takes up how different art forms make variant environmental interventions.

A future study might examine more fully how the process philosophy of Alfred North Whitehead influenced or otherwise corresponds with the thinking of these three figures (and can influence our reading of them now), especially how his relational ontology inflected their theorizing of creativity and worldmaking. Certainly, Whitehead's influence on McLuhan, direct and indirect, is evident but seldom remarked. The final page of *The Medium is the Massage* includes a stand-alone sentence from Whitehead that would have intrigued McLuhan for being at once inspirational and ominous: "It is the business of the future to be dangerous" (p. 160). Moreover, an extended passage earlier in the text gives Whitehead's view of the indeterminate nature of knowledge: "In the study of ideas, it is necessary to remember that insistence on hard-headed clarity issues from sentimental feeling, as it were a mist, cloaking the perplexities of fact.... Our reasonings grasp at straws for premises and float on gossamers for deductions" (*Medium*, p.10).[10]

Reading all three figures through Whitehead might serve to extend a key premise of this book which holds that earlier scholarship modelled fruitful ways to speak to crisis: that those before us were neither unwitting pawns of exploitative systems nor unduly optimistic about human progress and power. Reading the ideas and practices of the three through Whitehead would undoubtedly layer our understanding of them: Tyrwhitt's description of the appeal of design that fostered affect and cognition; Kepes's use of technology to enhance sensory encounter and experience; and McLuhan's desire for forms of art to deliberately break up word systems or image patterns, giving new and poly-sensual forms as in Joycean talk or Mondrian's canvases of music and colour. All rejected Cartesian duality as the ragged remains of Westernism and saw openings in this ending, bringing to mind McLuhan's casting of "Breakdown as Breakthrough" (*Culture*, 1970, p. 27). They explored art and design as commanding attention and capable of touching us—of "conferring on what touches us the power of making us feel and think" (Stengers, 2023, p. 175)—and as provocative of possibility and adventure—positions still expressed by many who imagine various stands against crisis.

Notes

1. McLuhan's recognition of the role of capitalism, industry and governance in product research and development is detailed in *The Mechanical Bride*; he also speaks the link between capitalism and control in *Understanding Media*: "Once we have surrendered our senses and nervous systems to the private manipulation of those who would try to benefit from taking a lease on our eyes and ears and nerves, we don't really have any rights left" (*Understanding*, p. 99). Representing technology as the product of scientists-as-makers was a strategy that helped buoy his argument that technologies were not locked down by ownership but available to be curtailed and controlled by skilled technocians informed by humanist values. To emphasize government and corporate influence—to make this the figure—would have been to detract from the residual power of scientist and creatives—power, residing in the background and seldom considered.
2. Donna Haraway tells us the term "Anthropocene" was "coined in the early 1980s by ecologist Eugene Stoermer" and made a star appearance "in 2000 when Dutch atmospheric chemist Paul Crutzen joined Stoermer to propose that human activities had been of such a kind and magnitude as to merit the use of a new geological term for a new epoch" (From "Tentacular Thinking: Anthropocene, Capitalocene, Chthulucene"(September 2016), *E-Flux*, vol. 75, p. 201).
3. Along similar lines, Ryan McCullogh has recently explored Neil Postman's critical position as that of "loving resistance fighter" [Duquesne University Duquesne Scholarship Collection

Electronic Theses and Dissertations (Spring 5-5-2023) *Neil Postman's Loving Resistance Fighter: A Philosophy of Communication in the Age of Technopoly*: 1-366. https://dsc.duq.edu/cgi/viewcontent.cgi?article=3204&context=etd]

4 Post-colonial studies have questioned McLuhan's role as a foundational theorist of media studies in a restructured canon (see Faiza, H., Jiwani, Y., McAllister, K., and Russill, C., "Putting Race at the Forefront of Communication Studies." *Canadian Journal of Communication* 46(*3*) 2021, p. 701); for another approach, see Sarah Sharma who explores the "ever-expanding possibility of a refreshed engagement with McLuhan's thought, the archives, and the library" ("Many McLuhans or None at All." *Canadian Journal of Communication* 44(*4*) 2019, p. 487).

5 This connection between Malraux and Kepes is resonant in McLuhan studies, given that McLuhan often hailed Malraux's idea by attaching the phrase "without walls" to varied nouns, such as his description in *Understanding Media* of photography as a "brothel without walls" (p. 255) and his comparison of "new possibilities for architectural and artistic modulation of space" to "housing-without-walls" (p. 176).

6 All three figures use "man" as a generic term to apply to humans, jarring to readers now but common when they wrote. I have left it in titles and in passages where changes disrupt textual integrity. When possible, I have tried to insert "human" in place of "man" to facilitate the process of reading and connecting then to now.

7 See *The Mechanical Bride: Folklore of Industrial Man* (1951) that looks at visible effects of mechanization on physical activity, which are unlike the less obvious effects of the electric age, that McLuhan said affected inner change: "In the electronic age with the outering of all five senses we turn to the outering of mental operations in computers" ("Electronic Age," p. 29); see also *Understanding Media* looking at how gadgetry—enacting reversal—return some tasks to human hands, so that for example, we do not have cooks and tailors but own stoves and sewing machines and do work for ourselves (p. 56).

8 Whereas Nagel contends that McLuhan knew but never fully articulated the contrast between medieval guild craftsman and modernist notions of individual creativity, I would counter that he may have avoided definitive statements because he himself never totally committed to one mode over the other. He was reluctant to abandon values of individualism, privacy, and personal authority associated with the modernist approach—for these are values he preferred "as a man molded within the literate Western tradition" (*Playboy*, p. 21).

9 In personal correspondence, David Howes, a McLuhan scholar in the field of sensory studies, reminded me that Harold Innes should be credited with using the term "mosaic" and that "McLuhan picked it up and developed it in his practice."

10 The Whitehead reference may not have been one McLuhan contributed to the co-written volume *The Medium is the Massage* (1967). I am grateful to William Buxton for pointing out "that McLuhan's contribution to the volume [*The Medium is the Massage*] was minimal." (Marshall McLuhan: Avant-Garde Beacon and/or Urban Futurist? *Canadian Journal of Communication*, 48(*2*), doi:10.3138/cjc.2022-0076, p. 413). With this reservation in mind, I none the less offer the quotation as evidence of McLuhan's interest in Whitehead, noting that the final page of a book is usually reserved for something of import; the first quote in this book is also from Whitehead (pp. 6–7). As further evidence, there is another passage from Whitehead in *Take Today* (1972, p. 135) and two full paragraphs in "The Electronic Age" (1961, in Moos, p. 37). These references span more than a decade.

References

Baker, C., & McPherson, G. (2014). *Extinction dialogs: How to live with death in mind*. New Revelation Press.

Barad, K. (2007). *Meeting the universe halfway*. Duke University Press.

Barad, K. (2010). Quantum entanglements and hauntological relations. *Derrida Today, 3*(2), 240–268. https://doi.org/10.3366/drt.2010.0206

Barad, K. (2018). [Video]. Troubling time/s and ecologies of nothingness. *European Graduate School of Video Lectures*. https://www.youtube.com/watch?v=RZHurGcoRmQ&t=7s

Blakinger, J. R. (2019). *György Kepes: Undreaming the Bauhaus*. MIT Press.

Bell, G., & Tyrwhitt, J. (Eds.). (1972). *Human identity in the urban environment*. Penguin Books.

Connolly, W. E. (2018). Extinction events and entangled humanism. In R. Grusin (Ed.), *After extinction*. University of Minnesota Press.

Darroch, M. (2008). Bridging urban and media studies: Jaqueline Tyrwhitt and the Explorations group, 1951–1957. *Canadian Journal of Communications, 33*(2), 147–169.

Dolphijn, R., & van der Tuin, I. (2012). [Interview with K. Barad]. Matter feels, converses, suffers, desires, yearns and remembers. *New Materialism: Interviews & Cartographies*. https://quod.lib.umich.edu/o/ohp/11515701.0001.001/1:4.3/--new-materialism-interviews-cartographies?rgn=div2;view=fulltext

Durham Peters, J. (2015). *The marvellous clouds: Toward a philosophy of elemental media*. University of Chicago Press.

Genosko, G. (2017). The designscapes of Harley Parker: Print and build environments. *Imaginations, 8*(3), 153–164.

Grosswiler, P. (1994). The convergence of William Stephenson's and Marshall McLuhan's communication theories. *Operant Subjectivity, 17*(3/4), 2–16.

Grusin, R. (2018). Introduction. *After extinction*. University of Minnesota Press.

Guittari, F. (2001). *The three ecologies* (I. Pindar & P. Suttin, Trans.). The Athlone Press. (Original work published in 1989)

Hamilton, C. The theodicy of the "Good Anthropocene." *Environmental Humanities, 7*, 233–238.

Haraway, D. J. (2016). *Staying with the trouble: Making kin in the Chthulucene*. Duke University Press.

Hayles, N. K. (2017). [video]. *Why we are (still) postmodern*. https://www.youtube.com/watch?v=14LdB1eDoS4

Kepes, G. (1944). *Language of vision*. Paul Theobald.

Kepes, G. (1953). Art and science. *Explorations, 1*, 72–78.

Kepes, G. (1956). *The new landscape in art and science*. Paul Theobald.

Kepes, G. (Ed.). (1966). Vision + Value Series. *The man-made object*. George Braziller.

Kepes, G. (Ed.). (1972). Vision + Value Series. *Arts of the environment*. George Braziller.

Kitnick, A. (2021). *Distant early warning: Marshall McLuhan and the transformation of the avant-garde*. University of Chicago Press.

Klein, N. (2014). *This changes everything*. Simon & Schuster.

Lamberti, E. (2012). *Marshall McLuhan's mosaic: Probing the literary origin of media studies*. University of Toronto Press.

Latour, B. (2018). *Down to Earth: Politics in the new climatic regime* (C. Porter, Trans.). Polity. (Original work published 2017)

Lear, J. (2007). *Radical Hope: Ethics in the face of cultural devastation*. Harvard University Press.

Marshall McLuhan in Conversation with Norman Mailer. (2006). [Video]. The Summer Way. https://www.youtube.com/watch?v=PtrJntaTlic

Maus, N. (2022). On Werner Schroeter. *October* (179), 132–136. https://doi.org/10.1162/octo_a_00451

Marchand, P. (1989). *Marshall McLuhan: The medium and the messenger*. Vintage.

McLeod Rogers, J. (2021). *McLuhan's techno-sensorium city: Coming to our senses in a programmed environment*. Lexington.

McLuhan, M. (1951). *The mechanical bride: Folklore of industrial man*. Beacon.

McLuhan, M. (1966). The emperor's old clothes. In G. Kepes (Ed.), *The man-made object* (pp. 90–95). George Braziller.

McLuhan, M. (1970). *Culture is our business*. McGraw-Hill.

McLuhan, M. *The medium is the message [1977 lecture] part 1 v3 around 14:23 into ABC TV, Monday Conference*. http://www.youtube.com/watch?v=ImaH51F4HBw&feature=player_embedded.1970s.

McLuhan, M. (1987). *Letters of Marshall McLuhan* (M. Molinaro, C. McLuhan, & W. Toye, Eds.). Oxford University Press.

McLuhan, M. (1995). The *Playboy* interview. In E. McLuhan, & F. Zingrone (Eds.), *Essential McLuhan* (pp. 233–69). House of Anansi Press Inc. (Original work published 1969)

McLuhan, M. (1997). The electronic age—the age of implosion. In M. Moos (Ed.), *Media research: Technology, art, and communication* (pp. 16–38). G & B Arts International. (Original work published 1973)

McLuhan, M. (2003). *Understanding media: The extensions of man* (Critical ed.), (W. Terrence Gordon, Ed.). Gingko Press. (Original work published 1964)

McLuhan, M. (2011) The relation of the environment to the anti-environment. In M. McLuhan & E. McLuhan (Eds.), *Media and formal cause* (pp. 11–26). NeoPoiesis Press. (Original work published in 1966)

McLuhan, M., & Fiore, Q., with Agel, J. (1967). *The medium is the massage: An inventory of effects*. Gingko Press.

McLuhan, M., & Fiore, Q., with Agel, J. (1968). *War and peace in the global village*. Bantam.

McLuhan, M., Hutchon, K., & McLuhan, E. (1977). *City as classroom: Understanding language and media*. Book Society of Canada.

McLuhan, M., & Mailer, N. (1968). *The summer way* CBC, https://marshallmcluhanspeaks.com/interviews/in-conversation-with-norman-mailer

McLuhan, M., & McLuhan, E. (1992). *Laws of media: The new science*. University of Toronto Press.

McLuhan, M., & McLuhan E. (2011). *Media and formal cause*. NeoPoiesis Press.
McLuhan M., & Nevitt, B. (1972). *Take today: The executive as dropout*. Harcourt Brace Jovanovich.
Nagel, A. (2012). *Medieval modern: Art out of time*. Thames & Hudson.
Nevitt, B., & McLuhan, M[aurice]. (1994). *Who was Marshall McLuhan?* Stoddart.
Norwood, B. E. (2015). [Review of the book *Mechanization takes a command: A contribution to anonymous history*, by S. Giedion]. *Culture Machine*, 1–12. https://culturemachine.net/wp-content/uploads/2019/05/576-1383-1-PB.pdf
O'Gorman, M. (2022). Revisiting the pharmakon: Why media theory needs queer theory. *Media Theory*, 6(2), pp. 234–252.
Richardson, M. (2024). *Non-Human witnessing: War data and ecology after the end of the world*. Duke University Press.
Savransky, M. (2021). After progress: Notes for an ecology of perhaps. *Ephemera: Theory & Politics in Political Organization*, 21(1), pp. 267–81.
Shoshkes, E. (2013). *Jaqueline Tyrwhitt: A transnational life in urban planning and design*. Routledge.
Snow, C. P. (1965). *The two cultures: and a second look*. Cambridge University Press. (Original work published 1959)
Sontag, S. (1965, October). The imagination of disaster. *Culture and Civilization*. https://www.commentary.org/articles/susan-sontag/the-imagination-of-disaster/.
Stengers, I. (2015). *In catastrophic times: Resisting the coming barbarism* (A. Goffey, Trans.). Open Humanities Press/Meson Press. (Original work published 2009)
Stengers, I. (2018). *Another science is possible: A manifesto for slow science* (S. Muecke, Trans.). Polity. (Original work published in 2013)
Stengers, I. (2023). *Making sense in common: A reading of Whitehead in times of collapse* (T. Lamarre, Trans.). University of Minnesota Press. (Original work published 2020)
Stimson, B., & Sholette, G. (2006). *Collectivism after modernism: The art of social imagination after 1945*. University of Minnesota Press.
Strate, L. (2017). *Media ecology: An approach to understanding the human condition*. Peter Lang.
Taylor, C. (2007) *A different kind of courage*. https://www.nybooks.com/articles/2007/04/26/a-different-kind-of-courage/?lp_txn_id=1544419
Terranova, C. N. (2016). *Art as organism: Biology and the evolution of the digital image*. I.B. Taurus.
Tsing, A. L., Mathews, A. S., & Bubandt, N. (2019, August). Patchy Anthropocene: Landscape structure, multispecies history, and the retooling of anthropology (an Introduction to supplement 20). *Current Anthropology*, 60, s186–s197.
Turner, F. (2013). *The democratic surround: Multimedia and American liberalism from World War II to the psychedelic sixties*. University of Chicago Press.
Van der Tuin, I. (2014). Without analytical divorce from the total environment. *Humanities*, 3(2), 244–263. https://doi.org/10.3390/h3020244
Van der Tuin, I. (2019). On research 'Worthy of the Present.' *Simon Fraser University Educational Review*, 12(1), 8–20. https://journals.lib.sfu.ca/index.php/sfuer/article/view/860/530

Wigley, M. (2001). Network fever. *Grey Room* (4), 82–122. https://doi.org/10.1162/1526381
   01750420825

CHAPTER 1

McLuhan and Environmental Crises

"... [I]f we keep our cool during the descent into the maelstrom, studying the process as it happens to us and what we can do about it, we can come through."
—McLuhan, 1969, *Playboy* Interview, p. 268

This chapter begins by considering McLuhan's sense of crisis and survival strategies. It then focuses on his retellings of Poe's Mariner story as resonant survival parable—one that reveals McLuhan's understanding of threat and survival as requiring relational thinking, as well as recognition of the need to combine science and art epistemologies, to merge figure and ground perception, and to be alert to the role of spirit or mystery. The chapter then examines McLuhan's view of crisis as provoked by our move from the forms of visual culture that modernism and attendant losses in areas like nature, individualism and privacy, language, and state governance. The chapter ends by assessing his sense of hope and its current relevance.

In McLuhan's view, incoming aural culture was introducing a variety of effects that had served as the latent ground of visual culture, such as loss of nature (with signs of human activity everywhere); language drift (as computers become chief agents of literacy and communication); dissolution of borders (as we shift attention from material to digital spaces); breakdown of governance arrangements (as nations and states become anachronistic in a connected environment). For

McLuhan, these trouble spots of radical change were not discrete, but interrelated, often in subtle, under-the-surface ways. Technology, culture, and politics are inter-influential; mind, culture and technology are inter-influential. In a long single paragraph from "The Invisible Environment" (1967), he explores how everything we know is dematerializing or dissolving, eroding "the future of" current forms "of work," "of consciousness," "of the child," "of the city," "of language" (p. 167). These paratactic leaps from one sector to another invite readers to consider what connections might adhere. Michael Moos has called this a "hypertext" approach which McLuhan employed to signal the limits of language itself and to create a textual "anti- or counter environment" for readers to navigate (1997, pp. 155, 164). McLuhan was less interested in pinning down relationships in flux than in sparking recognition of change across sectors. He spoke out against immersive regulatory propaganda ("Invisible Environment," 1967, p. 164) and showed no interest in intensifying this discursive climate.

Also key to McLuhan's rhetoric was avoidance of binaries. He did not insist on success or defeat as planetary outcome, unlike other modernists described by Alex Kitnick as making "utopian all-or-nothing pronouncements" (2021, p. 9). He cited "grounds for both optimism and pessimism" in imagining the likelihood of human agency shaping a livable future (*Playboy*, 1969, p. 268): things might go well if we build an environment that supports life and badly without strategic interventions. His overarching mission was to explore the "dynamics" (not the dialectics) of environmental change, for in his view figures move forward and recede, changing value and visibility but still constellated in "complementary process" (*Media and Formal Cause*, 2011, p. 45). Interviewed in 1969, he admitted preferring the ordered values of visual and literate culture, such as privacy, authority, and order—to deriving "no joy from observing the traumatic effects of media on man" (*Playboy*, p. 267). Yet with change inevitable, he hoped a transformed cosmos might offer new possibilities such as the planet transformed "into an art form" and humans "linked in a cosmic harmony that transcends time and space" (*Playboy*, p. 268). Rather than staging the future in detail, he offered speculations that—far from glib—were grounded in penetrating observation and perception, exercise of which he considered key to apt predictions (*Media and Formal Cause*, p. 55). Thinking with McLuhan resembles how Isabelle Stengers describes thinking with Alfred North Whitehead. Both provoke readers to be more considerate and involved readers, asking of text "what it renders important and what it makes remain silent" (*Thinking with Whitehead*, 2011, p. 22). We are not furnished with anything so simple as "a new way of seeing" but offered "the transformation of experience" that implies "reciprocal influence... that puts to the test both what brings about and what is brought about" (*Thinking with Whitehead*, p. 22).

A letter to Innis (1951) provides other evidence of McLuhan's deliberate avoidance of reductive dialectics that lock out interactive agents. He dismissed "the Deutsch-Wiener fallacy" as a failure within cybernetics to connect the arts and technology; by leaving out the arts, cybernetics was "unable of itself to see beyond or around technology" (*Letters*, 1987, p. 222). Countering such single vision, he worked with a figure-ground approach aimed at surmounting the limitations of perceptual habits that privilege recognizable figures to leave "a very much larger area of inattention: The two [figure and ground] are in a continual state of abrasive interplay, with an outline or boundary or interval between them that serves to define both simultaneously" (*Global Village*, 1989, p. 5). In "a continual state of abrasive interplay," figure and ground arrangements are unstable assemblages; misinterpreted by groups as stable and reduced to dogma, they create clash and conflict.

In McLuhan's view, habit and dogma attempt to impose stabilities that deny the constant play and transformative energy of multifarious visible and invisible influences. Indeed, he values artists for seeing beyond or beneath the visible environment; artists produce "counter-environments" by bringing formerly hidden agents to new light in new company, exposing new patterns. He noted that contemporary art—literature, painting, sculpture—has abandoned representational projects that "began for Western art in fifth-century Athens", stressing "the visual sense usually at the expense of the other senses" ("Emperor's New Clothes," 1968, p. 239). Meaningful contemporary work aims at activating a broader sensorium, retraining expanded perceptual activity and acuity, in this way more about medium than message for art as medium alters how and how much we notice, process, and value; artists can "teach human perception … not that you may know this or that, but that you may have the means of perceiving" ("Medium is the Massage," 1966, in *Understanding Me*, p. 93). Supportive of McLuhan's discussions of selectivity in perception and knowing is N. Katherine Hayles' account of cognitive assemblage that describes human consciousness forming after the filtering (not blocking) of perceptual and cognitive acts, so that "information is *transduced* as it moves from environment to organism" ("Detoxifying Cybernetics," 2024, p. 93). Supportive of McLuhan's view of perception as untapped resource is sensory expert David Howes's redefinition of the human sensorium as composed of more than 5 senses and of sensory activity as variable across cultural fields so that its "ever shifting divisions and relations" can be understood "by analogy to a kaleidoscope" (2022, p. 69). Howes goes on to assert, following McLuhan and Ong, that if the senses are best understood not as "localized in the brain" but as "socialized and technologized"—with perception both taught and directed—then "the senses are our first media" (2024, p. 9).

McLuhan's drive to increase perceptual activity was not to foster private learning—his own or that of individual readers—but to promote an involved citizenry whose decisions in the present would alter the future, for "the future of the future is the present" (*Medium is the Massage*, 1966, in *Understanding Me*, p. 93). Speculatively, he often referred to a programmed environment—one dominated not by self-correcting AI, skimming information from loops of feedback, but imagined as human-adjusted, calibrated by human hands and minds to support human needs. As I explored in *McLuhan's Techno-Sensorium City* (2021), he designated to artists the task of adjusting environmental conditions (pp. 63–64). Yet he defined the term "artist" capaciously, including creative thinkers "in any field, scientific or humanistic who grasps the implication of his actions and of new knowledge in his own time" (*Understanding Media*, 2003/1964, p. 96). Moreover, in the governance model McLuhan imagined, artists were not a tight cadre of technocrats but responsive to and informed by citizen input. Indeed, to avoid technocratic formations, productive "public participation becomes a sort of technological imperative" ("At the Moment," 1974, p. 57). He believed all of us had the perceptual equipment to shape the interactive environment, which he referred to by using defamiliarizing terms such as "Spaceship Earth" or "global theatre" invoking place and culture where "the audience and the crew become actors, producers rather than consumers. They seek to program events rather than to watch them" ("At the Moment," p. 57).

While McLuhan sometimes spoke of art as material and substantive or as creative production—as thing or act capable of revealing unknown patterns—other times he used the term more symbolically, as when he paired it with science and it stood for creative, insightful and humane purpose. Pairing "art" with "science" values, he referred to the interaction or exchanges between human making and computational media. Human activity, in all aspects of ingenuity, have changed the human body and all ecologies. If we fail to bring art (as in humane values) together with computational science, we are making a dangerous environment and apocalyptic now/future.

We might consider McLuhan as a futurist rather than a critical theorist for he had little interest in revising extant economic and political systems. He deliberately avoided, as "rear-view mirror" thinking, applying correctives to visible economic and social problems—problems that do not address "the new situation" but stay attached to "the most recent past," confining us to "march backwards into the future" (*Medium is Massage*, 1967, pp. 74–75). Defusing the position that avant-garde-ism is an evacuation of responsibility for improving present conditions, political philosopher Mark Fisher reminds us that for McLuhan "Being ahead of your time means seeing what's in front of you" ("Misrecognizing Narcissus,"

2010–11, para 10 and 11). He supports McLuhan's position that "the possibilities for a different politics depend on waking from narcissus trance and seeing the new potentials in what is in front of us" ("Flatness," n.p.). As an example of looking ahead, McLuhan imagined feedback potential beyond merely performative populism, involving citizens in world-making and conditions. There are also links between his position and current iterations of "Acceleration," a form of global humanism that advocates for letting go of leftist fantasies of return to "folk politics of localism" to navigate "complexity, globality, and technology" (Williams & Srnicek, 2014, p. 354). McLuhan wanted wider acknowledgement of the effects of artifice and technology on humans and planet and from this to put management and salvage strategies in place, repurposed toward common ends rather than destroyed as part of outworn modernism.

In a letter to international affairs expert Barbara Ward (1973), McLuhan espoused his opinion that political and economic theory and systems are always outmoded, reactive rather than properly responsive, as every "technological change or innovation brings in new dogma and politics" (*Letters*, 1987, p. 468). He saw international politics as failing to recognize affiliative principles sweeping the planet and with this failing to engage emerging technologies for social good or future optimization. In lieu of seeking labour and wage equity, for example, he was interested in theorizing the revised nature of work itself, with "roles" replacing "jobs." In a world encouraging "dropouts"—through disaffection and "disincarnation" (digitization)—human *doing* was less important than *being* and *being seen* ("The End of the Work Ethic", 2003/1972, p. 204)—foresight now recognizable as part of work- from- home reality and digital culture. His letter to Ward conveyed his limited interest in the prospect of international cooperation and questions "of what strategies" might be deployed "in propping up this or that portion of worldly culture at any given time" (*Letters*, p. 468). As stated elsewhere, he believed the geopolitics of nationalism were at end (*Playboy*, p. 258).

He did not enter popular debates about controlling "population explosion" but imagined the corrective potential of environmental programming. To McLuhan, such programming had potential to respond to regional needs and operate on several scales: on a small scale, altering material conditions like light and heat and the flow of information, and on a large scale, programming "whole environments. . . to accommodate the sensory preference and needs of entire communities" (*War and Peace*, 1968, p. 179). He did not furnish political models to guide global-scale "Total Change" (*Medium*, 1967, p. 16), but spoke of preserving personal freedom and liberty—cornerstone human values he feared were threatened if media and technology were allowed to accelerate and dominate—cutting off access to direct experience of the world: "Once we have surrendered our senses and nervous systems to the private manipulation of those who would benefit from taking a lease on our eyes, ears, and nerves, we don't really have any rights left. Leasing our eyes and ears and nerves to commercial interests is like handing over the common speech to a private corporation, or like giving the earth's atmosphere to a company as a monopoly" (*Understanding Media*, p. 99). He did not protest particular policies or government strategies but had a more sweeping mission, resisting corporate or government technocracy through reigniting human perceptual activity to enable its fuller range and involve citizens involvement in world culture and development.

McLuhan's reliance on the concept of "formal cause" helps explain his sense of the process of change as multi-directional and multi-relational, dynamic and instantaneous—and thus, unlike cause-and-effect thinking, neither easily applied nor comprehended. McLuhan used "formal cause" to upend our usual pattern of thinking by which cause precedes effect, offering that "effects precede causes" ("The Argument," 1973, p. 10). Formal cause is related to figure ground thinking, for it often resides unnoticed in the background, as McLuhan's description of formal cause developments indicate:

> many of the effects of the telephone had been anticipated by the general speedup of information that centered in the telegraph … The new effects through new uses of any innovation are realized only after it becomes obsolescent through fresh innovation. The old hidden ground then emerges as a new rear-view figure for all to see. (The Argument, p. 10)

In a recent text, *Formal Cause in Marshall McLuhan's Thinking*, Laura Trujillo Linan (2022) uses the theory of media as extensions to explore formal cause as residing in "perpetual changes" (p. 120) we ourselves provoke but fail to understand. There is a rhetorical element to formal cause thinking, for via the selectivity of perception we can be said to impose order. Yet what we discern as pattern is not merely a construction for, as Lance Strate reminds us (2017), McLuhan's use of the term "recognition" implies that patterns "are not merely in the mind of the beholder but have an objective existence." Beyond this, he notes that such patterns—"not simply subjective constructs" but in recognition "of objective phenomena"—can be found in both inorganic and organic things, as the "product of human ingenuity, or physical processes" ("The Effects That Give Cause," p. 110, 112). He argues that for McLuhan, pattern seeking is inherent in all "transactions with the environment," whether we read words, consider historical events, or study the physical universe (p. 113). While patterns reconfigure, there are within them elements of consistency. Formal cause thinking, as in the Mariner's story that links survival to pattern recognition, infused McLuhan's philosophy: driving his hopeful speculations that studying the present provides clues and connections and that everything (human and nonhuman, past/ present/ and future) connects to and influences everything else.

Understanding McLuhan as Mariner

To convey the inescapability of danger and reveal strategies for survival that combine scientific method with artistic/creative insight, McLuhan often cited Poe's Mariner from "A Descent into the Maelstrom" (1840). In Poe's story, the Mariner encounters a storm and powerful whirlpool off the Norwegian coast. The Mariner survives by controlling his fear and exercising intense concentration to determine what floats and sinks (p. 11). Immersive concentration alone leads "to invariable miscalculation" but leads to an imaginative leap that connects present to past. He remembers a beach littered with cylindrical objects and, observing the current situation, notices that cylinders remain afloat whereas other objects disappear into the vortex. To test his idea, he attaches himself to a cylindrical water cask, and stays afloat while the boat sinks.

McLuhan tells us the Mariner provides "a possible stratagem for understanding our predicament, our electrically configured whirl" (*Medium*, p. 150), even if we forces of danger are amplified in the current environment by increased human-made interference: "the strom of which Poe spoke in 1850 was nothing compared to the stroms in which we are involved at the present moment" ("Art as Survival," 2003/1973, p. 212). He is imagining resonance between then and now, not identical matching and flawless transfer. Indeed there are several layers of mediation between the Mariner's experience (if ever actual) and how we experience it. First, the Mariner recreates his experience for the listener-figure within the tale, using both narrative and performative/immersive elements. He leads a trembling listener-figure to a precarious cliff overlooking the sea, "A panorama more deplorably desolate no human imagination can conceive" ("Maelstrom," p. 2); apart from visual scene, wind and wave are "howling and shrieking" ("Maelstrom," p. 2). This retelling comes as close as possible to the actual experience, attempting to surmount the gap built into remediation to maximize connection between experience and mediated account. As readers, we are at further remove as we receive the written version of Poe's story, so that the whole is mediated through language. As McLuhan's reader's, the gap widens as we encounter excerpts of the tale filtered and recontextualized as references in McLuhan's texts. This reliance on the practice of telling and referential citing conveys McLuhan's sense that remediations allow for important transfer between original moment or event and later reception, although many elements are lost or changed in transmission.

McLuhan believed (along with Poe's Mariner) in the educative efficacy of sharing stories. Between moments and events then and now, there are abiding continuities—along the lines of Gregory Bateson's "pattern of patterns" (1979, p. 11)—so that there is resonance with repetition. By directing readers to find valuable insights in Poe's tale, McLuhan conveys that pattern finding is not confined to probing immediate experience but involves reviewing the past for clues and precedents, bringing to mind Alfred Korzybski's "time-binding" theory, which Lance Strate tells us refers "to the distinctly human capability to preserve and pass on what we learn from one generation to the next ... made possible by the fact that we have at our disposal the tools of language and symbolic communication, which allow us to store and transmit information from one individual to another, and within groups of individuals" (*Concerning Communication*, 2022, pp. 70–71). In Poe's tale, McLuhan provides a teaching guide rather than exact model, one involving readers in meaning making, so that to borrow another General Semantics theme, map is not territory. McLuhan assumes that the epistemic power of story is such that even when time, place, and scale change, we can none the less make connections and identify patterns that speak to us, providing a sense of continuity that, as the Mariner states, can "introduce the dawn of a more exciting hope" ("Maelstrom," p. 11). The connection McLuhan set up between crisis and hope in the Mariner's day and his own is much like the connection considered here between McLuhan's day and ours. Connections across time also arise when he conflates the setting of Poe's story with antiquity by referring to "whirlpool" as "labyrinth" (*Mechanical Bride*, 1951, p. v), indicating the tale has roots in Ancient dilemmas as well as reaching forward with meaning now. This transfer backward and forward across time comes with both links and gaps and implicitly call upon readers to determine similarity and difference.

According to the tale, all technologies can be managed but introduce laddered dangers—and we need to remember that media and technology for McLuhan are everything that is a product of human ingenuity, from language to clothing and cars to computers. The boat and sea journeys are, as John Durham Peters explains, "an enduring metaphor of the ways in which we stake our survival on artificial habitats amid hostile elements—that is of our radical dependence on technics" (*Clouds*, 2015, p. 101). Here, the boat—media in McLuhan's sense of being something built—puts the human body at sea and at risk; the body only survives by attaching itself to another human-made artifact, the cask. Technology introduces risks, but also options and opportunities. We must use what we have: the Mariner must select the best options so that he survives with technology rather than being sunk by it. Adapting to evolving circumstances is a McLuhan axiom: *Understanding the world is an ongoing process, trumping faulty and incomplete explanations* that depend on the limitations of language systems ("The Argument," p. 4) and the assumptions that truth is fixed rather than resonant and something made and remade.

The Mariner's parable offers hope. His survival shows that adjustment is possible and crisis will eventually abate. The cost of survival is steep, however. The survivor loses everything formerly cherished—others, objects, and occupation—and must take on the heavy burden of mentoring others. His jagged journey is resonant with Blake's poetic explorations of moving from innocence to experience. Signifying transformation, the Mariner's raven-black hair turns white ("Maelstrom," p. 11). While McLuhan often dodged summative pronouncements—as strategy to draw readers into the sense-making process—this sentence crystallizes his and the Mariner's undertaking: "Truth is something we make with all our senses in a conscious process of remaking the world as the world remakes us physically, psychically and socially" ("The Argument," p. 17).

Transcending the Maelstrom: Art and Science

In McLuhan's summary, the Mariner survived "by studying the action of the whirlpool and by cooperating with it" (*Mechanical Bride*, p. v). The everyman Mariner as problem-solver brings to life McLuhan's concerns about the limited knowledge of experts and those working from within disciplinary confines. They can mistake accumulated wisdom for "facts." A layperson is more likely to think on their feet, like Poe's Mariner "to explore actual processes from every side" ("Maelstrom," p. 11). The drive of traditional Western science to provide answers and impose systemic order can be its weakness, and McLuhan quotes Kuhn to further explain discovery as occurring when the assertions of science are overturned: "Discovery comes with the awareness of anomaly i.e., with the recognition that nature has somehow violated the paradigm, induced expectations that govern normal science" (qtd. in "The Argument," p. 4). The Mariner unlocks formulates the idea that shape rather than size accounts for buoyancy in a counterintuitive leap based on the memory that cylinders are "absorbed the more slowly" ("Maelstrom," p. 12).

The Mariner succeeds by "re-cognizing process patterns in the ground of existence" ("The Argument," p. 6). He must abandon his common-sense assumption that larger items offer protection—an assumption that kills his brother. Describing the need to test one's own personal beliefs, McLuhan cited the British Romantic poet Samuel Taylor Coleridge on the narrow-mindedness of experiential thinking alone: "To most men, experience is like the stern lights of a ship, which illumine only the track it has passed" ("The Argument," p. 6). The Mariner enacts "formal cause" thinking which for McLuhan means taking notice of what is hidden from view: "The effects come before the causes in all situations. The *ground* comes before the *figure in* all situations. With any new innovation, people are always able to say, 'The time is ripe,' meaning the *ground* and the effects have come long before the causes" ("Art as Survival," p. 212). The Mariner succeeds by responding to a dynamic environmental situation: observing, sensing, and making fresh connections.

This process of discovery does not counter scientific method but reveals this method alone is not enough. Scientific method combined with artistic insight aligns observation and measurement with intuition and imagination. Like an artist, the Mariner calls on finely tuned "perceptual apparatus" that enable him "to survive in a rapidly developing environment" ("Art as Survival," p. 208). The artist also melds scientific inquiry with creativity to enable "pattern recognition"; the Mariner's story provides "a parable of the artist's role in descending into dangerous waters" ("Art as Survival," p. 212) to emerge with insight that challenges quotidian experience and practices.

Transcending the Maelstrom: Spirit and Matter

The Mariner is transfixed by moment and scene, even melded into it. The distinction between human and environment, inner and outer, erodes, as being bonds with the elements and the material environment. Giving into "unnatural curiosity" and even "deleterious" speculation ("Maelstrom," p. 11), the Mariner ultimately relaxes intentional thinking to have an out-of-body experience—transforming ordinary consciousness. The transformative effects are clearly visible: after the Mariner "breaks through" and survives, he is unrecognizable, his black hair whitened; he says his old companions "knew me no more than they would have known a traveler from the spirit-land" ("Maelstrom," p. 13).

This brings us to the part of the story that is harder to analyze, the part depicting spiritual journey, so that like Wordsworth's speaker in "Tintern Abbey," the Mariner is able "to see into the life of things" (stanza 2). Isabelle Stengers laments the "ban" on talking about God driving post-Kantian Western philosophy, so that before-Kant philosophers felt "free to speculate about God," but after-Kant avoid "ultimate realities" that defy reason and proof (*Thinking With Whitehead*, 2011, p. 8). She says if we do not reintroduce irrational powers of faith and magic that were part of consciousness and cosmos before modernist rationality, we will "experience a certain shame and great sadness at having dismissed the age-old traditions—from the auguries of antiquity to those of seers, Taro readers, or cowrie shell diviners—as superstition" (*Catastrophe*, 2015, p. 149). A Whitehead scholar, she argues that Whitehead's relational vision drove his refusal to rule anything out, and that he embarked on speculative thought adventure that gave up sureties "to 'trust' in the possibility of a solution that remains to be created" (*Thinking With Whitehead*, p. 15). While Whitehead's may be a conceptual adventure and the Mariner's more directly experiential, they share trust in creativity and the possibility of an emergent solution beyond the powers of human reason alone. McLuhan's explorations link to theirs. While McLuhan talked about human technology as figure, the ground of this discussion was faith in the possibility of identifying pattern continuity. He never tired of telling us to pay attention to the unseen—to open our senses to take in more and to open ourselves to the presence of magic and spirit, also operant as invisible elements. Germane here to the transformative aspects of the Mariner's experience is Eric McLuhan's discussion of transformation in Catholic faith tradition, whose sacraments, involving faith and participation, "instantly transform the participant" and make "permanent and indelible marks on the soul of the participant" ("*The Sensus Communis*," 2015, p. 114).

In *Down to Earth* (2017), Bruno Latour contemporizes the reading of the Mariner as salutary figure. His Mariner is one who gives up both local (communal and place-based) and global (capitalist and colonial) values to assume more broad-based understanding of Terrestrial responsibility: "How can anyone agree voluntarily to turn toward the third attractor [the terrestrial] when one was headed tranquilly toward the horizon of universal modernization? To agree to look unblinkingly at such a situation is to position oneself like the hero of Edgar Allen Poe's short story, 'Descent into the Maelstrom'" (p. 44). Although Latour is unfamiliar with McLuhan's fascination with Poe's story, his enthusiasm for the Mariner's survival skills and valour strike similar notes: "One has to be as astute as the old sailor to believe that escape is possible, to keep playing close attention to the wreckage as it drifts: such attention may make it possible to understand suddenly why some of the debris is sucked toward the bottom while other objects, because of their form, can serve as preservers" (*Down to Earth*, p. 45). Along with sharing McLuhan's appreciation of Poe's story, Latour attends to Alfred North Whitehead's God and cosmology in a way that can inform reading McLuhan. As McLuhan did, Whitehead refused the modernist "bifurcation of nature," bifurcation being, as Latour tells us, what happens whenever we think "the world is divided into two sets of things," one composed of "the fundamental constituents of the universe—invisible to the eye, known to science, real and yet valueless" and another constituted by what the mind adds to make sense of these basic building blocks ("Foreword," "*Thinking With Whitehead*," 2011, p. xii). To illustrate he provides an example from Whitehead's *Concept of Nature*, where Whitehead pointed out that fire means little to us if we describe it as "molecules, electrons and ether" rather than in perceptual terms like "warmth and redness". Here is Whitehead's stated objection to bifurcation as leading to false cause-and effect thinking and dividing scientific thinking from artistic creativity and expression: "Unless we produce the all-embracing relations, we are faced with a bifurcated nature; namely warmth and redness one side, and molecules, electrons, and ether on the other side. Then the two factors are explained as being respectively the cause and the mind's reaction to the cause" (*Concept*, 1964, p. 32). We can trace in McLuhan's work the "God-function" Latour says is imbedded in Whitehead's philosophical propositions; "if nature can't be seen as bifurcated, if actual occasions are the stuff out of which the world is made... if eternal objects are there as guardians against the shift back to substance and foundations, then a God-function is implied" ("Foreword," *Thinking with Whitehead*, p. xiii). Latour points out that most modern philosophers contend there is no need for God, yet there is evidence of "their crossed out god" in the gaps of their reasoning ("Foreword," *Thinking with Whitehead*, p. xv). McLuhan deliberately limits his references to his Christian God—presumably to widen the range of his appeal to readers. Yet his belief in eternal if reconfiguring elements—and in our ability to recognize emergent patterns as objective formations rather than subjective constructions—points to a God principle or function implicated in the work of world-making.

All this sketches how the spiritual dimension of Poe's story was part of the story's appeal for McLuhan and Latour. Poe's epigraph addresses God not only as spiritual guide but as active and implicated principle: "The ways of God in Nature, as in Providence, are not as our ways; nor are the models that we frame any way commensurate to the vastness, profundity, and unsearchableness of His works" ("Maelstrom," p. 1). The Mariner's experience is unified or monistic—"non-bifurcated" in Whitehead's terms—in a "spirit-world" ("Maelstrom," p. 13) where opposites collide and co-exist, as given in the image of the terrible beauty of the whirlpool, a black hole lit on the surface by overhead moon rays and rainbow radiance: "The rays of the moon seemed to search the very bottom of the profound gulf; but still I could make out nothing distinctly on account of a thick mist in which everything there was enveloped, and over which there hung a magnificent rainbow, like that narrow and tottering bridge which Musselmen say is the only pathway between Time and eternity" ("Maelstrom," p. 10). The Mariner's journey is in this way spiritual and revelatory of eternal principles.

Are We All in the Same Boat?

Whether we face crisis together, united as human species, or whether there is room for disparate responses—many boats and journeys—has been debated by those resisting humanism as a category errant in clustering all humans together as if experiences are shared and equitable. Theorists as varied as public intellectual

Jared Diamond (in Gardels, 2020) and radical design theorist Benjamin Bratton (2022) have pointed to the recent world health crisis as urging recognition that we are all in the same boat and need to take collective action. If they see ours as a provocative transition moment requiring political strategies favoring universalism, others warn against the unfairness of collective solutions and universalizing logic. Marginalized people who have contributed least to global climate degradation and economic disparity should not be burdened with payback and asked to assume solidarity with colonizing perpetrators. In *Designs for the Pluriverse*, Arturo Escobar describes how the global south is resisting the imposition of universalist hegemonic-friendly approaches to pursue local cultural and economic programs, development he defines as guided by "design autonomy" (2018, pp. 184–85). He argues we are not in the same boat—that any such ride sharing would involve endorsing oppressive values of capitalism and colonialism rather than providing liberatory opportunities.

McLuhan took a "both/and" view of the commons as planetary and localized. Sketching incoming political change, he envisioned some form of planetary union, with "ministates" in "a totally retribalized world" (*Playboy*, p. 258). A successful transition would require allowing diverse practices within a common compact, so that "throughout the world" people would be "united into a single tribe [yet] they will forge a diversity of viable decentralized political and social institutions" (*Playboy*, p. 258). There is a universalism in his call, yet in speculating about its roll out, he speaks of regional implementation: sub-groups or tribes that are in tune with local needs. Also notable is that recent theorists are less prone to imagining a heroic loner figure like the Mariner—perhaps making McLuhan's point that we are moving from foregrounding autonomy and individuality to relational identity. Offsetting the individual quest figure, McLuhan often envisions futurity as collective undertaking. His images of "spaceship earth," for example, emphasized meeting challenge collectively, with all passengers contributing to the journey as crew ("End of Work Ethic," p. 193). There are two story arcs at play: individuals need to exercise autonomous responsibilities and improve self-understanding; there are also collaborative and cooperate obligations, to establish commonalities and caring. We save ourselves and we save others.

Picking up many McLuhanesque strands, Latour and Stengers continue exploring the possibility of exercising personal responsibility as well as exercising communal consciousness. What can a human do to survive? What does survival require and deliver? What are the survivor's responsibilities? What is owed to others and to earth? Poe's Mariner as survivor does more than live to see another day or earn more earthly time. Transformed, the Mariner gains a sense of awe. He sees relationship, process and interconnection where there had been fragmentation and disunity. McLuhan would agree with Stengers that we need "all peoples acknowledging that we are in the same boat," not with universalized claims and histories but envisioning a shared future that is still in the making "liable to political reinvention" (*Another Science*, 2013, p. 151). His view also endorses—as variant of his mosaic imagery—Stengers' call for storytelling as sharing perspectives such that there is "a weaving of regenerative, slightly transgressive Imaginations ... for reclaiming a future worth living" (p. 156).

Changing: Incoming Aurality

McLuhan saw the electric age introducing figure/ground shifts in every domain; as he said in *The Medium is the Massage* (1967): "Electric circuitry has overthrown the regime of 'time' and 'space' and pours upon us instantly and continuously the concerns of other men. . . Its message is Total Change" (p. 16). Media ecologist Christine Nystrom puts the problem of too much information this way: "Like the Sorcerer's Apprentice, we are awash in a flood of information. And all the sorcerer has left is a broom ... We are swamped in information, drowning in it. And we don't know how to reduce it to manageable propositions, or organize it coherently, or sort the relevant from the irrelevant" ("The Crisis," 1989, pp. 183–84). Loss of framework or ordering principles incited McLuhan's claim that humanity is in the process of abandoning principles of visual order in moving to less structured aurality. Moving into aurality, nothing is established, stable, and predictable—we live "without fixed boundaries" and assume that self and world are "dynamic, always in flux creating its own dimensions moment by moment" ("Acoustic Space," 1997/1960, in Moos, p. 39). To navigate, he described exercising immersive sentience rather than mere watchfulness; we do not want to depend on the eye that "focuses, pinpoints, abstracts, locating each object in physical space, against a background," but want to use the ear that "favors sound from any direction" ("Acoustic Space," p. 41).

The visual culture of modernity was anchored in print literacy, relying on a "process of uniformization" to circulate ideas or "instructions" as a kind of cultural propaganda (*Gutenberg*, 1962, pp. 196–97). As we move out of Gutenberg-fashioned culture, we can more readily discern its primary features of homogeneity, uniformity, and continuity—empire building features, McLuhan argued, enabling consolidation, unlike oral cultures that "defy definitions and orderly categories" and "no uniform processing" (*Understanding Media*, p. 123). For individuals, Gutenberg culture nurtured a sense of privacy, a sense of being distinct from others and even unique, which led to achievements requiring concentration and specialization. Before this, in preliterate cultures—without print to disconnect and distance thought from things—humans engaged the total sensorium, connecting action /thought/ feeling and attached to human and non-human lives around them. Words spoken in oral cultures were seen as active and alive "natural forces"—incantatory or magical—until print literacy changed "the notion of words as 'meaning' or 'significance' for minds" (*Gutenberg*, 1962, p. 23).

As we enter "new aurality," individuality recedes. The major ache of the new mode of collective being is loss of definition; the major advantage is the opportunity to reactivate the sensorium, putting more senses into interactive play and connecting us more intensely to the world and others, to expand our sense of consciousness, finding it more than "a verbal process" (*Understanding Media*, p. 121). Whereas literacy as a system supports analysis and separation for the imposition of order, the new way forward offers opportunities for "wholeness"—for a more integrated "imaginative, emotional, and sense life" (*Understanding Media*, p. 124).

In McLuhan's view, the process of responding to environmental change was work for all of us. Rather than continuing business as usual—shoring up boundaries, developing regulations and documents (however aspirational of protecting rights and freedoms), continuing to build cities as of old—he called on humans to begin reactivating the sensorium and finding new ways of understanding and communicating. Binaries and divisions would become like outworn index cards or shelving. Part of defining ourselves as relational creatures would mean discarding anthropocentric exceptionalism and instead conceiving of ourselves as part of earth and cosmos.

Breaking: End of Nature

McLuhan claimed nature ended once we ringed the planet with satellites, "placing it inside a man-made environment" (*Take Today*, 1972, p. 294). He meant there was no non-mediated wilderness left, no portion of earth, sea, or air free of human touch/taint. Yet for McLuhan "nature" was never more than a concept "invented" by the Greeks to abstract it "from total existence" ("The Argument", p. 2). In his view, we develop the language we need for the concepts we have in mind. With quantum relations, we no longer need neat divisions between nature and culture, nor between what is natural and artificial; the new model needs vocabulary for crossing and collision. He was aware of entropy principles holding that differences and definitions are destined to weaken as things slide together: as the principle of relationality trumps differentiation.

For McLuhan, the "end of nature" was one of many endings, in a world where one thing affects all others. He forecast the collapse of print and literacy, of cities and nations and political systems: "The end of the line" (*Medium*, 1967, p. 72). He foresaw a potential end to autonomy and experiencing the world directly, described this way in *From Cliché to Archetype*: "The results of living inside a proscenium arch of satellites is that the young now accept the public spaces of earth as role playing arenas. Sensing this they adopt costumes and roles and are ready to 'do their thing' everywhere" (1970, p. 10). He saw "staged happenings" demonstrating such roleplay, where participants assume group identity in an environment of electric artifice designed to stimulate the human sensorium in ways that can energize or shock and overwhelm. In a world of screens and stimulus directing what we see and feel, there is less room for comedy and tragedy that rest on human-to-human exchange; we inhabit a mediated world McLuhan called "the rag and bone shop of the global wasteland of Shakespeare & Co" (*From Cliché,* p. 10). (Shakespeare's Globe Theatre contemporized for McLuhan as the "global theatre.") In all cases, rather than elegizing collapse, McLuhan invited recognition of what might be saved or salvaged. This world shattering can be the end or a new direction.

The final pages of *War and Peace in the Global Village* (1968) dig into how loss of traditional evolutionary science requires new linguistic terms and categories. In a dark take on the "End of Nature" theme, McLuhan swapped the logics of Darwinian evolution for technological innovation shorn of biological purpose or urge. He cited biologist Ernst Mayr's description of evolution—a "well-integrated co-adapted system" (p. 188)—threatened by technological development driven by mere convenience and availability: "There is no mechanism [as technology develops] that would prevent such a destruction of genetically superior combinations and there is, therefore, no possibility of gradual improvement of genetic combinations" (Mayr, qtd. in *War and Peace*, p. 188). For humans who have "outered" limbs, nerves and mind, McLuhan speculated that evolutionary energy now resides outside the body in external elements, as we meld with techno-artifice (p. 190). No longer a species evolving within an ecology, we are buffeted by technological innovations and conditions.

He urged two (related) defenses. First, we need to reactivate the human sensorium. The second line of defense is more exploratory: if mind is now outside as well as inside the body, we need will and process to protect inner operations and bridge inner and outer zones. The sensorium is powerful in ways unknown to most. Exemplifying this, McLuhan cited blind WWII French War hero, Jacques Lusseyran, who wrote of "sensing" in place of "seeing" as enabling him to know of enemy presence and save lives under siege (*And There was Light*, 1963). If the senses can do more than we know—if they are not entirely bounded by brain and body, as commonly conceived, but capable of roaming in ways we disregard—such sensory operation may engender new intensities and affect, rather than allowing technologies outside the body to filter and feed information (as dreaded in our current AI scare).

Making: Art, Sensorium and New Commons

For McLuhan, artists possess elevated sensory capabilities—their senses are more active, multiple, and balanced, attuned to "high perception and interplay of all the senses" to create art that "to the visually oriented and literary, seems haunted, magical, and often incomprehensible" ("Five Sense Sensorium," 1961, p. 50). Such art can reveal "each object as a world and the world as an object," in lieu of reproducing the rational world of visual thinking. In "Art as Survival in the Electric Age" (2003/1973), McLuhan proposed that because we now live in an "artificial environment"—with technologies subduing brain and neural activity that had served as "natural equipment"—art can provide "a liaison between biology and technology" (p. 207). The artist's role is to give sustenance to "the perceptual apparatus that enables us to survive in a rapidly developing environment" (p. 208).

While artists can be guides, McLuhan wanted everyone more mindful of how to resist the pressures of technology. *City as Classroom* (1977) is a primer pushing young adults to train and deepen perceptual activity. It gives directions for taking in more of the material environment, for looking/listening/smelling and sensing one's surroundings, and for multi-sensory apprehension of both obvious figures and recessive background features. Less literal are directions for identifying environmental propaganda that shapes language and habits and hopes. As Philip Marchand notes in his biography, McLuhan wanted to correct radical educator Ivan Illich who recommended abandoning schools by counter arguing for schools as places to study "the *real education* children were receiving from the electronic media" (pp. 274—75). Along with extending perceptual activity, McLuhan's curriculum called for identifying how various media act for us in ways that block sensory and cognitive opportunities. McLuhan relied on figure and ground from Gestalt theory to convey the vastness of untapped perceptual potential: we exclude more of the environment than we take in by failing to engage sensory organs and nerves. In *War and Peace in the Global Village* (1968), he quoted extensively from Otto Lowenstein's *The Senses* to explain seeing as calculated, inculcated with habit, and regulated by language and naming: "The saying 'seeing is believing' may fittingly be reversed in this context into 'believing is seeing'" (qtd. in *War and Peace*, p. 11).

Rather than taking in fresh sensory information, we too often operate robotically with "unconscious and automatic ... reflex reactions" (qtd. in *War and Peace*, p. 19).

In McLuhan's model of futuristic governance, artists lead and teach, but there is two-way communication with citizens. In imagining a forum for experts and publics to pool insights, McLuhan was exploring the power of collectivity as many did in his day. In *Technocrats of the Imagination* (2020), Beck and Bishop explore mid-century fascination with collectivity as a force promoting creative energy and a power balance. This urge extends into our century, according to Stimson and Shollette (2006), who examine the growth of collectivism in late- and postmodernism when "culture was everywhere, no longer the property of the cultured or cultivated"; they contend that the desire to speak collectively "has long fueled the social imagination of artists," continuing from postwar culture "to pry open the social narratives of today" (p. 9). McLuhan's envisioned incoming "tribalism" as a potentially unifying cultural form, yet he also cautioned that, unmarshalled, it could provoke factionalism and blood and soil territoriality. By harnessing "here comes everybody" spirit, we can cultivate a sense of shared planetary (even cosmic) membership, while still honoring localized affiliation based on particularized affinities. As part of our new collectivism, we can be both planetary citizens and members of local communities *(War and Peace*, p. 23), and thus experience new levels of relational identity and commitment.

McLuhan's artists in control tower positions contribute to new civic order and governance. They also control the sensory climate of a networked environment by influencing a collective audience: they can spark "sensuous involvement" for a new cultural dispensation that replaces self-involvement. To direct culture from a "control tower" position (*Understanding Media*, p. 96) was not to tower over others but to be alert to environmental impacts and interactions and adjust these for benign purposes: "The computer will be in a position to carry out orchestrated programming for the sensory life of entire populations. It can be programmed in terms of their total needs...[and] of the total experience as picked up and patterned by all the senses at once" ("Invisible Environment," 1967, p. 166). If science delivers advances in computer technology, artists advise on sensory experience, to "program the entire environment responsively as a work of art" ("Emperor's Old," 1966, p. 93). Control tower positioning meant abandoning "the shaping of art objects, in order to program the environment itself" ("Emperor's Old," p. 94). To parse this is to say that art works with science and technology to create a responsive environment, whose purpose is to involve and inform publics who assume participatory and interactive roles.

McLuhan imagined the interplay of art, science and citizen awareness as capable of creating new forms of community and consciousness. As I explored in

McLuhan's Techno-Sensorium City (2021), one of the ways he described new planetary unity and human consciousness was by referring to a merger of Eastern and Western values, "creating conditions that favour equality—that do not discriminate on the basis of race, gender or wealth, since these categories of identity will lose their meaning" (p. 15). On both project and governance levels, artists "create optimal levels of interaction between media and the human senses" (*McLuhan's Techno-Sensorium*, p. 64) in ways that promote happiness and health in local and planetary community (p. 64).

Hoping: "nothing is inevitable" ("Foreword," Postman on McLuhan, 1997, xii)

Cultivating "understanding" and encouraging it to salvage and shape the future was, according to Neil Postman, McLuhan's true legacy ("Foreword," 1997, in Marchand, p. xii). According to Postman, McLuhan was a "prophet of hope" in dark times when many of his contemporaries despaired of stalled progress, stale and shallow conformity, media exploitation and ecological pollution. McLuhan's vision appealed to young people for encouraging citizen involvement in preparing for a future laden with changes—for arguing as anti-determinist "Nothing is inevitable" (p. xii).

Recent critical reception has cooled, particularly in areas of critical theory that dispute McLuhan's contribution and fit to progressive projects. For those seeking social change, McLuhan is sometimes dismissed as conservative, even reactionary, for advocating understanding in place of change making. For generating ways to play safe with technologies he saw as embedded, he is said to have failed to resist corporate media interests (now swollen into global platforms) and, wittingly or not, served as confederate. Political theorist Jodi Dean is impatient with approaches like his that assume the equalizing effects of citizen participation, which she argues are performative gestures masking the ongoing concentration of power: "Rhetorics of access, participation, and democracy work ideologically to secure the technological infrastructure of neoliberalism, an invidious and predatory politico-economic project that concentrates assets and power in the hands of the very rich, devastating the planet, and destroying the lives of billions of people" (2009, p. 23). Another objection is McLuhan's lack of advocacy for non-human species or habitat. Ignoring resource exploitation and dismissing nature as nothing other than an "invented" linguistic concept ("The Argument," p. 1) can sound glib. As noted earlier in this chapter, his frequent allusions to the end of nature mean primarily that nothing remains wild and unmediated. While he usually pronounced this death in neutral terms, dismay occasionally breaks in, as in saying our heavy imprint on earth has made a "junk yard of environmental change," littered with device detritus (*Playboy*, p. 158). His short film, *A Burning Woulde*, made with Jane Jacobs to stop expansion of a Toronto freeway, revealed his layered understanding of environmental deterioration (McLeod Rogers, *Techno-Sensorium*, pp. 116–19)—with references to the blight of roads and tracks cutting across green fields, to noise pollutants, waste and crowding.

There is also uneasiness about McLuhan on matters of race and gender. He did not engage with feminist issues. His race consciousness has been seen as inflected with the thoughtless racism of mid-century colonialism—othering BIPOC people in the guise of praising perceived qualities of difference (Towns, 2022). There's little question that McLuhan's language that uses "civilization" to refer to literate culture and "tribalism" as throwback practice is problematic, especially with principled inclusivity now part of scholarly work supporting reconciliation and respect for diverse cultural experiences and voices. There are also problems with his "us and them" references to East and West divisions, heard now as exoticizing "the other" in attempted praise.

Whether and what role McLuhan will play as canon, culture, and epistemic practice are reformulated and reimagined is still being explored as scholars look for productive vectors between traditional and non-traditional epistemologies. John Durham Peters suggests we might "take his analysis without taking his attitude" ("Reading," 2019, p. 496); Sarah Sharma points out we can "travel with McLuhan without necessarily taking him along for the entire ride" (2019, p. 484). In recent dialogue, rhetoricians Kristin Arola and Thomas Rickert challenge dominant Euro-centric and settler scripts and voices focusing on Latour. They move from questioning why he does not invoke Indigenous theory to whether non-Indigenous scholars should avoid representing Indigenous perspectives to avoid appropriation and flattening. Arola asks: "Are we really looking for Latour to weigh in on Indigenous thoughts on the climate? He's a French intellectual steeped in the sciences, grounded in some interesting strains of Catholicism with antimodern tendencies" (2022, p. 194). In its main points, this description of Latour characterizes McLuhan; how these tendencies affect reader response and determinations of relevance remain at issue. For some, their theory will be tainted and time worn; others want a big tent and deliberately look for generative connections. Something that may be worth bearing in mind is that in his day, McLuhan challenged traditional Western views by adopting principles of relationality. For example, he did not essentialize West and East, but imagined shared qualities as foregrounded and recessive in characterizing each. Perhaps this book can contribute to scholarly reconsiderations of McLuhan's place in developing theoretical models.

For McLuhan, the struggle to survive faces heavy odds. Human action and ingenuity are hugely influential, with potential to be productive or destructive. Human understanding is partial and limited. Add to this we live in a time of change and innovation, so what we do understand needs constant updating. No wonder, then, he urged expanding the process of understanding by activating the tapped and unused human sensorium. A dynamic formal cause environment of the sort he imagined can never be fully known; we need to perform as lifelong learners, tuning our sensorium to take in and integrate responses. McLuhan advocated for using methods of science and art: all of us engaged in inquiry using the fullest range of our senses, making connections and "sense" and then sharing what we learn and know with others. In the vein of current theorists who acknowledge our irreversible dependencies on machines—like Joi Ito in "Resisting Reduction" (2017) and those continuing his arguments in *Against Reduction* (2021)—he foresaw the need to resist computational reductions by asserting human and relational values.

McLuhan's program was short on proposals for ameliorative and immediate social change yet value-oriented in defending against a future of profit-driven and potentially rogue technologies. His exploratory inquiry studied emergent conditions, shaped by multiple pressures such as waves of technological innovation and less visibly by flights and limits of human apprehension. His way forward was neither to adjust current systems nor propose a definite alternative but to speculate about possible futures using a flexible framework. For him, positive future direction ruled out being controlled by science and the rigid predictabilities of AI regulation. He hoped artists could share information about and contribute to shaping technologies in support of complex humanistic values. Such values were not necessarily human-centered, but those promoting peaceful connections amongst planetary groups and between human and non-human realms—perhaps even between earth and the universes beyond. For McLuhan hoped for nothing less than a path to "cosmic harmony" (*Playboy*, p. 268).

References

Arista, N. et al. (2021). *Against reduction: Designing a human future with machines*. MIT Press.

Arola, K., & Rickert, T. (2022). The ancestors we claim: Conversations toward a future new materialism across boundaries. *Rhetoric Society Quarterly, 52*(2), 190–198. https://doi.org/10.1080/02773945.2022.2032815

Bateson, G. (1979). *Mind and nature*. Dutton.

Beck, J., & Bishop, R. (2020). *Technocrats of the imagination: Art, technology, and the military-industrial avant-garde.* Duke University Press.

Bratton, B. H. (2022). *Revenge of the real: Politics for a post-pandemic world.* Verso.

Dean J. (2009). *Democracy and other neo-liberal fantasies: Communicative capitalism and left politics.* Duke University Press.

Escobar, A. (2018). *Designs for the pluriverse: Radical interdependence, autonomy, and the making of worlds.* Duke University Press.

Gardels, N. (2020, July 28). Jared Diamond: Why nations fail or succeed when facing a crisis. *Noēma.* https://www.noemamag.com/jared-diamond-why-nations-fail-or-succeed-when-facing-a-crisis/

Hayles, N. K. (2024). Detoxifying cybernetics: From homeostasis to autopoiesis and beyond. In Yuk Hui (Ed.), *Cybernetics for the 21st century* (pp. 85–100). Hanart Press.

Howes, D. (2022). *The sensory studies manifesto: Tracking the sensorial revolution in the arts and human sciences.* University of Toronto Press.

Howes, D. (2024). *Sensorium: Contextualizing the senses and cognition in history and across cultures.* Cambridge University Press.

Ito, J. (2017). *Resisting reduction: A manifesto: designing our complex future with machines.* MIT. https://jods.mitpress.mit.edu/pub/resisting-reduction/release/19

Kitnick, A. (2021). *Distant early warning: Marshall McLuhan and the transformation of the avant-garde.* The University of Chicago Press.

Latour, B. (2011). What is given in experience? [Foreword]. In I. Stenger (Ed.), *Thinking with Whitehead: A free and wild creation of concepts* (pp. ix–xix, M. Chase, Trans.). Harvard UP (Original work published 2002).

Latour, B. (2018). *Down to Earth: Politics in the new climatic regime* (C. Porter, Trans.). Polity. (Original work published 2017)

Lusseyran, J. (1968). *And there was light: Autobiography of Jacques Lusseyran: Hero of the* French Revolution. New World Library. (Original work published in 1963).

McLeod Rogers, J. (2021). *McLuhan's techno-sensorium city: Coming to our senses in a programmed environment.* Lexington Books.

McLuhan, M. (1951). *The mechanical bride: Folklore of industrial man.* Beacon Press.

McLuhan, M. (1961). Inside the five sense sensorium. *The Canadian Architect.* (June), 49–51.

McLuhan, M. (1962). *The Gutenberg galaxy: The making of a typographic man.* University of Toronto Press.

McLuhan, M. (1966). The emperor's old clothes. In G. Kepes (Ed.), The *man-made object* (pp. 90–95). George Braziller.

McLuhan, M. (1967). The invisible environment: The future of an erosion. *Perspecta, 11,* 161–167. http://www.jstor.org/stable/1566945 .

McLuhan, M. (1974). At the Moment of Sputnik the planet became a global theatre in which there are no spectators but only actors. *Journal of Communications.* March. https://doi.org/10.1111/j.1460-2466.1974.tb00354.x

McLuhan, M. (1987). *Letters of Marshall McLuhan*. In M. Molinaro, C. McLuhan, & W. Toye (Eds.), Oxford University Press.

McLuhan, M. (1997). Acoustic space. In M. Moos (Ed.), *Media research: Technology, art and communication* (pp. 86–90). G+B Arts International. (Original work published 1960).

McLuhan, M. (1997). Notes on Burroughs. In M. Moos (Ed.), *Media research: Technology, art and communication* (pp. 86–90). G+B Arts International. (Original work published 1964).

McLuhan, M. (1997). The *Playboy* Interview: A candid conversation with the high priest of popcult and metaphysician of media. In F. Zingrone & E. McLuhan (Eds.), *Essential McLuhan* (pp. 233–269). Routledge. (Original published in 1969).

McLuhan, M. (2003). [Lecture, 1966]. The medium is the massage. In S. McLuhan & D. Staines (Eds.), *Understanding me: Lectures/interviews* (pp. 76–97). McClelland &Stewart.

McLuhan, M. (2003). [Address, given 1972]. The end of the work ethic. In S. McLuhan & D. Staines (Eds.), *Understanding me: Lectures/interviews* (pp. 187–205). McClelland & Stewart.

McLuhan, M. (2003). [Lecture, 1973]. Art as survival in the electric age. In S. McLuhan & D. Staines (Eds.), *Understanding me: Lectures/interviews* (pp. 206–224). McClelland & Stewart.

McLuhan, M. (2003). *Understanding media: The extensions of man* (Critical ed.), (W. Terrence Gordon, Ed.). Gingko Press. (Original work published 1964).

McLuhan, E. (2015). *The sensus communis, synesthesia, and the soul: An odyssey*. BPS Books.

McLuhan, M., & Fiore, Q. (1967). *The medium is the massage: An inventory of effects*. Gingko Press.

McLuhan, M., Fiore, Q., & Agel, J. (1968). *War and peace in the global village*. Bantam.

McLuhan, M., & McLuhan E. (2011). *Media and formal cause*. NeoPoiesis Press.

McLuhan, M., McLuhan, E., & Huchon, K. (1977). *City as classroom: Understanding language and media*. Book Society of Canada.

McLuhan, M., & Nevitt, B. (1973). The argument: Causality in the electric world. *Technology and Culture, 14*(1), 1, 1–18.

McLuhan, M., & Parker, H. (1968). The emperor's new clothes. *Through the vanishing point: Space and poetry and painting*. Harper & Row.

McLuhan M., & Powers, B. R. (1989). *The global village: Transformations in world life and media in the 21st Century*. Oxford University Press.

McLuhan, M., & Watson, W. (1970). *From cliché to archetype*. Viking.

Moos, M. A. (1997). McLuhan's language for awareness under electronic conditions. *Marshall McLhan Essays: Media research; technology, art, communication*. G+B Arts, pp. 140–166.

Nystrom, C. (2020). The crisis of narrative. In C. Wiebe & S. Maushart (Eds.) *The genes of culture: Towards a theory of symbols, meaning, and media, volume 1*. Peter Lang. (Original work published 1989)

Peters, J. D. (2015). *The marvelous clouds: Toward a philosophy of elemental media*. University of Chicago Press.

Peters, J. D. (2019). Reading over McLuhan's shoulder. *Canadian Journal of Communication, 44*(4), 489–501.

Poe, E. A. (1841). *Descent into the maelström.* file: https://ia601906.us.archive.org/14/items/TheWorksOfEdgarAllanPoe/TheWorksOfEdgarAllanPoe.pdf

Postman, N. (1998). Foreword. In P. Marchand (Ed.), *Marshall McLuhan: The medium and the messenger*. Vintage Canada.

Sharma, S. (2019). Many McLuhans or none at all. *Canadian Journal of Communication, 44*(4), 483–488. http://doi.org/10.22230/cjc.2019v44n4a3621

Srnicek, N., & Williams, A. (2014). #Accelerate: Manifesto for an accelerationist politics. In A. Avanessian & R. Mackay (Eds.), *#Accelerate#: The accelerationist reader* (pp. 347–362). Urbanomic.

Stengers, I. (2014). *Thinking with Whitehead: A free and wild creation of concepts* (M. Chase, Trans.). Harvard University Press. (Original work published 2011)

Stengers, I. (2015). *In catastrophic times: Resisting the coming barbarism* (A. Goffey, Trans.). Open Humanities Press/Meson Press. (Original work published 2009)

Stengers, I. (2018). *Another science is possible: A manifesto for slow science* (S. Muecke, Trans.). Polity. (Original work published in 2013)

Stimson, B., & Shollette, G. (2006). *Collectivism after modernism: The art of social imagination after 1945*. University of Minnesota Press.

Strate, L. (2017). The effects that give cause, and the patten that divides. Anton, C., Logan R. K., & Strate, L. (Eds.). *Taking up McLuhan's cause: Perspectives on media and formal causality*. Intellect. pp. 93–119.

Strate, L. (2022). *Concerning communication: Epic quests and lyric excursions within the human lifeworld*. Institute of General Semantics.

Trujillo Linan, L. (2022). *Formal cause in Marshall McLuhan's thinking: An aristotelian perspective*. Institute of General Semantics.

Towns, A. R. (2022). *On Black media philosophy*. University of California Press.

Whitehead, A. N. (1964). *The concept of nature*. Cambridge University Press.

CHAPTER 2

McLuhan's Collaboration with Jaqueline Tyrwhitt: Humanizing Visual and Acoustic Space

"We need to resist the tendency to develop everything that technology makes possible."
—Bell & Tyrwhitt, 1972, p. 144.

McLuhan met urban planner Jaqueline Tyrwhitt through a letter of introduction from art historian and architecture critic Siegfried Giedion (Gordon, 1967 p. 160; *Letters*, 1987, p. 233), when Tyrwhitt came from Europe to assume a faculty position initiating an Urban Planning program at the University of Toronto in 1952. At McLuhan's invitation, she became an active affiliate of the interdisciplinary *Explorations* theory group, formed in 1953 with political economist Tom Easterbrook, psychologist D. Carl Williams and anthropologist Edmund [Ted] Carpenter (Darroch, 2008, p. 148). She forged some connection between Giedion and the group (spurred on by McLuhan who admired Giedion's spatial theorizing), contributed several articles to the journal, and focused the group by recording and archiving meetings, working with McLuhan who was leading the collective.

Her article "The City Unseen" (1955, co-written for *Explorations* with Carl Williams) documented how students move from point "a" to "b" guided more by preconceptions than by actual encounters with visual objects and landscape. McLuhan referred to it as the crowning achievement of the Explorations group—demonstrating an interdisciplinary approach and investigating claims about blinkered perception and cultural propaganda (Shoshkes, 2013, *Transnational*, p. 175).[1]

I will explore how his *City as Classroom* (1977) is both homage to and extension of this groundwork study. Her concern with improving social conditions was related to her commitment to adjusting the urban environment to improve its human appeal and encourage sensory involvement. McLuhan shared this commitment, although over time he grew dismissive of planning activities for improving place and material conditions and wanted more attention paid to the transition from real to virtual and acoustic space. For him, the unseen and unknown futuristic environment became the figure of interest. He established the need for such study in *The Medium is the Massage* (1967): "Environments are invisible. Their ground rules, pervasive structures and overall patterns elude easy perception" (pp. 84–85). He was aware that literacy and attendant visual values retained cultural influence but took these as longstanding cliches compared to the effects of incoming aurality, emergent, amplifying, and for the most part unobserved. He believed if aural culture simply took shape without designed interventions to balance new with old qualities, we would suffer from catastrophic change—lose all sense of order and of agency.

Accord: Turning On the Human Sensorium/Balancing Inner and Outer Fields

McLuhan imagined humans in transition: no longer using bodies or physical places to conduct daily business, and relying more fully on screens, programs, and virtual communication—in a world much like ours now, one reliant on computers more than face-to-face contact. He knew, of course, that housing and social spaces in the built environment would continue to matter—yet found them relatively unimportant compared to the new challenge of imagining an environment for disembodied, dematerialized conditions. Figure-ground Gestalt theory—important to both McLuhan and Tyrwhitt—helps explain McLuhan's sense of the relationship between visible real-life conditions and incoming changes. Our current world is analytical, literate, and visual, with hearing and all other senses in the background, so that we also limit the range of our feelings. We are in the process of flipping this, so that acoustic and virtual life becomes dominant. It is notable that in such figure and ground thinking, nothing is static and essential, but interactive and formative, with mobility and focus determined by viewer positionality and perspective.

Aware of calling for work that lacked precedent or formula, McLuhan charged planners and architects with the difficult task of staging an environment for beings who no longer defined themselves as independent bodies, but as complex organisms balancing multi-level points of exchange within the body and, simultaneously, within the environment. He wanted design that would support a changing "structure of experience," where there would be nothing in isolation, lifting barriers such as those establishing subjective and objective positions and a sense of division between inner and outer being.[2] While he advised accommodating massive incoming changes, he further advised detecting valuable qualities in our current environment and protecting these. Honoring continuity alongside change, he urged preservation and salvaging operations to stave off "cataclysmic" destruction of valuable establishments and practices:

> [If] we diagnose what is happening to us, we can reduce the ferocity of the winds of change and bring the best elements of the old visual culture, during this transitional period, into peaceful coexistence with the new retribalized society. If we persist, however, in our conventional rearview-mirror approach to these cataclysmic developments, all of Western culture will be destroyed and swept into the dustbin of history. (*Playboy*, 1969, p. 265)

Theorizing aside, there's little question he understood the "felt" impact of design and place attributes on quality of life—apparent in his expressed appreciation of his Wychwood Park home in Toronto. He admired the variety of landscape features—with a rippling pond "fed by an artesian spring" and without the dull symmetries such as those imposed to organize newer suburbs—and the fact that "a heavily treed neighbourhood of twenty-three acres and fifty-four houses" existed "in the heart of Toronto" (*Letters*, 1987, p. 375). He especially recommended its circular (as opposed to linear) layout, a spatial arrangement with both aesthetic and social impact. To McLuhan, such circular patterns promote a sense of community without forcing face-to-face contact, gently widening "the family circle" (*Medium is Massage*, p. 14), whereas "lineality is not compatible with community," keeping neighbours apart:

> The community character of Wychwood Park is a direct result of the circular composition of the houses, resulting from Wychwood pond. When houses interface by their circular or oval compositioning, a kind of social resonance develops that does not depend on a high degree of social life or visiting amongst occupants. Rather there occurs a sense of theatre, as if all occupants were in varying degrees, on a stage. Something of the sort happens in any small village, and builders and planners could easily achieve rich community effects (even without a pond) simply by locating dwellings in non-lineal patterns. (qtd. in Gordon, p. 234)

For McLuhan, Wychwood represented an ideal. He valued the combination of privacy and sociability: one can be with neighbours without forced interaction. The landscape, full of life and motion, nurtured inner life and sensory response: rich green spaces, water patterns, and the play of dappled light, all stimulating feelings of beauty and calm. His description of it provides a non-formulaic instantiation of his (at times) abstract directives to designers to engage and involve people and to harmonize conflicts.

McLuhan admired Tyrwhitt's experience-based accomplishments and understanding of the human place within urban structure and culture—insights potentially valuable in educating a public trained to go through life in somnambulant acceptance, pictured in images of faceless, opaque and inattentive urban ghost throngs (See illustrations accompanying "The Invisible Environment," 1967, pp. 161–63). Two articles Tyrwhitt published in 1955 in the *Explorations* journal—"The Moving Eye" and "The City Unseen"—are particularly strong on addressing—even informing—McLuhan's understanding of the underused human capacity to sense the world. He often challenged humans to awaken to a world that holds so much more than we allow our senses to comprehend; in what for him was a corollary, he described the prime obstacle to sensory awakening as rampant technologies whose every innovative appearance squeezes out another form of sensory activity. Tyrwhitt spoke strongly to the first part of this problem, the human dimension; for the most part curbing technology was not central to her argument, yet the epigraph to this chapter signals her awareness of the need to resist developing "everything that technology makes possible."

In "The Moving Eye," Tyrwhitt studied the visual biases of Western design in contrast to the multisensory appeal of Eastern composition, a theme McLuhan often canvassed (see for example, "Emperor's New," *Vanishing*, (1968), p. 265). She explored the differences between the viewing and visual practices exercised by Eastern and Western citizens as they navigate urban spaces. For instance, she noted of the late-sixteenth century, Northern Indian city of Fatehpur Sikri that its structural elements were designed to avoid drawing the eye to any one fixed focal point. Because there is no "fixed centre," visitors never exhaust the possibilities of thoughtful observation, for "nowhere [is there] a point from which the observer can dominate the whole" (p. 90); the experience is immersive, and a visitor "becomes an intimate part of the scene, which does not impose itself" (p. 90). The architecture of Western cities, by contrast, directs the eye to certain points, often based on strong linear arrangements. Tyrwhitt defined "linear perspective" as key to an aggressive Western way of looking: viewers are provided with clear directions for easy consumption, and with a "single 'vanishing point'" allowing for "the penetration of landscape by a single piercing eye—my eye, my dominating eye" (p. 91). She presented sight as one of a suite of senses, trained by Western bias to dominate, even obliterate the others. This resonates with arguments McLuhan often made about the Gutenberg-induced tyranny of visualization, and the need to balance seeing with other sensory experience.

In the article, Tyrwhitt presented linearity as a design concept for establishing "the view" which Westerners expect, locate, and then rely on, often established by "a guided line—usually an avenue of trees or a symmetrical street" (p. 91). An organized view tells the viewer where to stand and what is important in the central object they are confronting; an important or central object is often an "elaborately symmetrical façade of a large building," and to see it in full it must be "beheld from a central point at some distance from it" (p. 91). These regulatory perceptual constructs lead Westerners to believe, "consciously or unconsciously," that non-linear perspectives with more integrated elements are "wrong" or crowded. We know to read symmetrical and imposing buildings as figures and to ignore elements that might detract from the standard view.

McLuhan's appreciation of the non-linearity of Wychwood Park connects to the excitement of irregularity that Tyrwhitt described as integral to Fatehpur Sikri. Western design directs the gaze and calls on the visual sense above others. More than simply a mode of perception, Tyrwhitt observed, Western-style vision was an "intellectual approach," whose regime is human-centred and offers viewers a static universe of objects, fixed in a grid. This way of making, seeing and knowing invokes shared norms rather than stimulating imaginative intelligence of "vision in motion" (p. 94)—a reference notable for seamlessly invoking the title of Moholy-Nagy's 1947 study of Bauhaus principles. Referring to the "seemingly solid" city of Fatehpur Sikri as resembling a transparent screen for its capacity to engage the sensations and feelings of those who make their way through it, Tyrwhitt praised it for allowing visitors to take in more than a single object, to feel as well as to see, and to have a unique and creative encounter with buildings and space. The Eastern city is not inexorably mapped out, nor are citizens/visitors expected to respond programmatically. It does not dictate what one sees or disregards, nor the order in which one takes in the field or moves through it, nor the speed and direction of one's passage.

The points Tyrwhitt raised about the need to exercise new forms of vision and to unite seeing with other sensory activity align with those McLuhan raised in his frequent disputations about rejuvenating the human sensorium. The words "perspective" and "perception" appear often across McLuhan works that examine seeing and sensing, serving as central topics of *Through the Vanishing Point*, *City as Classroom* and "The Invisible Environment." McLuhan's aim in *Through the Vanishing Point* (co-written with artist and art curator, Harley Parker) was much like Tyrwhitt's in "The Moving Eye": to point out the limitations of the organizational principles of linearity. He also addressed the contrasts between Eastern and

Western aesthetics, suggesting the desirability of balancing the two approaches (*Vanishing*, p. 7). His position diverged somewhat from hers by so firmly attributing the linear principles guiding Western cultural style and habits to the rise of literacy. He believed we are witnessing the dissolution of linearity and literacy dominant from the Renaissance to modernity. Ocular-centric representational values and fixed perspectives disappeared from avant-garde twentieth-century art that features abstraction, multiplicity and complexity and engages the viewer in perceptual responsivity; there was also a fading of literate practices, including slippage between word and meaning, in symbolist poetry and in Joycean prose refusing denotative surety.

Leaving the principle of linearity behind affects more than how we shape and take in the physical environment. Appreciating abstractions and intersections means adopting new cultural practices and attitudes. Giving up linearity means loosening our sense of the need for borders and division, and our desire for everything to have a particular place and a fixed meaning. In "Inside the Five Sense Sensorium" (1961), he playfully sketched the cross-cultural affects of loss of linearity, influencing entertainment, romance, work and domestic practices: "The chorus line, the stag line, the assembly line, all have gone the way of the clothesline" (p. 49). For McLuhan, if Westerners accepted Tyrwhitt's invitation to see beauty in the multiplicity and irregularity of Eastern design, they might gain access to dormant feelings, emotions and imagination, correcting blinkered for more fully-informed reason. Rather than depressing our senses by offering cliches, the built environment should, he urged, challenge the full human sensorium and expand consciousness, drawing on multiple and even integrated senses.

At the end of "The Moving Eye," Tyrwhitt suggested West can learn from East to build structures meant to stimulate the senses and feelings of pleasure and ease—challenging and involving citizens, rather than channeling them through a maze. Yet she urged us to avoid thoughtlessly introducing Eastern principles in ways that might be too extreme and lead participants to feel overwhelmed by indirection or confusion. For her, the challenge of planning and design was to allow for freedom as well as offer collective appeal:

> Here is our contemporary urban planning problem: how to find the key to an intellectual system that will help us to organize buildings, color, and movement in space, without relying entirely upon either introspective "intuition" ("I *feel* it to be right that way") or upon the obsolete and static single viewpoint based on the limited optical science of the Renaissance (p. 95).

Picking up on her definition of the problem facing planning, McLuhan wrote a paraphrase of it in a 1960 letter to her: "The problem of urban planning today ...

that we have now to face [is] in the management of inner and outer space, not fixed but ever new-made ratios, shifting always to maintain a maximal focal point of consciousness" (*Letters*, p. 278). His gloss aligns the process of attaining balance with instability, an allostatic rather than homeostatic regulatory process requiring constant adjustment to shifts in both inner and outer conditions. In "Inside the Five Sense Sensorium," McLuhan charged architects with adapting linear patterns to emergent, more organic and free-flowing patterns: "How to breathe new life into the lineal forms of the past five centuries while admitting the relevance of the new organic forms of spatial organization...is not this the task of the architect at present?" (p. 54). Tyrwhitt and McLuhan were in agreement about mobilizing a balance principle for designing space to engage publics. Both cited the need to overcome Western design limitations by consulting the practices of other cultures. Along with balancing Eastern and Western approaches, they also speak to repurposing or revising what already exists, of meshing old and new. None of this is mechanized or predictable, but more in the form of dynamic concatenation.

In a second *Explorations* article, "The City Unseen" (1955), Tyrwhitt collaborated with psychologist Carl Williams on a study of 823 Ryerson students that demonstrated their limited awareness of their day-to-day surroundings. As Darroch describes (2008), the experiment involved "24 questions, distributed to students attending the Ryerson Institute ... The questionnaire asked general questions about students' background and interests (especially their use of various media during the day and as pastimes), their perceptions of how they commonly approach the Ryerson Institute, and a series of questions detailing their perceptions of the visual environment in the vicinity" (p. 162). The results demonstrated that student subjects noticed only what they found useful, identifying afterwards only "those sensory impressions that interest or serve" them and remaining otherwise "unaware" of other objects ("City," p. 95). The article concluded with the regretful finding that respondents refuse "to see what lies about them" (p. 95). Their pragmatic orientation leaves them "supremely uninterested in critical appreciation of the environment," and, lacking aesthetic engagement or appreciation, "beauty passes them unseen" ("City," p. 96).

The title "The City Unseen" anticipates the title of a 1967 McLuhan article, "The Invisible Environment." The Tyrwhitt/Williams' piece also reads as precursor to McLuhan's *City as Classroom*, a co-authored textbook premised on the assumption students need to be more perceptually aware of their surroundings. Instead of recording, as Tyrwhitt and Willians did, the proclivity of students to move by rote and look only at figural features, *City as Classroom* advised students to confront actual scenes, objects and activities and deliberately use a variety of senses to take these in. After monitoring their sensory activity and inventorying material conditions, McLuhan's students were invited to question how media affects and alters their response to their surroundings: "What happens to our sensory lives with the advent of television, the motor car, or the radio?" (p. 166).

In a 1964 letter to Tyrwhitt, McLuhan noted in relation to city planning "that the city has become a teaching machine." He explained that by this, he meant planners were positioned to design the built environment to stimulate underused senses, thinking of it as a sort of "CARE package dispatched to undernourished areas of the human sensorium" (*Letters*, p. 299). Planners should avoid single or standalone projects to join design efforts to "program the entire environment by an artistic modulation of sensory usage" (*Letters*, p. 299). One such modulation would be to re-establish sensory balance. As he framed the dilemma in "Inside the Five Sense Sensorium," alphabet literacy introduced "a peculiar monopoly and separation of visual experience. At the expense of the other senses" (p. 51). Ignoring non-visual data that reveals details about the world numbs us to the sense of touch and sensory-induced feelings. Our experience is visual and cerebral—disembodied and incomplete. We need, McLuhan argued, to engage in sensorium rebalancing: having given up orality for literacy and community for individualism, many moderns feel isolated from a world of others and otherness. We need to exert conscious effort to activate all the senses and then blend their inputs to attain an inter-sensorial or synaesthetic understanding.

If literacy trained us to rely on linear vision, technological developments that extend our senses only exacerbate such sensory impairment. Without balance or proportion—indeed with explosions of new media continually eroding balances we attempt to strike—we are losing our balance and wits. In a 1960 letter to Tyrwhitt, he made his case that our attention is drawn to and absorbed by media images and gadgetry, and that we have lost both ability and inclination to be aware of surroundings for "we have not been driven out of our senses so much that our senses have been driven out of us" (*Letters*, p. 278).

McLuhan and Tyrwhitt shared many key ideas: the dominance of limited and regulated vision; the need to stimulate human awareness of environmental surroundings (to abandon attitudes of lethargy and unconscious); the value of balancing Eastern and Western approaches to environmental design. Both also used metaphor to convey outer and inner world relations—McLuhan more dire in warning of the dangers of outered limbs and nerves as "amputations" than Tyrwhitt who spoke of strengthening the "heart" of communities in a way that was not rule-driven but, humanized, responsive to scale and character (Tyrwhitt et al., 1952, "Cores Within the Urban Constellation," *Heart*, p. 103).

Discord: Continuing Visual Installations or Imagining an Acoustic Environment?

In 1963 and 1972, Tyrwhitt was instrumental in drawing McLuhan into participating in two of the annual Delos Symposiums convened by the Ekistics planning movement, led by architect Constantinos Doxiadis to study global settlement patterns and principles. The first event occurred in 1963, when a group of intellectuals—Tyrwhitt and McLuhan, alongside accomplished transdisciplinary figures like Margaret Mead, Buckminster Fuller, and Barbara Ward—boarded a yacht in the Mediterranean for eight days of "radical mixing of intellectual activity and sensual pleasure" (Wigley, 2001, p. 84). While the symposia were held yearly for the next decade, McLuhan did not attend another until Delos 10 in 1972, and by that point he no longer embraced the interests of the group, complaining of it in follow-up correspondence as a "complex social event" undervaluing "scholarship and knowledge" (*Letters*, p. 452). He dismissed the group as small minded and unadventurous in a letter to Margaret Mead: "I may say that I consider the Delos meeting of a very dubious quality and performance. The participants of all such gatherings seek reassurance for their convictions rather than new awareness of their inadequacy" (*Letters*, p. 464).

Given the focus of this book on McLuhan/Kepes/Tyrwhitt, it is intriguing that McLuhan confided his sharpest criticism of the event to fellow attendee Gyory Kepes, telling him that "we already live... far outside the ken of Doxiadis..." (*Letters*, p. 453). He spoke of his common ground with Kepes, dismissing the others as "19th century types" (*Letters*, p. 453). This acerbic tone is uncharacteristic of other McLuhan correspondence. He may have felt conference participants paid insufficient attention to him. Yet worse than being ignored during the proceedings would have been evidence of others ignoring his Dew Line warning—the "Distant Early Warning System" advising of the need for vigilance to avoid exposure to incoming technological threats ("Emperor's New," *Vanishing*, p. 244). For McLuhan, transitioning from visual to aural society meant leaving seeing and doing behind and moving to a stage of listening and connecting via electronic networks. He was chagrined to find international intellectuals coalesced around responding to actual and foreseeable worldly problems rather than joining his efforts to control the creep of technology in the new and forming environment. They wanted to secure worldly moorings, while he wanted to humanize something resembling what we call meta life.

Nor was his contribution highly esteemed by attendees he criticized, judging from the archived minutes assembled by Tyrwhitt categorizing McLuhan's assertion that *Ulysses* by James Joyce was "the best piece of city planning and building of this century" as "Communication via Humour" (Wigley, 2001, p. 113). To widen the gap, she is on record saying she remained unconvinced by McLuhan's argument that acoustic space was replacing visual space—that humanity was giving up real for virtual experiences as they accepted the mediating interventions of electronic devices. In a letter to McLuhan in 1974, Tyrwhitt shared her reservations about taking the shift from visual space too far, especially in building and planning matters wherein visual space "is the only space architects can handle": "I have never commented on your structures of Visual Space versus other aspects of space. Of course you are right, but the only space architects can handle is physical space, which is basically visual space" (qtd. in Darroch, 2008, p. 166).

What happened in the decade between Delos 1 and 10? Arguably the main shift was in the force of McLuhan's commitment to studying "electric" change, so that he wanted the environmental effects of media and the computer to stand forward as central in planning conversations. He was not interested in planning human-scale settlements, not even those aimed at community building to meet social needs; nor was he interested in planning for the equitable roll out of hardware infrastructure and physical networks to facilitate world-wide media distribution—graphic work Mark Wigley says increasingly captivated designers and urbanists who attended Ekistics meetings (2001, p. 89).

Prior to Delos 1, McLuhan and Doxiadis bonded over the idea of a prosthetic environment—the idea that human limbs and senses have been outered with increasing innovations, popularized if not originated by McLuhan. Yet if for McLuhan this meant creating an environment designed to restore sensory life and balance, for Doxiades and followers this idea led to planning infrastructural networks to enable more, and more equitable, distribution. Wigley reports Doxiades increasingly gravitated to a model of buildings as networks, "call[ing] a house 'a network of walls'" (2001, p. 91). This phrase underscores his disconnect from McLuhan, who attached the phrase "without walls" to a variety of phenomena—houses and photographs in *Understanding Media* (1964), for example (pp. 76, 255). He was adapting Malraux's observation that art should happen outside galleries to fit his own vision of various life experiences beginning to unfold in electronic and mediated ways, without physicality or spatial borders. Concerns with roads and transportation, with water, waste and food management, seemed too literal. He wanted safety plans for an electronic and mediated environment; he wanted to consider how our transformation into increasingly ethereal substances or virtual forms might take place without entirely ending humanity and life as we know it.[3]

Hailing Joyce as paramount city planner had to do with his assessment of Joyce as playing with words and word arrangements in ways that revealed their rich variety and flexibility and by so doing opening up more ways to think and communicate: "This updating of language is really an updating of sensibility of awareness of perception" ("Art as Survival," 2005/1973, p. 223). McLuhan was concerned that precise denotative diction and coherent and sequential discursive style—effective for the transfer of ideas and information in modernist industrial culture—were no longer viable in a technologized world of instantaneous connectivity, where "everything does relate to everything" and "the language of industrialized areas has lost its oral quality and oral rhythms and seems to be incapable of translating the new sounds of technology or humanizing the new sounds through that language" ("Art as Survival," pp. 223, 217).

McLuhan's disconnection from planning efforts and Ekistics' goals may also have been rooted in his North American background and experience. While not parochial, McLuhan as a North American did not share the post-war European hands-on experience of reconstruction and building as essential to safety and social relations. He was more familiar with the relative indulgence of unfettered North American expansionism, resulting in bigger buildings and roadways and suburban playgrounds. To McLuhan, planning and architecture meant "bricks and mortar" solutions, fixing current problems by improving buildings and infrastructure. This was part of what he dismissed as rear-view mirror thinking.

His North American experience may also have blunted his appreciation of the city "Core" which for Tyrwhitt was "the heart of the city." Her co-edited volume, *The Heart of the City* (1952), represented the views of distinguished architects who met in 1951 for CIAM 8[4] to explore the value of cities having a defined Core, designed to promote sociability—with restrictions on car traffic, advertising, and other media—and culture—with inclusion of sculpture and art (Giedion "A Short Outline," in *Heart*, p. 164). Tyrwhitt's piece in the collection makes clear that she used the word "heart" as a metaphor to present the Core as essential to urban life, enabling the expression of human feeling and cultivation of fellow feeling: "The Core is not the seat of civic dignity: the Core is the gathering place of the people …The location of the Core can be most easily seen when some collective emotion is aroused"; it "provides a physical setting for the expression of collective emotion … the place where the people of these communities turn out to greet their acquaintances, observe their neighbors, gossip with friends, and meet their sweethearts" (p. 103). McLuhan is on record dismissing the need for a hub as physical gathering or governance place. In his mind, North Americans were not interested in importing European Piazza life, having lived with something of a reverse pattern which he explained in the form of a question in a 1972 letter to Margaret Atwood: "Why do North Americans, unlike all other people on the planet, go outside to be alone and inside to be with people?" (*Letters*, p. 457).[5]

Whereas for CIAM discussants the Core was significant and worthy of "revitalization" (Giedion, in *Heart*, p. 137), for McLuhan the principle of decentralization was already evident. As I examined in an earlier article (2015), McLuhan saw North American cities as having already sprawled out from cores enabled by transportation routes ("McLuhan and the City," p. 141). By his day, alongside visible infrastructure like roads and trains, cities were further dispersed by "invisible interconnectivity, such as flight paths and digital networks" ("McLuhan and the City," p. 137). In sum, he referred to the core as having museum status ("Emperor's New," *Vanishing*, p. 243) and did not support revival efforts: "What the town planners call 'the human scale' in discussing ideal urban spaces is equally unrelated to these electric forms. Our electric extensions of ourselves simply bypass space and time, and create problems of human involvement and organization for which there is no precedent" (*Understanding Media*, p. 144).

McLuhan's engagement with Doxiadis was relatively fleeting, and it is perhaps more revealing to consider the trajectory of his intellectual relationship with Tyrwhitt and even Giedion. There is some evidence he believed they were overly committed to visual and architectural components against his arguments about our transition from literate and visual to acoustic space—our ever-increasing withdrawal from actual place and encounters and migration to electronic media (seeing the world through television, communicating by phone, listening to recorded and broadcast voice and music). As Richard Cavell notes, McLuhan understood his world was in "a transitional moment, when primarily literate culture was experiencing aspects of oral culture as they were being retrieved by electronic media" (*Space*, 2002, p. 137). As his career advanced, he honed in on what he called "acoustic space"—a de-materialized environment, similar to what we now call the metaverse, involving online or "discarnate" interaction shorn of visible, material components, rendering speech, walls and bodies invisible. He warned we were becoming discarnate by reliance on devices and living through mediated rather than first-hand encounters. His way of thinking also anthropomorphized the outer environment—granted life energy via human transfer and now evolving at will, having assumed the formerly human capacity to adapt and change.

His attitude to our transition from literacy is crucial to understanding his position on incoming "acoustic space" as posing opportunities and potential disasters: "I do see the prospect of a rich and creative retribalized society—free of the fragmentation and alienation of the mechanical age—emerging from this traumatic period of culture clash; but I have nothing but distaste for the *process* of change. As a man molded within the literate Western tradition, I do not personally cheer the dissolution of that tradition through the electric involvement of all the senses" (*Playboy*, p. 267). He maintained that still-hidden but emergent conditions needed to be understood to be managed to advantage, allowing for both adjustment and salvage. With electronic energy, with an uptick in the speed of change, we were newly positioned to witness change: "Because of today's terrific speed-up of information moving, we have a chance to apprehend, predict and influence the environmental forces shaping us–and thus win back control of our own destinies ... [recognizing] what it does to us and with us" (*Playboy*, p. 239). Thus for him the building of cities and attendant cultures was a secondary—even outmoded—activity, since our primary energies should be directed toward managing the arrangements of "electric" technologies—powerful enough to do more than physical, mechanical work, performing complex nervous and neural activity.

While McLuhan became increasingly committed to understanding the world as acoustic or aural, replacing the visual mode accompanying literacy, Tyrwhitt, urbanist and planner, never gave up valuing and shaping social conditions and external place, both landscape and built environment. She sought to make an inviting human-scale environment, recommending the nurturance of local organic and community connections. In short, working with visual space—imagining bodies continuing to need human-scale accommodation on an earth needing our care—she was committed to improving material living conditions.

McLuhan was likely disappointed that Giedion and Tyrwhitt did not take up his vision of incoming acoustic space. Their continued interest in components of "visual space"—Tyrwhitt's interests, for example, in forming coalitions to improve various elements of modernist life, from architecture and infrastructure to global equity and ecology—was counterproductive to his speculative project of planning for a future shorn of current systems and practices, a future forming if not fully visible. According to Darroch, McLuhan's awareness that Tyrwhitt and Giedion did not fully accept his aurality thesis may have led him to the inaccurate conclusion that Giedion was insensitive to language and soundscapes. In a letter presumed penned in 1954, McLuhan downplayed Giedion's insights as those that "supplemented" his own and chastised him for being "oblivious to the role of words, spoken or written, as part of the greater communication nexus" (qtd. in Darroch, 2008, p. 157). Yet, his intellectual rancor did not last. In a 1967 interview he roundly acknowledged Giedion's acuity and influence:

> Giedion influenced me profoundly. *Space, Time and Architecture* was one of the great events of my lifetime. Giedion gave us a language for tackling the structural world of architecture and artifacts of many kinds in the ordinary environment... Giedion began to study the environment as a structural work –he saw language in streets, buildings, the very texture of form. ("Hot and cool interview," 1997/1967, p. 48)

Later still in a 1972 address, he recalled Tyrwhitt as influential in formulating the term "acoustic space" at an Explorations group meeting: "Jaqueline Tyrwhitt … was explaining how Giedion presented the fact that the Romans were the first people to enclose space … a genuine enclosed space, namely, a visual space" ("The End of the Work Ethic," 1997/1972, p. 101).

Tyrwhitt's scholarship also retained references to McLuhan. In *Human Identity in the Urban Environment*, she hailed a position he advanced: "McLuhan says that a kind of cultural law suggests that the greater the density, the greater the social distance" (1972, p. 232). In another section, she reproduced a long passage of his (only part of which follows) exploring how technology has turned us into lifelong learners rather than wage laborers, and with this dematerializing settlement needs to place new demands on planners to design digital spaces and interfaces (rather than for in-person community gathering as of old):

> The electronic extension of the brain involves each of us totally in the family of man, an involvement which constitutes a new kind of continuous learning as involuntary as seeing when one's eyes are open. The global extension of the human brain is an enormous upgrading of man. We must not fail to exploit it. The most important task of the planner is to prepare the environments for the exploitation of this new tremendous opportunity.
>
> What does this mean in terms of human settlement when learning a living supplants earning a living? Production itself is left to automated machines and the work force withdraws from the factory to the seminars … that can be dispersed decentralized, without need for large agglomerations of population.
>
> Since the central purpose of human settlement in the electronic age becomes learning, human settlement must be a projection, a multidimensional model of our new global consciousness (p. 527).

Interesting, too, is that Part Two of this volume, called "Man: Balancing Inner and Outer Realities" rephrases what McLuhan said in a 1960 letter to her about urban planners needing to balance the "shifting rations of inner and outer space" to adjust for expanded consciousness enabled by global communications (*Letters*, p. 278). Tyrwhitt and Bell divide Part Two into four units, whose titles bring to mind themes that engaged both Kepes and McLuhan [see Chapter 4]: "Balance Between the Human Body and Natural Forces," "Balance Between Reason and Emotion," Balance between Specialization and a Comprehensive Approach, and Balance Between Man's Private Life and the Welfare of community" (pp. 143–149). To demonstrate some of these links, we might think of McLuhan's Mariner meeting the universe, of his and Kepes's arguments for process and monism rather than dialectic and dualism, of their interest in interdisciplinarity, and of their (albeit nascent) consideration of local claims in a global world. McLuhan made multiple calls for balance and unity, Kepes for scale and proportion—these as synonymous with Giedion's term "equipoise" (*Mechanization takes Command*, 1948). In Tyrwhitt's gloss of the shared mindset of Doxiadis and Giedion we can hear echoes of McLuhan and Kepes: "Doxiadis takes us swiftly through an analysis of the interrelation of man's body, senses, mind and soul and—like Giedion he concludes that only when these are all in equilibrium can am feel and perform at his best ... we need to resist the tendency to develop everything that technology makes possible" (*Human Identity*, 1972, p. 144). Conclusions attributed to her colleagues Giedion and Doxiadis are likely those she herself held; if so, Tyrwhitt, Kepes and McLuhan all proposed rebalancing schemes to avoid threats to identity, community, and earth.

While they explored similar ideas, their lives were also knit together by interactive moments that spanned several decades, from early-to-mid 50's to the mid 70's. In their "Introduction" to the 2016 reissue of *Explorations, 1953–57*, describing how the Explorations group defined as a key challenge "the creation of a new language of vision," Darroch and Marchessault provide an example of the intertwined life and work of all three of our lead figures—McLuhan, Kepes and Tyrwhitt:

> The notion of a new "language of vision" recalls in particular Gyorgy Kepes's 1944 classic essay by the same title. *Language of Vision* proposed a radical revamping of art and design pedagogy in terms of visual communication, committed to identifying common patterns of unity across varied approaches to human experience. Kepes, a Hungarian-born professor of visual design at MIT associated with László Moholy-Nagy and the New Bauhaus, had in 1950 staged an exhibition "The New Landscape," a constellation of images of natural and scientific phenomena that attempted to shift our view from the static object to a method of pattern seeing. Jaqueline Tyrwhitt visited the exhibit while working with Giedion and most likely brought it to the attention of the Toronto faculty members. The group would publish an early draft of Kepes's introduction to his 1956 book *The New Landscape in Art and Science*. (p. xv)

McLuhan/Tyrwhitt and Urban Change: Visual, Aural, or Both?

Some may be familiar with McLuhan's brief and effective urban activism, when he joined forces with Jane Jacobs to oppose the expansion of the Spadina Expressway in Toronto (McLeod Rogers, 2021, p. 116). The two lobbied then-Premier Bill

Davis to "Stop the Spadina" and collaborated on a film, *The Burning Would* (1970), opposing expressway expansion by showcasing its deleterious impacts: noise pollution foremost, but other degradations as well. His advocacy of green-minded politics and community protection prevailed and development stopped. Yet this activism was something of an anomaly. While McLuhan likely opposed exploitative over-development on principle, this campaign served self-interest in saving his Wychwood home and neighborhood from proposed development.

Overall, McLuhan was no acolyte of urban planning or activism, which he believed used today's technological tools and social standards to address tomorrow's needs. He did not rally to support pressing social-impact issues like waste management, food supply, and healthy living. Neither was he supportive of international coalition building aimed at establishing universal standards. A gap separated him from his contemporaries—Jacobs, Tyrwhitt, and Kepes—all of whom struggled to improve material conditions. Compared to them, McLuhan was more idealist than materialist, studying conditions for nurturing inner life and mind, "trying to understand our technological environment and its psychic and social consequences" (*Playboy*, 1969, p. 236). His tendency to privilege inner over outer life is noted by the editors of his letters who contrast Innis's work on media resources and cultural impacts—studying the effects of "the oral tradition, parchment, papyrus, paper and the printing press in disseminating information, and the impetus these media provided for cultural change"—to McLuhan's interest in media's effects on human life and psyche "concentrating on the effect of the media on the senses rather than on social organization" (*Letters*, p. 220). Whatever we build shapes and changes us; before building more we need to inventory the effects of media. Otherwise, he feared, we may be overwhelmed, anesthetized, and annihilated, fated to the suffering implied by Bertrand Russell's observation that "if the bath water got only half a degree warmer every hour, we would never know when to scream." ("Emperor's New," *Vanishing*, p. 253).

Rather than replicating more of what we already have and attempting to ballast a way of life already outgrown, McLuhan wanted artists to devise environments designed to optimize new patterns of sociability and communication. Artists, not planners, should take the lead, for the artist "is especially aware of the challenge and dangers of new environments presented to human sensibility": "The artist studies the distortion of sensory life produced by new environmental programming and tends to create artistic situations that correct the sensory bias and derangement brought about by the new form" ("Emperor's New," *Vanishing*, p. 238). Artists can counter current trends by provoking involvement. He argued that current conditions left unaddressed would lead to further disorientation, fully "outering" bodies and senses, leaving us with little to no control. He hoped for the creation of counter environments, allowing for the repatriation of the sense life and an expansion of consciousness and community. He further hoped that technology might be used to support this goal. Such hope did not cast him as techno-utopian dreamer, disseminating what James Carey dismisses as "New Jerusalem" promises of "the restorative powers of media" that attempt "*a justification of optimism*" ("Innis," p. 38, emphasis mine). Instead, much as Kepes did, he argued that technologies can be harnessed to offer new ideas and once understood, can be used to restore balance or equipoise.

Many of McLuhan's predictions about incoming aurality have come into play. We rely less on print books, more on virtual lives and dialogue, and define ourselves in relational contexts on the principle "that everything is connected with everything" ("Art as Survival," p. 223). Attached to smaller self-selected breakaway groups, we may be less vulnerable to generic conformist pressures, but we are relentlessly shaped by AI and algorithms, "becoming a servo-mechanism of our own environment by adjustment" ("Art as Survival," p. 223). The sorts of warning signals McLuhan sent out are expounded in the recent text *Your Computer is on Fire* (2021) that studies the various ways electronic communication has narrowed what we think, say, and know: from the provision of a QWERTY keyboard that disallows some forms of thought and expression (pp. 337–62), to search engine optimization, that furnishes and blocks information according to AI traffic signals (pp. 199–212).

McLuhan's reservations aside, Tyrwhitt and those interested in settlement questions were responding to a sophisticated interactive model of urbanism exceeding traditional forms of planning affecting physical place. Tyrwhitt with Ekistics and other cohorts of global intellectuals and practitioners grappled with what we have learned to call "wicked problems," those that are clustered, indeterminate, and resistant to solutions, created by the intersectional systemic problems (Buchanan, 2021, p. 15). Housing and dwelling continue as huge challenges on a global scale provoked by the interplay of such factors as health, poverty, and climate disaster; shelter aside, there is attendant human and social turmoil. We still live in houses, in cities, in nations, and are still sorting out belonging and boundary claims and are attempting to balance advantages and protections. Tyrwhitt's contribution to addressing human, local and global needs, convening coalitions to do so, established a model for what continues to be the challenging work of brokering international discussions and agreements.

Examining what he calls an *Ethics for the City* (2018), Richard Sennett gives currency to some of the complexities addressed in Delian dialogues: interested not only in how we build the city but "how people dwell in it" and asking whether "urbanism should represent society as it is or seek to change it" (pp. 1, 4). Tyrwhitt herself characterized Ekistics as a form of urban studies considering complexity and scale. She viewed physical planning as "one of a number of processes to be considered" amongst others such as "the developed and the undeveloped, the individual and the mass, the natural and the man-made, the spontaneous and planned" as well as "how universal issues may be distinguished from parochial ones" (Bell & Tyrwhitt, 1972, pp. 27–28). The sort of planning Tyrwhitt advocated for aimed at ethical as well as physical outcomes, securing food supply, air, land and water supply safety, protection of green spaces (Bell & Tyrwhitt, pp. 44, 46). She saw population increase and urbanization as "a major problem of the last third of this century, one to which 'No one, nowhere can remain immune' as such large increases in the numbers of people and in the sizes of settlements may lead to a more regimented form of human existence" (Bell & Tyrwhitt, p. 35). Her concerns continue to play out. The overrepresentation of our species and planetary imbalance has indeed prompted plans for "wilding" that comes with a "more regimented form of human existence" that Tyrwhitt hoped to stave off. Speculative filmmaker and architect Liam Young, for example, explores quarantining the human population in a dense enclave in his *Planet City* project. Looking at his proposals to minimize the human footprint underscores the urgency of the dilemma Tyrwhitt hoped to forestall.

We continue to face real challenges, exacerbated by human activities, with accelerant technologies chief among these and, as McLuhan argued, interactant. Arguments for balancing the human population that Tyrwhitt and other serious planners made in her day went away for a time, feared as oppressive and attached to genocidal schemes. Yet thoughtful feminists are now reopening such arguments to test how they might be separated from oppressive politics and introduce new freedoms (Haraway & Clarke, 2018). Renewed interest in moderating human impact and spread are evidenced in recent urban development models that champion the creation of dense and mixed-use communities, such as in the "10-min City" model (Moreno, 2021). Such a model is again rooted in ideas about efficiency, walkability and density conspiring to support "human community" and scale as explored by Tyrwhitt and other planners (Tyrwhitt, 1972, "The Pedestrian," *Human Identity*, p. 595). Similarly, there are also calls to harness extractive technologies in ways that manage resources to rebalance the planet, underscoring that "managed decline, managed retreat, managed rejection" are not evidence of defeat but of "taking control of our own destiny" (*Ending*, 2021, p. 22). Despite frustrations many now express against the interventionist efficacy of supranational governance bodies,[6] many problems of world-wide scope continue to demand immediate attention and action, based on some form of planetary alliance and oversight. Tyrwhitt modelled this kind of consensual work addressing shared global problems. In McLuhan, we find more mercurial and future-oriented thinking. To take inspiration from this legacy, we might consider points of complementarity in these two approaches, and how they can contribute to a model for action and vision.

Notes

1. In "The Ford Foundation and Communication Studies: The University of Toronto Program (1953–1955)," William Buxton describes how the Explorations group accessed Ford Funding. He notes that for the most part McLuhan reported results somewhat whimsically by citing his own probes and interests. "The City Unseen" enabled him to bolster the report with its more solid experimental design and evidence.
2. I would like to acknowledge Veronica Dakota's work on Susanne Langer's art theory and philosophy of mind. Her unpublished online presentation "I feel, therefore I am" showcased Langer's philosophical theory—"a logico-aesthetic analysis of experience"—as addressing many issues related to giving form to perception and feeling via art communication. Dakota's presentation revealed that Langer theorized many of the points raised by figures studied here. (Online presentation, *Langer Circle*, Sept 28, 2024). I have studied overlap between McLuhan and Langer in the article, "Susanne Langer, Marshall McLuhan and Media Ecology. Feminist principles in humanist projects," *Explorations in Media Ecology*, 20 *Issue Gender and Media Ecology*, June 2021, pp. 131—149. https://doi.org/10.1386/eme_00081_1
3. A loose yet fascinating connection is to Margaret Sheldrik's *Visceral Prostheses: Somatechnics and Posthuman Embodiment* (London: Bloomsbury, 2022) that explores humans as always having lived beyond the bounds of the physical body, doing so now in ways "greatly complicated by the realisation that biotechnologies, nanotechnologies, information technologies and cognitive science are potentially mutually implicated in a model that raises the fundamental philosophical question of what constitutes the human as such" (p. 7). She notes that a new concept like "microchimerism" supports the view that we are "all always already prosthetic" (p. 5), becoming increasingly aware of this now that the effects are more visible and multiple. The book takes our prosthetic condition as opportunity rather than woe, and thus corresponds with McLuhan's view that changes to our originary condition can be positive if understood and managed (*Playboy*, p. 268).
4. Le Corbusier's definition of CIAM [International Congresses of Modern Architecture], given July 1951 and reproduced in *The Heart of the City*, emphasized its international character, "made up of architects and town planners from all the five continents; troublesome fellows with independent minds, who have been working and meeting together for twenty-three years" (p. xii).
5. It is of historic interest that Margaret Atwood disagreed with this formula (see ftn. 1, *Letters*, p. 457), whereas Walter Gropius espoused a form of it in his piece, "The Human Scale," in *The Heart of the City*, p. 53.
6. See Hardt and Negri, "Empire, Twenty Years On," [*New Left Review*, Nov/Dec. 2019 https://newleftreview.org/issues/ii120/articles/empire-twenty-years-on] assessing the failure of supranational institutions, and Benjamin Bratton, *Revenge of the Real*, [Verso, 2022] specifically on the failure of the World Health Organization to execute fair and effective Covid protocols.

References

Bell, G., & Tyrwhitt, J. (Eds.). (1972). *Human identity in the urban environment*. Penguin Books.

Buchanan, R. (1992). Wicked problems in design thinking. *Design Issues, 8*(2), 5–21. https://doi.org/10.2307/1511637

Buxton, W. J. (2018). The Ford Foundation and communication studies: The University of Toronto program (1953–1955). *Rockefeller Archive Research Reports*, 1–13. https://rockarch.issuelab.org/resource/the-ford-foundation-and-communication-studies-the-university-of-toronto-program-1953-1955.html

Carey, J. W. (1967). Harold Adams Innes and Marshall McLuhan. *The Antioch Review, 27*(1), 5–39. https://doi.org/10.2307/4610816

Cavell, R. (2002). *McLuhan in space*. University of Toronto Press.

Darroch, M. (2008). Bridging urban and media studies: Jaqueline Tyrwhitt and the Explorations group, 1951–57. *Canadian Journal of Communications, 33*(2), 147–170.

Darroch, M., & Marchessault, J. (2016). Introduction to the eight-volume series of the 2016 edition of Explorations, 1953–57. In *Explorations* (special ed., pp. v–xxxii). Wipf & Stock. (Original work published 1953)

Giedion, S. (1948). *Mechanization takes command*. Harvard University Press.

Giedion, S. (1952). A short outline of the core. In J. Tyrwhitt, J. L. Sert & E. N. Rogers (Eds.), *The heart of the city*. (pp. 164–168). Pellegrini & Cudahy.

Gordon, T. W. (1967). *Marshall McLuhan: Escape into understanding*. Stoddart.

Haraway, D., & Clarke, A. (Eds.). (2018). *Making kin not population: Reconceiving generations*. Prickly Paradigm Press.

McLeod Rogers, J. (2015). McLuhan and the City. In J. McLeod Rogers, C. Taylor & T. Whalen (Eds.), *Finding McLuhan: The mind/the man/the message* (pp. 135–156). University of Regina Press.

McLeod Rogers, J. (2021). *McLuhan's techno-sensorium city: Coming to our senses in a programmed environment*. Lexington.

McLuhan, M. (1961, June). Inside the five sense sensorium. *The Canadian Architect, 6*(6), 49–51.

McLuhan, M. ([1964], 2003). *Understanding media: The extensions of man* (Critical ed.), (Terrence Gordon, Ed.). Gingko.

McLuhan, M. (1967). The invisible environment: The future of an erosion. *Perspecta, 11*, 161–167.

McLuhan, M. (1997). The hot and cool interview. In M. Moos (Ed.), *Media research: technology, art, communication* (pp. 92–109). G+B Arts. (Original work published 1965)

McLuhan, M. (1997). The playboy interview. In E. McLuhan & F. Zingrone (Eds.), *Essential McLuhan* (pp. 233–269). Taylor & Francis. (Original work published 1969)

McLuhan, M. (1997). The end of the work ethic. In M. Moos (Ed.), *Media research: technology, art, communication* (pp. 92–109). G+B Arts. (Original work published 1972)

McLuhan, M. (2003). *Understanding media: The extensions of man* (Critical ed.) (W. T. Gordon, Ed.). Gingko Press. (Original work published 1964)

McLuhan, M. (2005). Art as survival in the electric age. In S. McLuhan & D. Staines (Eds.), *Understanding me: Lectures and interviews* (pp. 206–224). McClelland & Stewart. (Original work published 1973)

McLuhan, M., & Jacobs, J. (Directors). (1970). *The Burning Would*. https://www.youtube.com/watch?v=GDzkjL7r5zg

McLuhan, M., McLuhan, E., & Hutchon, K. (1977). *City as classroom: Understanding language and media*. Agincourt Book Society.

McLuhan, M., & Parker, H. (1968). Emperor's new clothes. In *Through the vanishing point: Space in poetry and painting* (pp. 237–261). Harper and Row.

Molinaro, M., McLuhan, C., & Toye, W. (Eds). (1987). *Letters of Marshall McLuhan*. Oxford University Press.

Moreno, C. (2021). Introducing the "15-Minute City": Sustainability, resilience and place identity in future post-pandemic cities. *Smart Cities*, *4*(1), 93–111. https://doi.org/10.3390/smartcities4010006

Mullaney, T. S., Peters, B., Hicks, M., & Philip, K. (Eds.). (2021). *Your computer is on fire*. MIT Press.

Sennett, R. (2018). *Building and dwelling: Ethics for the city*. Yale University Press.

Shoshkes, E. (2013). *Jaqueline Tyrwhitt: A transnational life in urban planning and design*. Routledge.

Tyrwhitt, J. (1955). The moving eye. *Explorations*, *4*, 115–119.

Tyrwhitt, J. (1972). The pedestrian in megalopolis: Tokyo. In G. Bell & J. Tyrwhitt (Eds.), *Human identity in the urban environment* (pp. 595–603). Penguin.

Tyrwhitt, J., & Williams, C. D. (1955). The city unseen. *Explorations*, *5*, 88–96.

Tyrwhitt, J., Sert, J. L., & Rogers, E. N. (1952). *The heart of the city: Towards the humanization of urban life*. Pellegrini and Cudahy.

Wigley, M. (2001, Summer). Network fever. *Grey Room* (4), 82–122.

Young, L. (n.d.). *Planet city*. https://planetcity.world/

CHAPTER 3

Jaqueline Tyrwhitt's Relations with Marshall McLuhan and Gyorgy Kepes

ELLEN SHOSHKES

"The meaning of history arises in the uncovering of relationships. That is why the writing of history has less to do with facts as such than with their relations. These relations will vary with the shifting point of view, for like constellations of stars, they are ceaselessly in change."
—Sigfried Giedion, Mechanization Takes Command

This chapter maps out the personal and professional relationships linking Jaqueline Tyrwhitt (1905–83) with Marshall McLuhan (1911–80) and György Kepes (1906–2001) and situates this network of exchange within the context of concerns that drove Tyrwhitt's work at various junctures in her career as a planner, educator, and editor. Their exchanges and mutual influence are noteworthy because Tyrwhitt's career serves as a touchstone for an era (1930s–70s) which saw the rise of broad conceptions of urban design and bioregional planning as scientific, humanistic techniques for guiding interrelated physical and social evolution.[1]

This utopian line of planning thought was first articulated by the visionary Scottish polymath Patrick Geddes (1854–1932) to guide civic reconstruction after World War I toward an emergent "biotechnic" society—based on cooperation and in harmony with nature. Bolstered by a new understanding of ecosystems, Geddes' planning ideas gained wide support during the Great Depression as a "third way" between unbridled capitalism and totalitarian political economies. Those ideas became firmly established in the context of post-World War Two reconstruction efforts, enriched by general systems theory and cybernetics, and embodied in the aspirations of welfare states and new transnational organizations such as the United Nations (UN). An overarching framework for the development of this line of planning thought at mid-century was the "generally positive philosophy of life … an ecological worldview grounded in the life sciences," that zoologist Julian Huxley (1961, pp. 282–3)—the first Secretary General of the UN Educational Scientific and Cultural Organization (UNESCO)—called "evolutionary humanism."

This chapter employs a chronological narrative to shed light on how Tyrwhitt's relationships with McLuhan and Kepes involved this discourse, notably as it was shaped at the Delos Symposia that Greek planner Constantinos Doxiadis (1913–75) hosted from 1963–72. McLuhan was initially attracted to these ideas, but ultimately rejected them. The chapter begins with an overview of Tyrwhitt's formative influences, charting corresponding paths in the lives of McLuhan and Kepes. Next, I discuss how Tyrwhitt's work evolved in the context for planning for the physical reconstruction of Britain in the years during and immediately after World War Two, and the concurrent encounters between McLuhan, Giedion and Kepes during the war years. I cover the expansion of Tyrwhitt's work to encompass issues of postwar reconstruction worldwide, as a transnational actor, leading to a teaching position at the University of Toronto, where she met McLuhan. I discuss Tyrwhitt's primary collaboration with McLuhan in the Culture and Communications seminar. Finally, I consider Tyrwhitt's role in connecting McLuhan to her work (alongside Kepes) at Harvard and with Doxiadis.

Tyrwhitt's Formative Influences

Tyrwhitt was raised in London and trained as a garden designer. She studied horticulture, completed a year (1924–5) at the Architectural Association (AA) school, then practiced for several years. Wanting to do more meaningful work during the depression, she studied economics and became an organizer for the League of Industry, promoting federated self-governing industries. This led her to become involved with PEP (Political and Economic Planning), a group co-formed by Julian Huxley to study components of a "national plan for Great Britain." Tyrwhitt was part of a sub-group studying the location of industry. In 1935 Tyrwhitt used her PEP connections to land a job at Dartington Hall, the estate rehabilitated by Leonard and Dorothy Elmhirst (PEP's primary funders) as an experiment in rural reconstruction, integrating industry with agriculture, the arts, and progressive education. Huxley (1961, p. 2) praised the Elmhirsts as "pioneers of humanist planning."

While at Dartington Hall Tyrwhitt probably discovered Geddes' *Cities in Evolution* (1915), which inspired her interest in town planning. She was particularly attracted to Geddes' use of biological metaphors to explain the evolution of cities and the transition underway from industrial civilization to one based on electric power, a healthier biotechnic society. Geddes—who had studied evolution with Julian's grandfather, Thomas Huxley—applied ecological concepts to study the interrelationships between people, their way of life, and place. In 1937 Tyrwhitt enrolled in the School of Planning and Research for National Development (SPRND), which opened under the direction of E.A.A. Rowse, a follower of Geddes, as an offshoot of AA in 1935 to teach Geddes's bioregional approach. By the time she completed her course in July 1939 Tyrwhitt had become "an ardent disciple" of Geddes.

Corresponding Paths: Kepes and McLuhan

Both McLuhan and Kepes lived briefly in England at this time and were influenced by similar ideas. McLuhan studied English at Cambridge University for two years (1934–6) after graduating from the University of Manitoba, in Winnipeg, Canada. At Cambridge McLuhan was impressed by the New Criticism's emphasis on "verbal analysis of literary texts," particularly the idea that "practical literary criticism could be associated with training in awareness of the environment" (Marchand, 1989, pp. 64, 40). There, McLuhan also deepened his attraction to literary critic G.K. Chesterton's Catholicism and related idea of Distributism. Notably, Distributism called for an anti-utopian (wait till the afterlife), culturally traditionalist variant of the Dartington Hall model of modernist communitarianism (DeBoer-Langworth, n.d.).

Kepes lived in London from 1935 to 1937, having followed his mentor, painter László Moholy-Nagy (1895–1946)—whose bio-technical social aesthetic ideals aligned with Geddes's—from Hungary via Berlin, where they had taught at the Bauhaus school of design. Kepes and Moholy-Nagy became part of the circle around Huxley and PEP. This diverse network of businessmen, scientists, academics, and designers included many members of the MARS (Modern

Architectural Research) group, the British chapter of CIAM (*Congres International d'Architecture Moderne*) (Weschler, 1978, p. 10), with ties to AA and SPRND.

In another parallel, both Kepes and McLuhan next relocated to the American Mid-West. In 1937 Kepes accepted an invitation to teach at the New Bauhaus school that Moholy-Nagy established in Chicago, Illinois. McLuhan was then working not far away as a teaching assistant at the University of Wisconsin, in Madison. In 1937, newly converted to Catholicism, McLuhan became an instructor of English at St. Louis University, a Jesuit institution in Missouri. In September 1939, McLuhan, now married to an American, returned to Cambridge to work on his doctorate. Despite the outbreak of war in Europe at that time, McLuhan spent "a pleasant year" at Cambridge, inspired by his discovery of the significance of the classical trivium (grammar, logic, and rhetoric) as a worldview (Marchand, 1989, pp. 60–2).

The War Years: Planning for Britain's Postwar Reconstruction

Meanwhile, Tyrwhitt's life was dramatically affected by England's entry into the war. SPRND closed in September 1949, when Rowse enlisted in the army; Tyrwhitt soon joined the Women's Land Army. However, she returned to London in February 1941 amid the Blitz to direct a new organization, the Association for Planning and Regional Reconstruction (APRR), created to carry on SPRND's research. Tyrwhitt modelled APRR on PEP and embarked on a comprehensive research agenda encompassing regional planning, industry, agriculture, nutrition, demography, housing, recreation, health, education, and uses of waste. This work involved developing practical applications for Geddes's principles: standardized methods for cross- disciplinary surveys and for visualizing and displaying survey data. Standardization to facilitate communication across specializations was a key aspect of APRR's effort to create a "composite mind"—Rowse's metaphor for the synthesis generated by multi-disciplinary teamwork.

Tyrwhitt was particularly proud of APRR's wartime correspondence course for armed forces personnel, for which she reorganized Rowse's school as the School of Planning and Research for Regional Development (SPRRD). The need to create a new curriculum provided a stimulus to formalizing the new scientific, humanistic concept of planning emerging from APRR's work. Tyrwhitt articulated APRR's approach in "Town Planning," in the inaugural issue of *The Architects'*

Yearbook (1945)—a journal showing how European modernism could be adapted to postwar conditions in England. Here Tyrwhitt (1945, pp. 11, 13–16, 23) invoked "the space-time scale of our generation [that] has been grandly set forth by Giedion and needs interpretation in all forms of physical planning"—referring to CIAM General Secretary and Swiss architectural historian Sigfried Giedion's already canonical book, *Space Time, and Architecture* (1941) [herein *STA*]. "The life of the future needs the two contrasts in scale expressed in the same plan: a sense of space, freedom of movement, scope for expression, together with closely knit neighborhood life." Humanistic mastery of our technical abilities—dramatically advanced by the war—depended on the "intimate neighborhood life ... [that] breeds social consciousness and civic responsibility." This lesson was confirmed by civil defense measures which demonstrated the value of "some form of common meeting-place" for neighbors. In such democratic civic centers "positive health ... is encouraged by the full and free development of the varied potentialities of each individual ... within the pattern of the community." Tyrwhitt continued to develop this creative synthesis of Geddes' bioregionalism and modernist ideals—notably as formulated by Giedion—in the years ahead.

Concurrent Encounters: McLuhan and Giedion in the 1940s

While McLuhan was in St. Louis (1940–4) he encountered the ideas of both Giedion and, indirectly, Geddes, via the writings of American social critic Lewis Mumford. As McLuhan biographer Philip Marchand (1989, p. 77) reports, "these two writers ... left him with important suggestions about technology that he would develop in his mature work." Significantly, McLuhan was particularly inspired by Mumford's book, *Technics and Civilization* (1934), which is based on Geddes's ideas. Marchand contends that Mumford's "description of a world bound by a communication network is not far from the vision behind" McLuhan's famous phrase "global village;" in fact Mumford acknowledges his intellectual debt to Geddes for this vision.

McLuhan met Giedion when he gave a lecture in St. Louis in 1943, while traveling to research his next book, *Mechanization Takes Command* (1948) [herein *MTC*]. Neither man had yet read the other, but they shared an interest in modernist poets, literature, and the unity of art and science. McLuhan soon read and was profoundly inspired by both *STA* and *MTC* (Marchand, 1989, p. 78); he corresponded with Giedion for several years (Toye, 1987, p. 131). To help advance McLuhan's career, in 1943 Giedion commended him to economic historian John Nef Jr., as a "promising young scholar" who would fit into Nef's interdisciplinary Committee on Social Thought at the University of Chicago (cited in McEwen,

2017). Giedion's introduction, while not immediately productive, was prescient. The work of Nef's protégé, political economist Harold Innes at the University of Toronto (UT), notably *Empire and Communications* (1950), "influenced McLuhan greatly" (Toye, 1987, p. 219).

Concurrent Encounters: Kepes and Giedion in the 1940s

Giedion, who was stranded in the US and based in New York City (NYC) during the war, made frequent trips to Chicago to visit his old friend Moholy-Nagy at the New Bauhaus school (later Institute of Design), where he got to know Kepes. They stayed in touch after Kepes moved to NYC in 1943 to teach at Brooklyn College (at the invitation of Tyrwhitt's MARS member colleague Serge Chermayeff). Giedion wrote an introduction to Kepes' *Language of Vision* (1944), which built on Kepes' work with Moholy-Nagy, adapting biotechnical modernist principles explicitly to support American democratic civic ideals (Turner, 2013, p. 95). In this book, historian Anna Vallye (2011, p. 279) explains, Kepes "advanced a philosophy of ... a visual technology of knowledge, oriented to training 'the creative imagination for positive social action.'" In 1945, William Wurster, then Dean of the School of Architecture at Massachusetts Institute of Technology (MIT), hired Kepes to establish this type of educational program as part of an initiative to modernize the architecture curriculum and bolster the humanities there. Giedion's friend, historian John Burchard was helping lead that effort, and later invited Giedion to contribute to it. But it is Tyrwhitt's transatlantic shift, beginning in 1945, that impelled Giedion to pursue such opportunities at MIT.

Post-War Planning for Reconstruction: Renewal of Transnational Exchange

Tyrwhitt's first trip to North America, in early spring 1945, was an official lecture tour to report on town planning for post-war Britain. In Canada she met practically everyone in the nascent Canadian planning movement. One leading planner, Humphrey Carter, was her close friend from their AA student days. In the U.S., thanks to her membership in the MARS group, she met many CIAM émigrés, among them Moholy-Nagy and Giedion. Tyrwhitt was particularly taken by Moholy-Nagy, who led her to a new appreciation for the aesthetics of planning. Back in London she continued her work, previously preoccupied with social and economic concerns, from this new perspective: "A plan is a design," she wrote in "Training the Planner" (1946, 210–11); "the planner must be ... a creative artist who not only sees what is in terms of what could be, but has the power to set this down in such a manner that his vision is shared and understood by others." She also reoriented APPR's Information Service to an international audience, offering subscribers a bimonthly bulletin reporting on the work of APRR as well as summary of "matters of interest in the planning world"—presaging her work for Doxiadis as co-founder and editor of the journal *Ekistics*, Doxiadis's term for the science of human settlements, discussed below.

Evolutionary Humanistic Planning

Tyrwhitt was immersed in the utopian optimism buoying those who converged in London in 1946 to re-establish pre-war ties in the context of the new UN organizations. Julian Huxley (1946, pp. 8, 7), who became the first General Secretary of the UN Educational, Scientific, and Cultural Organization (UNESCO) Preparatory Commission, voiced this spirit in proposing that the "general philosophy of UNESCO should ... be a scientific world humanism, global in extent and evolutionary in perspective." Notably, Huxley's evolutionary humanism was partly inspired by Geddes' ideas (Goujon, 2001, pp. 38–9). Tyrwhitt had this international audience in mind in producing *Patrick Geddes in India* (1947), an edited collection of excerpts from Geddes's town planning reports Geddes prepared for Indian cities 1915–19. Tyrwhitt selected texts to demonstrate the relevance of Geddes's town planning principles to the worldwide task of urban reconstruction and the realization of a new cooperative world order that the UNO would foster. These included "diagnosis before treatment" (survey before plan) and "conservative surgery," (rehabilitation rather than removal); and especially, "bioregionalism," (people and place are inseparable). That is "what makes this book particularly apt and timely for the days ahead," Lewis Mumford (1947, p. 9) affirmed: "One cannot appreciate Geddes's regionalism unless one also appreciates his internationalism, his universalism."

Tyrwhitt's growing involvement in the MARS group further enriched her new aesthetic perspective and internationalism. The MARS group hosted CIAM 6, the first post-war conference, in Bridgwater, England, in 1947. After a hiatus of ten years, CIAM members explicitly reformulated their goals in alignment with Huxley's vision for UNESCO in resolving to "undertake the task of imagining the new world of man as a whole," by engaging CIAM's "logical processes of evolution to town planning" (Thomas, 1951, p. 10). They also embraced Giedion's (1951, p. 30) call for a new focus on aesthetics as "a part of our attitude towards the world." Publication that year of Moholy-Nagy's *Vision in Motion* (1947)—a new edition of *The New Vision* (1928)—was a timely reminder that he'd previously formulated the link between planning and aesthetics: "Vision in motion also signifies planning, the projective dynamics of our visionary faculties" (Moholy-Nagy, 1947, p. 12). The process of planning CIAM 6 together fostered Tyrwhitt's and Giedion's personal connection. As their friendship deepened, she became drawn into his relationships with both Kepes and McLuhan.

Tyrwhitt's Trans-Atlantic Shift

Tyrwhitt began actively seeking international work in early 1948. She was nominated for a UN job, but Giedion felt "it as a kind of moral duty to help UNESCO," which then contemplated a community planning program (cited in Shoshkes, 2013, p. 104). Tyrwhitt's friend Catherine Bauer, an American housing expert now married to William Wurster and lecturing at the Harvard Graduate School of Design (GSD), agreed, as UNESCO was "the only outfit that could deliberately set out to *broaden the horizons of the housing and planning movement*, relating it to the other elements in development of a world culture" (cited in Shoshkes, 2013, pp. 104–5). Tyrwhitt didn't get the UN job, but when she took advantage of an opportunity to spend a month in the US in spring 1948, paying her way by giving lectures, she launched her career as a transnational actor.

Housing expert Charles Abrams (1902–70) hosted Tyrwhitt in New York and arranged for her to lecture at the New School for Social Research on Britain's post-war planning. She soon lined up lectures at Yale, Harvard, MIT, and Columbia. The Wursters hosted her visit to Harvard and MIT. There she was invited to contribute to the first post-war issue of the student journal *TASK* 7/8 (1948), which was dedicated to reconstruction worldwide. Kepes, now running a Visual Design program at MIT, designed the cover. In her Introduction Bauer Wurster (p. 6) hailed transnational organizations such as UN and UNESCO that were instigating the "revival and intensification" of "broad-based international fellowship and cross-fertilization in this field." Tyrwhitt was eager to engage in this network of exchange. Back in England she helped Giedion and MARS group chair Max Fry plan the CIAM's first educational effort, an international summer school, held in London that July, modelling a program for educational reform in architecture they hoped UNESCO would disseminate.

Tyrwhitt returned to New York in September to give a series of lectures at the New School, honing her synthesis of Geddes's bioregionalism and CIAM modernism. In between her weekly talks she travelled on speaking engagements, broadening her network and perspective. In Chicago, at the Institute of Design (formerly New Bauhaus, now led by Chermayeff) she encountered Buckminster

Fuller, whose "Dymaxion" ideas resonated with her background in botany. In Cambridge she participated in seminars at Harvard and MIT. Encouraged by her reception she felt inspired to develop her own voice and interpretation of Geddes. For her final New School lecture, she reprised one that Geddes gave there in 1923 which includes a description of the Valley Section, one of his key concepts.

Cities in Evolution

Tyrwhitt included part of her rendering of Geddes' talk on the Valley Section in the Introduction to the abridged edition of his *Cities in Evolution* (1915), which refers to this concept without defining it. Tyrwhitt produced this edition on behalf of APRR and Geddes' son, Arthur; they hoped this book, then out of print for more than a generation, would again serve, as Geddes had intended on the eve of World War One, as a guide for post-war reconstruction and renewal. Here Geddes (1915, p. xxx) affirmed: "Eutopia ... lies in the city around us; and it must be planned and realized, here or nowhere, by us as its citizens—each a citizen of both the actual and the ideal city seen increasingly as one." Tyrwhitt (1949, p. x) argued: "Perhaps it is only now ... that the time is ... ripe for ... this book. Now that simultaneous thinking—a process that seemed almost magical when demonstrated by Geddes with the aid of his ... [diagrams] has become insisted upon in the popular writings of every *philosophical scientist*." To that end APRR's edition includes appendices that analyze Geddes's Notation of Life diagram as "an early systems model;" and excerpts Geddes' explanation of how this diagram demonstrates the interrelation of environmental and socio-cultural evolution.

Mumford—tacitly acknowledging Tyrwhitt's new prominence as an authority on Geddes—used his review of APRR's edition of *Cities in Evolution* in the *Architectural Review* (1950, August, p. 82) as the occasion for his own reassessment Geddes's "contribution to city planning and civic philosophy," declaring that Geddes "is fast becoming a rallying center for the best minds of this generation." This was largely due to Tyrwhitt's efforts as editor, translator, and interpreter. As discussed below, Tyrwhitt will likewise bring the significance of Geddes's ideas to bear in both McLuhan's Communications and Culture Seminar and Doxiadis' Delos Symposia.

Tyrwhitt as Transnational Intermediary

Throughout her transatlantic activities Tyrwhitt remained in close contact with Giedion in Zurich. When she was in Cambridge, MA in 1948 Giedion wrote: "I would like to work next fall in USA if you are there. I would like to help to reform

MIT" (cited in Shoshkes, 2013, p. 115). Tyrwhitt tactfully explored that idea over lunch with Wurster and Burchard, now the first Dean of the MIT School of Humanities. Wurster then gave Tyrwhitt a tour of MIT's new dormitory designed by Finnish architect Alvar Aalto. Giedion relied on Tyrwhitt's account of her experience of this building for the new chapter he was writing about Aalto for the second (1949) edition of *STA*. Significantly, Tyrwhitt's account—which Giedion (1950) cited verbatim in an article based on the chapter—presaged her text on "vision in motion" in "The Moving Eye" in *Explorations 4* (1955) (see below). Historian Nicholas Bullock (2002, p. 48) asserts that Giedion's new Aalto chapter offered an "organic" aesthetic and integrative approach as "a powerful spur to thinking about an alternative to function" at a time when architects and planners were searching for a "new humanism." Significantly, this chapter, and most of Giedion's work in English after this time, was an unacknowledged *collaboration* with Tyrwhitt.

Giedion literally wanted Tyrwhitt to be "his eyes and ears" in the US to monitor the reception of *MTC* (1949). Tyrwhitt tracked and lined up reviews, so she would have read McLuhan's (1949, p. 599) joint assessment of *MTC* and *Vision in Motion* in *The Hudson Review*: "The present volumes suggest a variety of means whereby English might … resume the plenary functions of the older classical education." It was in this context of educational reform in architecture and the humanities that Giedion wrote Burchard, in 1949, about opportunities at MIT. Burchard, eager to strengthen MIT's new School of Humanities invited Giedion to give a series of public lectures in spring 1950 on "The Role of Art in Contemporary Life," as a Visiting Professor in the departments of History and English (Geiser, 2018, p. 418). Coincidentally, McLuhan, now teaching English at the University of Toronto (UT), spoke on this same topic at the multi-disciplinary "Values" Discussion Group chaired by Innis in spring 1949, as part of a parallel effort to bolster the humanities at UT (Buxton, 2004, pp. 191–2.)

In addition to his lectures at MIT lectures, Giedion led a seminar on "Civic Centers and Social Life." Tyrwhitt, back in the United Kingdom, translated and edited much of Giedion's MIT lectures (as well as his new material for the 1949 edition of *STA*). In April 1950 she managed to return to the US, initially staying with Giedion in Cambridge. This brought Tyrwhitt in close contact with Kepes, who was helping students in Giedion's seminar prepare their visual presentations. At this time Kepes was attending weekly discussions hosted by MIT mathematician Norbert Wiener on new developments in the sciences. Kepes was deeply impressed by Wiener's cybernetics synthesis, as well as related work suggesting that "one's capacity to orient oneself is based on the ability of the neurological system to discern invariance in continuous transformation," according to historian

Judith Weschler (1978, p. 12), who suggests that Kepes applied these ideas as *metaphors*. Thanks to Kepes, Giedion attended two of Wiener's discussion groups, where he, too, found confirmation for his own ideas—notably his notion of a new type of *man in equipoise*, or dynamic equilibrium in an environment of constant change (Martin, 1998, p. 109). Tyrwhitt was also excited by the cybernetic ideas percolating at MIT, as was McLuhan. Essentially, Giedion, Tyrwhitt, Kepes and McLuhan were moving ever closer within their shared constellation of ideas and growing proximity in the space of what we might call "greater New England" (encompassing Toronto).

The Core of the City: The Vital Center

Tyrwhitt can be seen applying cybernetic ideas as metaphors in "The Valley Section: Geddes' World Image" (1951), written in preparation for the 8th CIAM congress, on the theme of the urban core as a center for civic life, which the MARS group hosted in 1951. For this essay she combed Geddes' lectures to find passages that clarified the inter-relationship between his Valley Section and Notation of Life diagrams. Tyrwhitt demonstrated how they operated together to model processes of guided social evolution grounded in a particular city region, highlighting the vital role of centers of social activity in this cybernetic system. More broadly, in the context of the cold war, Tyrwhitt and the MARS group's focus on "the vital center" as a place (like historian Arthur Schlesinger's 1949 book of that title, addressing its political dimensions) echoed appeals in many arenas (e.g., psychological, cultural), "for cybernetics and scientific humanism … [as the basis for] individual autonomy within a collaborative society," in the words of communications scholar Fred Turner (2013, pp. 175–7). The concept of the core gave geographic specificity to these abstract political-social ideals.

CIAM president Jose Luis Sert wrote about the upcoming "CIAM 8: The core of the city" in the second issue (1951) of *trans/formations: art, communication, environment*, a short-lived journal founded by Harry Holzman and Martin James (*MTC*'s English translator), to advance discourse affirming "that art, science, and technology are interacting components of the total human enterprise" (Editorial, 1950, p. 1). Sert, Giedion and Tyrwhitt—then working with Sert in New York on CIAM and UN affairs while teaching at Yale—were consulting editors (Vallye, 2009, pp. 29, 50). Significantly, McLuhan (1987, p. 223) was then thinking along similar lines; in March 1951 he sent Innis his proposal for an "experiment in communication" inspired by Innis' work as well as the "method used by my friend Sigfried Giedion." This experiment became the

Culture and Communications seminar (1953–4) discussed below. *Explorations*, the "humanistic" journal associated with that seminar, was explicitly modelled on *trans/formations* (Carpenter, 2001, p. 240). Tyrwhitt's essay "Ideal Cities and the City Ideal," in *Explorations 2* in April 1954, was originally written for *trans/formations*, which folded in 1953.

The Core and the Urban Constellation

At this time Tyrwhitt was searching for an ideal conception of a city at the *metropolitan* scale, revitalizing the role of the central city (the core) as an alternative to growing calls for urban decentralization along English garden city lines. Her thinking crystalized when she met with Kepes at MIT in April 1951 (to collect illustrations from Giedion's seminar to display at CIAM 8). Kepes guided Tyrwhitt through his recently opened New Landscape exhibit, an assemblage of images created in MIT labs revealing what he described as "new frontiers of the visible world" that provided "new models of relatedness" (cited in Weschler, 1978, p. 12). This exhibit led Tyrwhitt to an original analytic insight: a further development of Geddes' concept of the conurbation. She recalled, the "photographs of the heavenly constellations ... of microscopic biological life ... of plant cells ... of whirlpools and deserts ... of inorganic crystalline formations" evoked an image of what she termed "the urban constellation" to describe the dynamic relationships of cities, villages and towns organized around "a vital city center" (cited in Shoshkes, 2013, p. 142.)

Tyrwhitt presented her new formulation in May 1951 at the American Institute of Architects (AIA) Conference in Chicago, where she moderated a prominent panel on new towns as a strategy for civil defense. Excerpts from her talk were subsequently published as "The Next Phase in City Growth—The Urban Constellation" and illustrated with images from Kepes's New Landscape exhibit in a special section on architecture for civil defense featured in *Progressive Architecture* (September 1951). Asked: Do decentralized new towns provide safety in the event of a nuclear attack? Tyrwhitt's (1951, p. 77) response was a resounding NO: "There must be a vital city center to which all parts of the [urban] constellation have access."

At CIAM 8 in July 1951 Tyrwhitt used the urban constellation to frame discussions of the urban core "at five 'scale levels' of community: housing group, neighborhood, town or city sector, city, and metropolis." In her remarks at the congress and in the accompanying book *CIAM 8: The heart of the city* (1952), for which she was the lead editor (which also included images from Kepes' exhibit) Tyrwhitt (1952, p. 104) emphasized: The Core wasn't "a group of civic buildings together with their related open spaces," but rather "the gathering place of the people ... a physical setting for the expression of collective emotion." The "cure for our ... amorphous modern cities" and urban decline was not to be found in urban decentralization along garden city lines but "by the creation of new Cores—new concentrations of activity—by a visual emphasis upon centers of integration rather than ... bands of separation."

Meanwhile, Tyrwhitt had been exploring job opportunities in Toronto with Humphrey Carver, who, in his capacity as chairman of the Research Committee of the Canada Mortgage and Housing Corporation (CMHC) was encouraging Canadian universities to create postgraduate planning education courses. CMHC was underwriting programs at three universities, however the University of Toronto's "President, Dr. Sydney Smith was hard to budge," Carver (1975, pp. 120, 123) recalled: "eventually an arrangement was made" to hire Tyrwhitt. She received the job offer in August and began work as Visiting Professor of Town Planning in September 1951.

1951–1955: Toronto Explorations

Tyrwhitt's main charge at UT was to set up a pilot one-year postgraduate certificate program in town planning that offered "students the opportunity to learn and to relate to one another the social, economic and aesthetic problems of community environments" (U. of Toronto, 1952, p. 31). She also gave a lecture course based on her Yale lectures. She had to juggle this job with continuing work editing the CIAM 8 book, which took another nine months. In November Giedion received a copy of McLuhan's recently published *The Mechanical Bride* (1951), prompting him to encourage McLuhan to contact Tyrwhitt, "one of his best friends" (cited in Shoshkes, 2013, p. 147); and he encouraged Tyrwhitt to meet McLuhan, who he considered "one of the few on the right way." Almost immediately McLuhan invited Tyrwhitt to his home for dinner and she soon became a family friend. But after returning to NY for winter break Tyrwhitt felt "exhilarated" to be back among people she had "something in common with," whereas she didn't yet feel connected to anyone in Toronto, even those she liked best, including McLuhan. Seeing Martin James reminded her of the article she'd promised him for *trans/formations*. Newly inspired, she quickly wrote "City Ideals and the Ideal City" based on her first two lectures in Toronto. This essay concludes with hope that a nascent "revolution of humanism ... can be glimpsed between the lines of S. Giedion's [*MTC*] and ... run[s] like a gleaming thread through the CIAM discussions on the 'Heart of the City'"—underscoring Tyrwhitt's (1954, p. 50) preoccupation then on her work with Giedion, Sert and CIAM.

By spring term Tyrwhitt was more involved in "the Canadian scene" and keen to "find a team that could really do something" (cited in Shoshkes, 2013, p. 148). Happily, her contract was renewed for another year. In her second year at UT, Tyrwhitt deepened her bond with McLuhan's family when she helped around the house after their sixth child was born in October 1952. She also became more established on the faculty and optimistically agreed to be part of a faculty team McLuhan formed for a proposal to the Ford Foundation for a two-year seminar to study "changing patterns of language and behavior and the new media of communication," based on the work of Innis, Giedion, Weiner, et. al. In addition to McLuhan (English), the other faculty sponsors were Edward Carpenter (anthropology), Tom Easterbrook (economic history) and Carl Williams (psychology). The proposal touted Tyrwhitt as a "pioneer of interdisciplinary studies in Britain ... long associated with the research projects of Sigfried Giedion" who was advancing inter-disciplinary efforts around town planning at Toronto (cited in Shoshkes, 2013, p. 148).

Concurrently Tyrwhitt had been working on inter-related CIAM and UN affairs in NY with Sert and CIAM member Ernest Weissmann, newly appointed Assistant Director of the new Town and Country Planning Section of the UN Division of Social Affairs. In early 1953, after Sert was named dean of the Harvard Graduate School of Design (GSD) and chair of the Architecture Department, he hinted he might need Tyrwhitt's help at Harvard in something "very interesting and right up her alley." Part of her felt "there is a good job to be done [in Toronto] IF ONE STAYS HERE and does the job thoroughly; another winces at the very idea," she wrote Giedion in Zurich (cited in Shoshkes, 2013, p. 153). She saw McLuhan's proposal as a way of getting Giedion invited to the university which would make her more willing to stay there.

Uncertainty in Toronto and a UN Mission to India

But Tyrwhitt's future and the fate of town planning at UT was uncertain, as permanent funding for the program wasn't yet secured. In March Weissmann recruited Tyrwhitt to lead a UN technical (TA) mission (a first for a woman) in India, as Project Director to advise the Indian government on an International Exhibition of Low-cost Housing, and to organize a concurrent Seminar on Housing and Community Improvement in Asia, to further promote information exchange. A main discussion topic at the seminar—the first of its kind—would be the education of planners. Without an offer from UT, she accepted the UN job, a ten-month assignment beginning in May. President Smith agreed to consider a three-year appointment starting in fall 1954, pending funding. Tyrwhitt left Toronto presuming she'd return.

Tyrwhitt was doing preparatory work in Geneva, Switzerland in July 1953 when she learned the Ford Foundation had funded McLuhan's proposal, and the seminar would commence that fall term. She promptly wrote McLuhan suggesting they begin by establishing a common vocabulary, then conduct a study along the lines of Giedion's "inter-faculty study of methodology," even possibly invite "Giedion over to frame the program" (cited in Shoshkes, 2013, p. 166). But she wondered: "Where do I fit in?" UT's announcement of this prestigious award noted Tyrwhitt's proficiency "at planning cooperation between academic departments"—a skill not attributed to any other team member. The need for someone with her skills soon became apparent. McLuhan wrote Tyrwhitt in India that they were struggling to find a common focus and were using some grant funds to publish a journal, *Explorations*, to foster collaboration. McLuhan also hoped that discussing Giedion's work (and Kepes's) over the summer would help the fractious group (later known as the Explorations Group) coalesce.

Meanwhile, in India, delegates at Tyrwhitt's UN seminar, which included Doxiadis (who had just launched his multidisciplinary consulting firm), affirmed the importance of comprehensive physical planning as a distinct profession. The challenge was how to introduce planning education in countries where the profession was not yet well established. That included Canada. In April 1954, while in London, Tyrwhitt learned that UT had eliminated both her position and the town planning program. Greatly distressed, Carver wrote Tyrwhitt that his efforts to consolidate support were "resented as the intrusion of a government official." He'd continue to advocate to set up the course, conceivably in 1955. But "this will require much conspiracy and effort—and where are the conspirators?" (cited in Shoshkes, 2013, p. 174). Tyrwhitt went to Toronto in June determined to help. With McLuhan's backing President Smith allowed reallocation of grant funds to support her as the seminar's secretary. This position provided a foothold for her to try to restore the planning program.

The Explorations Group Year 2

Tyrwhitt threw herself into her role as seminar secretary, proposing to begin by editing their existing material so "this winter we produce ... the results of some group work ... not just an interesting collection of essays but ... achieve some sort of synthesis and state some sort of theory" (cited in Shoshkes, 2013, p. 174). Her offer to work with Giedion to develop his contribution spurred the team to discuss *STA* that summer. Tyrwhitt probably suggested they read the third, expanded edition of *STA* (1954, pp. 785–6) for which she'd translated new content relevant to the seminar: a chapter on "Perspective and Urban Planning;" and a section—citing her edition of *Cities in Evolution*—that lauds Geddes' reading of a city plan as "a system of hieroglyphics, in which man has written the history of civilization" and equates Mumford's appreciation of Geddes' universalism with a passage from James Joyce. Tyrwhitt played a key role in the seminar as its liaison with Giedion as well as an interpreter and guide to his writings.

The seminar began its second year by discussing "models" in their fields. Tyrwhitt introduced the Core of the City as a model for town planning, and the seminar discussed readings from *CIAM 8: The Heart of the City*. At the second meeting she led a discussion of Giedion's work, using her copy of unpublished text, "The Study of Anonymous History," and *MTC*'s Epilogue, highlighting his concept of *man in equipoise*. For their third meeting the faculty attended an Institute on Culture and Communication at the University of Louisville (October 22–3), which notably included anthropologists Margaret Mead, who Tyrwhitt had met during the war, and Dorothy Lee. Tyrwhitt would have seen *Cultural Patterns and Technical Change* (1953), edited by Mead (1953, p. 9) with Lee for UNESCO, assessing the expansion of the UN TA program: a "new assumption on an international scale of responsibility for introducing changes which are needed among peoples in areas of the world which can visibly benefit from the knowledge which the people of other areas have." Mead, later a stalwart participant in the Delos Symposia, and Lee, later Tyrwhitt's colleague at Harvard and lifelong friend in Athens, helped Tyrwhitt understand the relevance of the Culture and Communications Seminar to her work with the UN, at Harvard and with Doxiadis.

The Moving Eye

That same week Tyrwhitt decided to write her seminar paper on "Architectural Space in India: Fatehpur Sikri," a Mughal city she'd visited in India, probably with Doxiadis. Furthermore, the faculty chose her proposal to organize a survey on Perception of the Visual Environment as one of four experiments to carry out with the Ryerson Institute. Carpenter countered that "LANGUAGE was the basic study of the seminar and ... discussions on Giedion's work [on architectural space] had ... thrown the group off the track." Tyrwhitt helped the group stay focused on the topic of media bias in which "VISION and SPACE" were important factors (Tyrwhitt, 1954a). By then Sert had invited Tyrwhitt to speak at GSD in January

1955 (essentially, a job talk). Tyrwhitt had this broader audience in mind as she helped design the Ryerson survey and wrote her paper, "Fatehpur Sikri: The Space Concept of a Moghul City Core" (published as "The Moving Eye" in *Explorations* 4). In this essay Tyrwhitt (1955, pp. 90, 93, 94) noted that once a spectator "steps within this urban core he becomes an intimate part of the scene, which … discloses itself gradually to him, at his own pace …" She found a key to this composition in Doxiadis' thesis—which she hadn't read yet so she probably learned it from him in India—that the Athenian Acropolis was designed to be seen from viewpoints along a processional path that present "a carefully balanced panoramic scene … or 'eyeful.'" Tyrwhitt posited that "this panoramic view presented to a moving eye" was closer to the principles underlying Fatehpur Sikri's design than linear perspective from a fixed viewpoint.

Tyrwhitt's paper, along with one Williams presented that day on "Auditory Space," famously prompted McLuhan to conceive of two-dimensional, centerless, "acoustic space" (versus visual space)—"an all-purpose tool that he used to the end of his career" (Marchand, 1989, p. 133). But neither Tyrwhitt nor Giedion, who visited the seminar in February 1954, engaged with McLuhan's concept of acoustic space. She was concerned with the physical space we inhabit: "dynamic space—remembered and anticipated, before and behind—but still 'physical'" (cited in Darroch, 2008. p. 166). That was the focus of the Ryerson survey.

The City Unseen

The Ryerson survey—considered the group's "major effort" that year—resulted from Tyrwhitt's determination that they "achieve some sort of synthesis and state some sort of theory." Tyrwhitt supplied a theoretical perspective for analyzing the results, presenting excerpts from "The Valley Section: Geddes' World Image" at a meeting in March. Tyrwhitt and William's paper on the Ryerson experiment featured a quote from Geddes that began: "Every modern city is only the most complex evolutionary expression and development of the life of nature." They concluded: "[A]s these students are without any concept with which they can assess the aesthetic values of their environment, beauty passes them by unseen" (Tyrwhitt & Williams, 1955, pp. 79, 95). Tyrwhitt brought that material with her to Harvard, where in February she'd been appointed Assistant Professor of City Planning, "so that it can be re-used if worthwhile," she wrote Giedion (cited in Shoshkes, 2013, p. 175). "But it's more in Kepes' line," she acknowledged, referring to Kepes's research along similar lines with Kevin Lynch at MIT on the perceptual form of the city.

1955–1964: Urban Design and Ekistics

By March 1955, Tyrwhitt's efforts in concert with Carver and CMHC president Stewart Bates, secured an endowment for the first chair of town and regional planning in Canada. In April the Explorations Group seminar came to an end, as did the most active phase of Tyrwhitt's collaboration with McLuhan. Meanwhile Tyrwhitt had sent her paper on Fatehpur Sikri to Doxiadis, who was impressed by her "ideas about the space concept" and wanted to work with her again. He asked Tyrwhitt, if, while at Harvard, she would prepare a monthly bulletin of international information, like APRR's Information Bulletin, for the far-flung staff of his growing international consulting firm. Tyrwhitt agreed, as long it would also go to UN TA. In October 1955 she published the first bulletin, which later became the journal *Ekistics*. She now sought to connect McLuhan to her work at both Harvard and with Doxiadis.

Urban Design at Harvard

Sert had recruited Tyrwhitt to join Giedion in helping him introduce a new urban design curriculum at GSD as "the meeting ground of architects, landscape architects, and city planners." Sert's vision was to adapt CIAM urbanism—notably Tyrwhitt's concept of the core and the urban constellation—to the growing urban crisis in America, i.e., uncontrolled sprawl and central city decline. Tyrwhitt was well-suited for this role, as she knew many members of Sert's predominantly new faculty, most of whom had ties to CIAM, as well as allied colleagues at MIT, such as Kepes. An important part of her job was to organize a major conference on urban design, in April 1956, to build support for the new curriculum "in view of the great interest in urban renewal and urban redevelopment and the continued growth of cities" in the US (Sert, 1956, p. 492). An incentive for this interest was federal and state funding for urban redevelopment, which was contingent on preparation of multi-sectoral plans. However, there was a shortage of planners trained to deal with multi-faceted urban problems. The premise of Sert's conference—and the new urban design curriculum—was that this work called for a comprehensive approach to *physical* planning, at a scale and complexity requiring a specially trained multi-disciplinary team. Sert hoped this conference, the first in a series, would build consensus among GSD's three disciplines on the *aesthetic* aspects of physical planning as a basis for such collaboration. Kepes supported Sert's approach. Kepes spoke at the first urban design conference and a follow-up roundtable during which participants decided to frame the field narrowly as "the design section of the planning process;" and to discuss issues raised by this definition at a second conference in April 1957. There Kepes and Lynch presented their research on the perceptual form of the city, Tyrwhitt's role in Harvard's urban design program and conferences (1956–64) brought her closer to Kepes, whom she saw often, as a friend with shared professional interests and values.

Connecting McLuhan to Harvard

Tyrwhitt re-connected with McLuhan in 1959 when she was involved in a design competition for a new Toronto City Hall (part of an urban renewal plan). That fall he began a sabbatical from UT to develop a syllabus for the study of media in high school. This led to the production of his "Report on Project in Understanding New Media," in June 1960. The strain of that work contributed to his suffering a near-fatal stroke (Marchand, 1989, p. 159). Concerned for his health, in late 1960 Tyrwhitt suggested he spend a recuperative term at Harvard, and possibly contribute to Harvard's new center for visual arts. The Committee on Visual Arts, chaired by Sert, decided that this center should focus on communications, aligned with urban design concerns about environmental legibility (Churchill, 1959). Their rationale resonated with McLuhan's warning, in the preface of his report on new media, "that media are capable of 'imposing' their 'own assumptions' on the people who use them" (Marchand, 1989, p. 155).

McLuhan (1960, 278) liked the idea of being at Harvard, and responded to Tyrwhitt by positioning his own theories in terms of urban planning: "The problem of urban planning today in the field of nuclei that *is* the global village is assuming more and more the character of language itself, in which all words at all times comprise *all* the senses, but in ever shifting ratios which permit ever new light to come through them." Unphased by the opacity of McLuhan's writing Tyrwhitt looked for ways to bring him to Harvard. In May 1961, she invited him to speak at her Freshman Seminar—a pilot program that Dorothy Lee helped launch "to confront freshmen with new ways of seeing and understanding." To bolster Tyrwhitt's efforts on his behalf McLuhan sent Tyrwhitt a letter from Roland Penrose, chairman of the Institute for Contemporary Art in London, endorsing a project McLuhan had proposed. Tyrwhitt used this letter, unsuccessfully, to rally support from Sert, who knew Penrose well. Tyrwhitt (1963, n.p.) gently flagged an obstacle McLuhan faced: "Roland recognized your value in the visual field—just ... from your writing (which means he is fairly hard working as a reader as well as perspicacious) while the chaps here just took you as an interesting passing phenomenon." At this time McLuhan was writing profusely but as Marchand (1989, p. 198) confirms, the "quality of his writing ... did not boost McLuhan's reputation, even among those sympathetic to his ideas." (Kepes was tapped to lead Harvard's visual arts center—named Carpenter Center when it opened in 1963—but declined as he was planning his own center at MIT).

Connecting McLuhan to Delos

Alongside her work at Harvard, Tyrwhitt spent summers in Athens, supporting Doxiadis's efforts to build an institutional base for ekistics as a new discipline. In the summer of 1962, she assumed a wider range of responsibilities for Doxiadis. Notably she joined the planning committee for what Doxiadis called the Delos Symposion: an "informal meeting with free exchange of bold ideas" on the "problems facing urban settlements today and, in the future" (Delos, 1963, p. 205). This gathering occurred during a two-week Aegean cruise in July 1963. Doxiadis relied on Tyrwhitt's organizational skills as well as her London, CIAM, Toronto, Harvard, and UN contacts to plan this event and the guest list. Many of the 34 attendees—from different countries, disciplines, backgrounds, and positions—were Tyrwhitt's connections. One was Stewart Bates, Tyrwhitt's ally in Toronto, who had seen "the extraordinary opportunity for CMHC to be an influence upon the evolution of Canadian society through shaping the urban environment" (Carver, 1975, p. 134). Another was McLuhan (1963, p. 289), who received a last-minute invitation in April 1963. In appealing to Bates for travel funds, McLuhan attested: "My concern with the crisis in the evolution of human settlements stems from years of study of the effects of media of communication and transportation on changing patterns of human association and living."

As the sole rapporteur Tyrwhitt captured the spirit of the discussions in the symposion in her report in *Ekistics* (October 1963). She analyzed the participants' "differing points of view ... [to] demonstrate how they found a common language that led to the synthesis" stated in the Declaration of Delos (Report, 1963, p. 205). Tyrwhitt noted McLuhan's caution: "Are we selecting as key problems things that are possibly about to disappear with the rise of information levels, such as congestion and confusion?" However, she also cited his optimistic vision that the electronic extension of the human brain "to embrace the globe," reduced "the planet to the scale of a village." McLuhan posited that this "involves each of us totally in the family of man, ... which constitutes a new kind of continuous learning. ... The most important task of the planner is to prepare the environment for the exploitation of this ... tremendous opportunity" (cited in Report, 1963, pp. 207, 206). Significantly, as noted above—and Tyrwhitt clearly knew—McLuhan's idea of a "global village" is close to Geddes's vision of the postindustrial, biotechnical world, as articulated by Mumford in *Technics and Civilization* (1934).

At the final session of the symposion participants unanimously adopted The Delos Declaration, which both defined the problem and suggested a solution:

> Science and technology determine more and more of the processes of human living ... What is not realized is that the failure to adapt human settlements to dynamic change may soon ... [present] the gravest risk, short of war, facing the human species. ... Thus, the need for rational and dynamic planning of human settlements ... (Report, 1963, pp. 205–6).

The Delians resolved to reconvene in a year. At this moment in time McLuhan shared their understanding of the nature of the global urban crisis and the need for scientific, humanistic planning—vision in motion. In signing the Delos Declaration, he declared: "I am about to ... organize a center this fall in Canada, and I hope that through it I will be able to keep in constant association with all of you. It was a wonderful experience" (cited in Report, 1963, p. 253).

Diverging Paths

After publication of *Understanding Media* in 1964 McLuhan was greatly in demand; he was too busy to accept Tyrwhitt's invitation to visit her Freshman Seminar that spring term or attend Delos 2 in July. It was at Delos 2 that Delians formed the World Society of Ekistics (WSE), which helped convince the Ford Foundation to award a grant enabling Doxiadis to host the Delos Symposia annually through 1972. McLuhan (1964, pp. 308, 309) wrote Fuller (who attended all the symposia and served as WSE president 1975–77) that he "was not at all happy about missing the [Delos] seminar." He was eager to share his latest thoughts on "technology as creator of environment," the environment as "artefact" and the consequences of a "prepared environment for learning." (McLuhan's tendency toward technological determinism diverged from the evolutionary theories of change shared by many Delians, among them prominent biologists, physicians, geneticists, and psychologists.)

While his fame grew, McLuhan's health deteriorated. After brain surgery to remove a tumor in late 1967, he took years to recuperate, and never fully recovered (Marchand, 1989, p. 213). McLuhan (1969, p. 392) declined the invitations he received to Delos 6, 7 and 8 (1968—70), but appreciated being included, writing Doxiadis: "I think of your cruise very much." He did attend Delos 10, in July 1963, intended to be the final symposion, but did not enjoy himself.

Unlike previous years, Delos 10 was a large gathering, including special guests, family members, friends, and student observers, to celebrate the Delians' accomplishments of the previous decade. As Tyrwhitt (1978, p. 131) declared, "Without the Delos Symposia, it is doubtful that the UN would have got world support for its conferences on the environment and human settlements," beginning in 1972. Delian discourse helped shape the agenda of that first UN Conference on the Environment, which had just taken place in June 1972, in Stockholm, which promoted the new concept of sustainable development and the ideal of planetary stewardship. At Delos 10, special guest Rene Dubos (cited in Report, 1972, p. 237), a leading microbiologist who was a delegate to the UN Conference (as was Delian Barbara Ward), affirmed: "A global approach is necessary for dealing with the ecological and economic problems of the spaceship earth which affect all of us, but each human settlement has problems of its own which require local solutions" (i.e., "think globally, act locally"). The UN had seemingly fulfilled Julien Huxley's earlier call for UNESCO to adopt a philosophy of "scientific world humanism, global in extent and evolutionary in perspective."

McLuhan didn't enjoy Delos 10. His vision of "the new acoustic world" was now rather apocalyptic, and he "felt unable to get his message through to the participants" (Marchand, 1989, p. 244). McLuhan (1972, p. 453) wrote Kepes, who had attended Delos 6 and 10, that he'd felt closest to him "if only because of your understanding of the world and design." (Kepes was now director of the Center for Advanced Visual Studies at MIT.) Oddly, given the diversity of participants at Delos 10, which included many prominent scientists, McLuhan complained: "The bulk of the people there were fairly brick and mortar or hardware men who belong almost entirely to the 19th century." McLuhan was more acerbic with Margaret Mead—WSE president 1969–71—disparaging "the Delos meetings as of a very dubious quality and performance.... My own concern is with the exploration of ignorance rather than the shoring-up of knowledge" (1973, p. 464). Mead however, extolled the symposia as an exemplar of "an innovation in communication:" an informal group of diverse intellects working simultaneously in pursuit of a shared intellectual goal (1968, pp. 26–7).

Nevertheless, McLuhan joined in signing the Declaration of Delos 10, which reaffirmed the validity of the first declaration, noting the persisting and worsening crisis in world settlements and the accelerating speed of urbanization. Now Delians presented specific proposals to be brought to "the urgent attention of those who are responsible for action" (Report, 1972, p. 230). At the signing ceremony McLuhan solemnly stated: "It has been the task of the Delians to confront the problems and pollution of the world by the human dialogue of the spirit into an invaluable treasure of discovery and vision" (cited in Report, 1972, p. 291). He was more tongue-in-cheek in offering his own proposals (i.e., to build cities in complementary pairs, like yin and yang). Tyrwhitt categorized his remarks as "Communication via humor."

End Note—Finding Connections

Tyrwhitt prepared a background document for Delos 10 consisting of excerpts from *Ekistics* representing themes discussed at Delos 1–9. This document, published as *Human Identity in the Built Environment* (1972), included a chapter based on a discussion of communications at Delos 4 (1966)—which McLuhan is mis-identified as having attended. Tyrwhitt added to that chapter the same extract of McLuhan's paper for Delos 1, discussed earlier, she'd published in *Ekistics* (Report, 1963, p. 257). In choosing this passage, signifying the connection between McLuhan's optimistic idea of a "global village" and Geddes's vision (which she considered "essentially ekistic"), Tyrwhitt honored McLuhan as part of the legacy of the dialogue at Delos. The Delian's hopefulness, affirmed in the Declaration of Delos 10 (Report, 1972, p. 232), about the human capacity to "understand and deal with the most important and difficult problems of his life on earth," and create a better world, is still relevant today.

Note

1 This chapter draws on some of my previous work, notably Shoshkes (2013, 2015, 2017, 2023).

References

Bullock, N. (2002). *Building the post-war world*. Routledge.
Buxton, W. (2004). The "Values Discussion Group" at the University of Toronto, February–May 1949. *Canadian Journal of Communication, 29*(2), 187–204.
Carpenter, E. (2001). The not-so-silent sea. In D. Theall (Ed.), *The Virtual Marshall McLuhan* (pp. 236–261). McGill-Queen's University Press.
Carver, H. (1975). *Compassionate landscape*. U of Toronto Press.
Churchill, M. (1959, April 11). Design school pioneers in creative approach. *The Harvard Crimson*. Retrieved from http://www.thecrimson.com/article/1959/4/11/design-school-pioneers-in-creative-approach/?page=single.
Darroch, M. (2008). Bridging urban and media studies: Jaqueline Tyrwhitt and the explorations group 1951–197. *Canadian Journal of Communication, 33*(2), 147–169.
DeBoer-Langworth, C. (n.d.). Distributism. *The Modernist Journals Project*. Retrieved from https://modjourn.org/essay/distributism/.

Doxiadis, C. (1955, April 8). [Letter to J. Tyrwhitt]. RIBA Library Archive (Tyrwhitt papers, Box 48 Folder 3), London, UK.

Geddes, P. (1949). *Cities in evolution* (Abridged ed., orig. 1915) (J. Tyrwhitt, Ed.). Williams & Norgate.

Geiser, R. (2018). *Giedion and America*. Gta Verlag.

Giedion, S. (1950, February). Alvar Aalto. *Architectural Record*, *107*(638), 77–84.

Giedion, S. (1951). Architect, painter and sculptor. In S. Giedion (Ed.), *A decade of new architecture* (vol. 30). Editions Girsberger.

Giedion, S. (1956). *Space time and architecture* (5th ed., orig. 1941). Harvard.

Goujon, P. (2001). *From biotechnology to genomes: The meaning of the double helix*. World Scientific.

Holzman, H., & James, M. (1950). Measure of man. *Trans/Formation*, *1*(1) 1.

Huxley, J. (1946). *UNESCO: It's purpose and philosophy*. UN.

Huxley, J. (1961). The humanist frame. In J. Huxley (Ed.), *The humanist frame* (pp. 13–48). Harper & Brothers.

Kepes, G. (1947). *Language of vision*. Paul Theobold.

Marchand, P. (1989). *Marshall McLuhan: The medium and the messenger* (1998 ed.). MIT.

Martin, R. (1998, December). The organizational complex: Cybernetics, space, discourse, *Assemblage*, *37*, 102–27.

McEwen, C. (2017, May). *Giedion to Nef re a 'promising young scholar,' McLuhan's New Sciences*. Retrieved from https://mcluhansnewsciences.com/mcluhan/2017/05/giedion-to-nef-re-a-promising-young-scholar/

McLuhan, M. (1949, Winter). Encyclopedic unities. *The Hudson Review*, *1*(4), 599–602.

McLuhan, M. (1960, December 23). [Letter to J. Tyrwhitt]. In M. McLuhan, *Letters*, 277–8.

McLuhan, M. (1963, June 17). [Letter to S. Bates]. In M. McLuhan, *Letters*, 289.

McLuhan, M. (1964, September 17). [Letter to B. Fuller]. In M. McLuhan, *Letters*, 308–9.

McLuhan, M. (1972, August 1). [Letter to G. Kepes]. In *Letters*, 453.

McLuhan, M. (1973, January 25). [Letter to M. Mead]. In *Letters*, 464.

McLuhan, M. (1987). *Letters of Marshall McLuhan* (M. Molinaro, C. McLuhan & W. Toye, Eds.). Oxford University.

Mead, M. (1968). The conference process. In M. Mead & P. Byers, (Eds.), *The small conference* (pp. 42–54). De Gruyter Mouton.

Mead, M., & Lee, D. (Eds.). (1953). *Cultural patterns and technical change*. UNESCO.

Moholy-Nagy, L. (1947). *Vision in motion*. Paul Theobold.

Mumford, L. (1934). *Technics and civilization*. U of Chicago.

Mumford, L. (1947). Introduction. In J. Tyrwhitt & P. Geddes (Eds.), *Geddes in India* (pp. 7–13). Lund Humphries.

Mumford, L. (1950, August). Mumford on Geddes. *Architectural Review*, *108*(644), 81–7.

Need for more balance in the flow of communications. (1972). In J. Tyrwhitt & G. Bell (Eds.), *Human identity in the built environment* (pp. 516–27). Penguin.

Report on Delos Ten. (1972, October). *Ekistics*, *34*(203), 224–303.

Report on Delos One. (1963, October). *Ekistics, 16*(95), 205–67.

Shoshkes, E. (2013). *Jaqueline Tyrwhitt: A transnational life in urban planning and design.* Ashgate.

Shoshkes, E. (2015). Introduction. In J. Tyrwhitt & E. Shoshkes (Eds.), *Society and environment a historical review* (pp. viii–xxvi). Routledge.

Shoshkes, E. (2017). Jaqueline Tyrwhitt translates Patrick Geddes for post-world war two planning. *Landscape and Urban Planning, 166*, 15–24.

Shoshkes, E. (2023). Bioregional urbanism: Reflecting on the legacy of the RPAA through the lens of Jaqueline Tyrwhitt. *Planning Perspectives, 38*(4), 759–77.

Thomas, M. H. (1951). The report of CIAM 6, Bridgwater 1947. In S. Giedion (Ed.), *A decade of new architecture* (vol. 8, pp. 8–11). Editions Girsberger.

Toye, W. (1987). Commentary. In M. Molinaro, C. McLuhan & W. Toye (Eds.), *Letters of Marshall McLuhan.* Oxford U.

Turner, F. (2013). *The democratic surround: Multimedia and American liberalism from World War II to the psychedelic sixties.* U Chicago.

Tyrwhitt, J. (1945). Town planning. *Architects Year Book* 1, 11–29.

Tyrwhitt, J. (1947, December). Training the planner in Britain. *IFHTP News Sheet*, 209–13.

Tyrwhitt, J. (1949). Introduction. In Geddes, P. (Ed.), *Cities in evolution* (Abridged ed., orig. 1915, pp. ix–xvi). Lund Humphries.

ADD SIZE AND SPACING 1949

Tyrwhitt, J. (1951). The valley section: Patrick Geddes' world image. *Journal of the Town Planning Institute, 37*(3), 61–6.

Tyrwhitt, J. (1951, September). Do new towns provide safety? No. *Progressive Architecture. 32*(9), 77, 79.

Tyrwhitt, J. (1952). Cores within the urban constellation. In J. Tyrwhitt, J. L. Sert & E. N. Rogers (Eds.), *CIAM 8: The heart of the city: Towards the humanisation of urban life,* (pp. 103–107). Pellegrini.

Tyrwhitt, J. (presumed). (1954, November 1). *Culture & communications seminar, U. of Toronto 1954/5: 5th meeting.* Culture and Communications Seminar, U. of Toronto papers. Archives of the Ford Foundation, New York, NY, USA.

Tyrwhitt, J. (1954, April). Ideal cities and the city ideal. *Explorations, 2*, 38–50.

Tyrwhitt, J. (1955). The moving eye. *Explorations, 4*, 90–95.

Tyrwhitt, J. (1960, February 14). [Letter to M. McLuhan]. RIBA Library Archive (Tyrwhitt papers, Box 49 Folder 2). London, UK.

Tyrwhitt. J., & Williams, D. C. (1955). The city unseen. *Explorations, 5* (1955), 88–96.

Vallye, A. (2009, Spring). The strategic universality of trans/formation, 1950–52. *Grey Room, 35*, 28–57.

Vallye, A. (2011). *Design and the politics of knowledge in America, 1937–1967: Walter Gropius, György Kepes* (PhD diss., Columbia University).

Weschler, J. (1978). *György Kepes: The MIT years, 1945–77.* MIT.

CHAPTER 4

McLuhan and Kepes: Art, Science, and Civics "in a new kind of world city" (McLuhan to Kepes, August 1972, *Letters*, p. 453)

In 1972, after attending the Delos 10 Ekistics symposium—and disengaging from the dominant conversation about improving global housing and settlement—McLuhan wrote to György Kepes acknowledging fellow feeling and shared perspective:

> You were certainly the person at the [Delos] conference most near my own interests and concerns, if only because of your understanding of the world of design. The bulk of the people there were fairly brick and mortar or hardware men who belong almost certainly in the 19th century. Ecology is the most they are prepared to concede to our time and their approach to that problem is almost entirely piecemeal. I think that *we are already living in a new kind of world city* that is far outside the ken of Doxiadis. (italics mine, *Letters*, 1987 p. 453)

McLuhan believed Kepes shared his view of the holistic and environmental influence of design, so that techne in one field was not autonomous but had intersectional resonances across ecologies. For both, "design" meant more than shaping place, space and things, for they recognized Anthropocentric consequences much as we do now, with human-led innovation and activity impacting organic along with inorganic elements. For both, since technological developments have altered conditions of being in the world, exchanging a natural for a human-made environment, the design problem is dynamic and future oriented. Artists and designers need to address psychological and social questions, such as how to overcome quietude and conformity by creating spaces of play and challenge that stimulate the human sensorium and enable citizen involvement.

Both built their thinking on principles of holism and relationality, best expressed in the term "unity." McLuhan stated, "Nothing has its meaning alone … The 'meaning of meaning' is relationship"; as relational creatures, human consciousness is built by "the translation of all the senses into each other" (*Take Today*, 1972, p. 3) . He further observed our interactive relationship with the world—we shape it and it in turn shapes us—so that an artefact is "not neutral or passive, but an active logos or utterance of the human mind or body that transforms the user and his ground" (*Laws*, 1992, p. 99). Kepes described our innately relational character in more storied form, narrating pre-literate life as having "no break in the spectrum of life [that was] everywhere in men, beasts, plants, stones and water":

> … the pearly iridescence of seashells, the sparkling of a crystal, the phosphorescent glow of the sea at night, and the sunlight caught in droplets above the waterfall are all signs of an embracing, living thing, the basic link seen as the great snake whose body arches across the sky in in the rainbow. Everything is permeated by life. Everything seems in contact, interacting, interliving. ("Toward Civic Art," 1970/1972, p. 92)

Modern humans, without access to this mode of perception and unaware of relational dynamics, need expanded perception to recognize a world not "of independently functioning discrete systems but of a total organism" ("Toward," p. 92). For both Kepes and McLuhan, losing our sense of connectivity to everything—of being part of an organic whole—was key to modern malaise. With everything named and sequenced, categorized and separated, we privilege individualism and compartmentalized order. They proposed radical reorientation: an ontology honouring our relation to others and things and, in epistemic support of this, using all the senses to take in the world, for expanded, expansive consciousness.

For both, recognizing connections across time is part of relational consciousness, linkages binding past and present, as well as to the future. Kepes recognized newness balanced by "the dynamics of evolutionary continuity" ("Toward," p. 71). He was fascinated, for example, by continuities of form and function in objects from different times, collaging them for us to discern contrasts and analogies–such as how a modern "electric range" compares to a "Railroad station coal stove"; how Pueblo pottery ("circa a.d") compares to contemporary Italian "Blown and molded glass vases" (*Man-Made Object*, 1965, pp. 9–15). Presenting image collages without explanatory narrative and inviting readers to observe analog and difference was a strategy McLuhan also used (evident in *Medium is the Massage* (1967), *War and Peace in the Global Village* (1968), and *Culture is our Business* (1970). McLuhan provided examples of old to new dynamism in his "four laws of media." In short form, the four laws hold that any media artifact can be understood as innovative for extending or enhancing certain capacities while obsolescing others, in this retrieving and even reversing former characteristics (*Laws*, pp. 98–100). To frame this in figure and ground terms familiar to both McLuhan and Kepes is to note that when something is foregrounded and eclipses a figure of former import, it is newly constellated (not constituted), so there is sameness and difference.

Understood in these terms, change involves translation rather than loss. Neither McLuhan nor Kepes accepted conventional scientific explanations of human progress. Instead, they spoke of patterning and "transformations" of past phenomena. Their take on how the past inflects the present relates to "time-binding" in Alfred Korzybski's General Semantics theory, which Lance Strate says refers "to the distinctly human capability to preserve and pass on what we learn from one generation to the next" (*Concerning Communication*, 2022, pp. 70–71). Yet if time-binding celebrates the principle of continuity, continuity for Kepes and McLuhan comes in translation, amid reconfigured contexts and across spectrums, making patterns hard to decipher.

Both argue that to understand pattern and order and re-establish equilibrium, we need to adjust our senses. Kepes warned of being overwhelmed by machinery and artifice as "we continue to develop ever more powerful tools and equipment without having the sense of values that tell us how to use them" ("Toward," p. 87). Kepes called for "a new way of seeing," a call we might imagine McLuhan broadening to "a new way of sensing"; for both perception, cognition and consciousness were joined. In "Culture Without Literacy" (1953), McLuhan expressed fear of sensory overload and quoted approvingly from Kepes's *Language of Vision* (1944), reproducing 200 plus words:

> The environment of man living today has a complexity which cannot be compared with any environment of any previous age. The skyscrapers, the street with its kaleidoscopic vibration of colors, the window-displays with their multiple mirroring images, the street cars and motor cars, produce a dynamic simultaneity of visual impression which cannot be perceived in the terms of inherited visual habits. In this optical turmoil the fixed objects appear utterly insufficient as the measuring tape of the events. The artificial light, the flashing of electric bulbs, and the mobile game of the many new types of light sources bombard man with kinetic color sensations having a keyboard never before experienced. Man, the spectator, is himself more mobile than ever before. He rides in streetcars, motorcars, and aeroplanes and his own motion gives to optical impacts a tempo far beyond the threshold of a clear object-perception. The machine man operates adds its own demand for a new way off seeing. The complicated interactions of its mechanical parts cannot be conceived in a static way; they must be perceived by understanding of their movements. The motion picture, television, and,

in a great degree, the radio, require a new thinking, i.e., seeing, that takes into account qualities of change, interpenetration and simultaneity. (Kepes, qtd. in "Culture," p. 136)

McLuhan—who often called for multisensory involvement to replace occularcentrism—may have felt Kepes over-emphasized vision in this passage. Yet he would have noted Kepes referred to "seeing" in varied contexts (linking seeing to hearing related to radio and noting the impacts of multiple motion) and spoke of interactant senses, as in "thinking" and "seeing" that take "into account qualities of change, interpenetration and simultaneity."

Kepes referred to accelerant technologized conditions in his day as composing "The New Landscape" (1956) and McLuhan referred to "a new environment for the planet" from the time of Sputnik in 1957, "the moment that the earth went inside this new artifact, [and] Nature ended" ("At the Moment of Sputnik," 1974, p. 49). According to McLuhan, technology and mediation involve "all of us, all at once" in an artificial environment that changes work, leisure, travel, and communication, information flows and value formation (*Medium*, p. 53). Kepes added the prefix "inter" to many words sensory words (e.g. inter-seeing) to convey multiplying imbrications, arguing that the time had come again for us to reestablish "dissolved and broken links, for a union of man and his surroundings, for concrete expression of new relationships" ("Toward," p. 89).

A formal cause perspective informed how McLuhan and Kepes viewed change: in place of instrumental cause-and-effect, they took a rhetorical and interpretive approach, wherein causes are factors we [eventually] recognize and name. Kepes quoted American pragmatist Charles Sanders Pierce on evolution as a process that, neither progressive nor finite, is dependent on "the future thought of the community" (qtd. in "Toward," p. 89). McLuhan shared a similar view of process-based reality, continually adjusted as "something we make in the encounter with the world that is making us" (*Take Today*, p. 3). From this perspective, cause and effect is a human-made device, developed to aid thinking and the work of establishing order and meaning. They moved away from imagining a world of sequenced and predicable arrangements and looked instead for hidden-change actants and emerging patterns.

Both looked to art to challenge convention. For both, alternative environments created by artists could make tangible—more intelligible—atmospheres and arrangements whose contents would otherwise remain recessive and hidden. Thought of in this way, art is less about its materiality, plasticity, or representational character than about impacting the viewer. McLuhan's retelling of the Narcissus myth is helpful here (*Understanding Media*, 2003/1964, p. 63). In his account, the tragedy involves not obsessive self-love, but failure to understand media—Narcissus "mistook his own reflection in the water for another person," and his dilemma symbolizes how fascination with mediation can lead to a disconnect from actual life—in this case, he is deaf to Echo's attempts to win his interest. Combatting our imbalanced attachment to media, McLuhan wanted art aimed at sensory attunement. In his chapter for Kepes's *Man-made Object* (1966), McLuhan underscored the goal of multisensory awareness, referring "to making a world in which all the senses participated at once"—geared ultimately to restoring "the unity of the imaginative life by creating a multisenuous interplay" ("Emperor's Old Clothes," p. 91). Neither were interested in representational art which they saw as supporting habitual and outmoded perceptual practices and thinking. They encouraged counter environments created to reveal invisible elements and emergent patterns, often assisted by powerful human-made tools able to open new perceptual channels.

The programs of each, using art as sensory training ground to expand and reshape human consciousness, had radical political and social implications. In a 1969 interview, McLuhan expressed some faith in fortuitous design: "I expect to see the coming decades transform the planet into an art form; the new man, linked in a cosmic harmony that transcends time and space, will sensuously caress and mold and pattern every facet of the terrestrial artifact as if it were a work of art, and man himself will become an organic art form" (*Playboy*, p. 268). A mere two years later, in 1971, Kepes expressed similar hope: "This developing, embracing vision of artists, we may hope is prophetic of a new world … The capacity of this [new technological] realm to guide us, mold us, and transform us is beyond calculation" ("Toward", p. 93). These are not techno-utopian nor technocratic visions. These expressions of optimism came with awareness that so far tools and technologies had been a source of upset and noise. Kepes described the imbalance of artifice and innovation this way:

> The wildly proliferating man-made environment rapidly shrank living space, polluted air and water, dimmed light, bleached color and relentlessly expanded mass, dirt, noise, speed, and complexity. The changing society exploded with problems in an immense scale: ecological disasters, social tragedies, eroded individuality, confused and impoverished human relationships. ("Toward," p. 85)

Both Kepes and McLuhan took as their mission sounding "Dewline" warnings,[1] to discourage lassitude and to excite sensory, intellectual, and emotional involvement. They aimed high. McLuhan hoped to "give indispensable orientation to future problems well before they become troublesome" ("Emperor's New Clothes," 1968, p. 245); Kepes wanted art to educate us away from social crisis and the devastation of climate and ecology. Facing an insecure future, McLuhan and Kepes hoped for a new compact and commons—for fuller exercise of perception, as well as for developing language or communicative practices adequate to sharing such new "visions." McLuhan sometimes speculated about moving from alphabet literacy to a form of thought transfer such as ESP (see "Invisible Environment," 1967, p. 165). For his part, as biographer John Blakinger notes, Kepes used "the phrase 'communication crisis' on the dustjackets of his seven Vision + Value volumes" (p. 418). Igniting community participation, making publics more conversant with science, and establishing trusted cultural leadership were ways to reduce human suffering and avoid "present ecological tragedies". He argued a more creative way of life required "the interaction of the whole community" involving "the intricately interconnected workings of its members." Much as McLuhan did, he imagined artists and "creative men in many fields" leading the community toward "a new 'common' property of all who seek a higher quality of life" ("Toward," p. 90). Plans like these remain aspirational for many among us who continue imagining a "commons" as fruit of collective action.

In Chapter 5, Terranova reads Kepes and McLuhan in relation to the Cybernetics movement of their day. Whereas Orit Halpern (2014) positions them as key actors or contributors, Terranova suggests they used some of the vocabulary rather than adopting wholesale a model of the world powered by self-regulating systems. Indeed, McLuhan spoke out against the limitations of such an approach in *Take Today*, wryly dismissing systematic theories for ignoring "primitive problems" like human needs and emotions (p. 135). As Terranova explores, both Kepes and McLuhan preferred a model requiring human decision-making and interventions, with human hands steering the works. Rather than imagining closed feedback loops, with technologies designed to be self-correcting, they imagined more reciprocity, with human users as designers able to refresh and improve existing arrangements.

Both also recognized ongoing interactive connections amongst human and non-human realms, including human-made objects. They were aligned with second order cybernetics, going beyond Bateson who looked for patterns connecting the world of the living to adhere more closely to the view espoused by his student Tyler Volk, who Lance Strate tells us expanded the concept "to include physics and chemistry, as well as biology, ecology and psychology, along with mythology and culture," imagining "pattern so wide-flung that it appears throughout the spectrum of reality" ("The Effects," 2017, p. 113). In McLuhan's interactive theory of extensions (*Understanding Media*, pp. 63–68), tools and media take on human tasks and qualities and in so doing create "new ratios of new equilibriums among the other organs and extensions of the body" (p. 67).

Kepes held a McLuhan-inflected notion of technology as extension, as Terranova summarizes in *Art as Organism* (2016): "Perception is essentially extended and prosthetic" (p. 107). Kepes presented this human/object transfer in a three-part collage, "Communities of Objects," presenting photographs narrativized as sharing features of human culture: a pawnshop window captioned "Tenement of objects," a repair shop captioned "Object hospital," and a wrecking yard, called "Car cemetery" (*Man-made Object*, 1966, 24–25). Moving beyond two-step interaction—"we shape our tools, and they shape us"—this visual narrative takes a "tools are us" turn, picking up on the vital role of humans in making and interpreting the world.

McLuhan and Kepes in Their Milieu

Biographically, McLuhan and György Kepes knew of each others' work and corresponded throughout their careers. These are direct points of contact: (1) McLuhan cited Kepes in several publications, notably in "Culture Without Literacy" (1997/1953, p. 136), "Inside the Five Sense Sensorium" (1961, p. 50), and *Understanding Media* (p. 145); (2) Kepes's article "Art and Science" appeared in the inaugural volume of University of Toronto's *Explorations* (December, 1953); (3) McLuhan's essay on art and culture, "The Emperor's Old Clothes," appeared in Kepes's edited collection, *The Man-Made Object*, (published in 1965, the most popular of his 6-volume Vision+Value series); and (4) McLuhan and Kepes exchanged a number of letters and interacted at Delos 10—a symposium convened in 1972 by architect Constantinos Doxiadis and his Ekistics group. This chapter opened with an excerpt from McLuhan's letter to Kepes expressing intellectual allegiance against forces he perceived as outmoded for seeking solutions to poverty, housing and global development. In all, they were aware of each others' projects and corresponded over the twenty-year span in which each made sizable contributions to theorizing art and technology.

An émigré from Hungary escaping WWII persecution, Kepes's grounding was in European Bauhaus theory. He joined Moholy-Nagy in Chicago in 1937 as a faculty member at the New Bauhaus school (Terranova, 2016, *Organism* 75). Bauhaus scholar Oliver Botar tells us that traditional readings of Bauhaus theory have emphasized its "rational approach" and "apolitical collaboration with industry," and overlooked what he calls "the biocentric Bauhaus" concerned with "the Romantic sense of wonder and unity with nature" and biologism, which privileges scientific concepts "such as evolution and survival of the fittest over other spheres of knowledge" ("Biocentric Bauhaus," 2017, p. 18). In *Art as Organism* (2016), Terranova looks at elements of biocentrism in Kepes. Linking the Bauhaus and

Kepes to biocentrism forms another bridge to McLuhan, a monist who likewise imagined oneness and unity. As his recitations of Poe's Mariner story encapsulate, he was fascinated by links between body and environment; he saw the relational and interactive character of everything and posited from this eventual cosmic unity. Like Kepes, he was fascinated by science, both its theory and practice—although both scholars veer away from evolutionary progress to imagine change as reconfiguration. Several recent studies provide further evidence of Bauhaus influence on McLuhan. Alexander Kitnick (2021) reminds us that McLuhan reviewed Moholy-Nagy's *Vision in Motion* in 1949 (p. 7). Alexander Nagel and Gary Genosko explore McLuhan's collaborations with Harley Parker (curator of Toronto's science-oriented ROM from 1957 to 1967)—Parker a graduate of Bauhaus-inflected Black Mountain trained by Josep Albers. The brand of biocentrism Botar and Terranova claim for Bauhaus figures can also be claimed for McLuhan.

As founding director of the Centre for Advanced Visual Studies [CAVS] at MIT (from 1967–72), Kepes positioned himself to promote the meeting of art and science. As early as 1953, in "Art and Science," his article for McLuhan's *Explorations*, he argued for the bridge-building power of art to bring theoretical and practical science to publics: "Art can make an important contribution by providing insights into structural correspondence common in the various disciplines of science but ignored because science of necessity isolates and limits its field and objectives" (p. 78). In the first collaborative exhibition held in 1970 by CAVS at MIT, Kepes offered viewers "an immersive group experience" in installation pieces that, according to biographer John Blakinger, attempted to transform the show's lifeless technical media, all the electronic equipment and clunky machines, into an environmental ecology. The show's phenomenological technics—interactive sculptures, responsive materials, and ephemeral sensation of flashing lights and frenzied motion—enveloped viewers in a sensory rich simulacrum of a natural landscape (2019, p. 295). In the written statement explaining the show, "Toward Civic Art," Kepes was clear on the potential of art to promote public education in "an apparently uncontrollable new-scale world, so big, strange, and explosive" (p. 84). In his view, malaise would linger so long as the extended world revealed by science remained inaccessible to ordinary human senses. Artists can engage technology to provide warnings and propose correctives, revealing patterns (amongst humans, between past and present, and between humans and the environment), conveying "that everything fits together" and "that the world is right and full of promise" (p. 91). Art and science together can bring balance and healing.

The following summary of a signature Kepes project outlines his key passions (passions also evident in McLuhan's work): casting (1) the artist as teacher, (2) art and science as interactive, and (3) art as productive of public engagement potentially expanding perception and consciousness. Biographer John Blakinger speculates that Kepes was likely the figure McLuhan had in mind when he pictured the socially-invested artist "leaving the ivory tower for the control tower" (2019, p. 11)[2] to guide incoming technological changes and make decisions about integrating media into the networked surround; if Kepes modelled control-tower artistry, McLuhan took him to have access to "precise advanced knowledge" pertaining to "the psychic and social consequences of the next technology," sharing insights "anticipating and avoiding the consequences of technological trauma" (*Understanding Media*, p. 97). Both McLuhan and Kepes were committed to public pedagogy for improving sensory life. With this would come recognition of one's connection to others and to the planet, fostering a new sense of unity. Their goals aimed at long-term and massive impact: changing psychic life and community structure.

We are, they argued, too much and too blindly driven by dependence on technologies. Yet this dependency brings opportunity. What has been invisible as hidden ground has recently come into view, as we communicate with others around the globe, as well as see telescopically into the universe or microscopically into the atom. Everything was always, already there, but now we have tools and technology for seeing and hearing more. Science has brought information but it must be art, both argued, that helps us discern configurations and make meaningful narratives. Huge shifts enable expanded perception and reveal new information, and this needs to be integrated into our collective habitus and story.

Thus occupied with public education, they felt some distance from contemporaries devoted to political activism, in particular to protests against the Vietnam War. Rather than join protests, they treated the war as symptomatic of a larger problem: as the outcome powerful technologies being directed by scientists inattentive to human values and by corporate leaders and officials whose tools and programs foster violence, compel obedience, and discourage citizen input or intervention. McLuhan and Kepes wanted holistic and deep structural change: they wanted a governance framework open to citizen input into decision-making about developing the artificial and electric environment. Their shared concern with bringing science to art and civics may explain why McLuhan felt linked to Kepes at the Delos 10 symposia, for alike they would have found some of the practical work aimed at improving human settlement and housing retrogressive—similar to patching or putting a fresh coat of paint on a deteriorating building rather than going deeper to transform perceptual habits and relational awareness to remake how we think and live.

Art/Science and Expanded Consciousness

McLuhan believed artists were iconoclasts, able to break through common habit and environmental "propaganda," the limited set of ideas and figures generally recognized as important ("Invisible Environment," p. 161). By mapping hidden elements—breaking the ground rules of old technologies and "habits of fragmented and specialized perception" ("Emperor's Old Clothes," p. 90)—artists can expand our sense of what is present in the world. The role of art, McLuhan said, "is to create the means of perception by creating counterenvironments that open the door of perception to people otherwise numbed in a non-perceivable situation" ("Emperor's New Clothes," p. 241). These "counterenvironments" provoke audience participation and interaction, unsettling figure and ground relations and enabling new patterns.

Kepes, likewise, believed in the power of art and "the artistic image" to create meaning and expand minds ("Visual Arts," 1960, p. 3). Such images—"symbolic form[s] grasped directly by the senses but reaching beyond them and connecting all the strata of our inner world of sense, feeling, and thought"—can inspire viewers to abandon outmoded habitual responses upon receiving "a significant message delivered simultaneously to our senses, our feelings, and our minds" ("Visual Arts," p. 4). These images fuse sensory and conceptual operations: "This essential unity of primary sense experience and intellectual evaluation makes the artistic form unique in human experience" ("Visual Arts," p. 4). Serious artists guide the process of pattern recognition and value production in a way that can unify cultures by providing a shared lexicon, bonding individuals together and making "our perceptual grasp of the world functional, meaningful, satisfying, and communicable" ("Visual Arts," p. 6).

Kepes viewed vision and insight in Western society as cramped by the predominance reason. He contrasted the West, a space of reason shorn of feeling or imagination, to the East, which he imagined as harmonizing realms of feelings: "The East has concerned itself not with the world's structure and has institutionalized as the West has not highly developed appreciation of its harmonies, its tastes and flavors" ("Art and Science," 1953, pp. 74–5). He avoided characterizing Western reason and Eastern feeling in essentialist terms by describing them as available and recessive qualities needing to be balanced in both zones: "The dynamic interdependence of the wisdom of the senses and the wisdom of reason is fundamental to a balanced growth" (*New Landscape*, 1956, p. 371).

Kepes also described the harmful split between artistic and scientific knowing, with the rule of science ascendent in our culture, "our powers of abstract analysis" having "outstripped our powers of visualization" ("Art and Science," 1953,

p. 77). We are preoccupied, he said, with superficial information and impressions without grasping the interactive worlds revealed by telescopic and magnifying technologies. Scientific advances expose things formerly unknown or unseen, yet a science producing only objective reports and measurements misses opportunities to understand more about life and our place within it: "The man-made world, after five centuries of accelerating scientific discovery and technical development, has expanded so explosively in so many directions that we seem unable to grasp its dimensions or assert authority over its dynamics. ... We have disrupted the atom and speared the moon, but, as we all know, there is as much apprehension over the unknown, unpredictable consequences" ("Visual Arts," 1965, p. 7). The rift between art and science needs bridging, to develop "common language" and "common symbols" (*New Landscape*, 1956, p. 20). Art informed by advances in science, can offer meaning in the face of cultural change: "Science, in a sense, has been the angel with a sword, evicting us from the smaller, friendlier world in which we once moved with a confidence born of familiarity, and plunging us into a bigger, alien world" ("Visual Arts," p. 7). Artists participating in world-making projects "contribute to the creative shaping of the earth's surface on a grand scale":

> Until now man was tied to the earth's crust: he could move only on the land or swim in or skim across the water. Except for the rare vantage points of high mountains our globe was given to us only in limited horizons. The new technology has freed us from the ancient bondage. ... we are shifting frames of reference and thus perspectives. (*Arts of the Environment*, 1972, p. 10)

Characterizing his time as "explosive" ("Toward," p. 84), Kepes imagined peace and healing dependent on the public's regaining a sense of proportion and scale, requiring individual and collective regulation. Perhaps more directly than McLuhan, he spoke of the need for a vital commons and the renewal of democratic ideals—and thus supported a movement that Fred Turner says animated contemporary figures like Margaret Mead and Gregory Bateson from 1940s onward, drawing many intellectuals post-World War II and through the Cold War years to the task of defining "the Democratic Personality" and cultivating a renewed and invigorated "Democratic Surround" (2013, p. 151). For Kepes, seeing was a learned function, a "cognitive act" affected by cultural conditions ("Visual Arts," p. 3). He believed the technologized world, while affording more to see and know, was vertiginous if not framed by art to "unify the experience of eye and mind" ("Visual Arts," p. 12).

McLuhan advocated similar bridging. He often spoke of an East/West divide—of disadvantaged Westerners who need to integrate Eastern practices—and of the art/science divide. Alike, they believed that technology could unlock insights and that publics needed artists to help guide new sensory awareness. To this end, McLuhan often coached "taking control" of new media, which meant more than holding an on /off switch. Instead, control was based on understanding how the reverberative energy of every advance alters everything else, freeing us to see that it is not "how a medium is used that counts" but "what it does to us and with us" (*Playboy*, p. 239). He was not thinking of "control" as instrumental mastery over tools. The control he had in mind would depend on individuals becoming aware of current and trending environmental conditions and their relation to place and others, in this way engaged in active "world making." Much as Kepes described the need to update and remake vision and consciousness, McLuhan referred to reshaping consciousness as the most important part of the human project. "The making and shaping of consciousness from moment to moment is the supreme artistic task of all individuals. To qualify and perfect this process on a world environmental scale is the inherent potential of each new technology." ("Emperor's Old Clothes," p. 95).

Patterns and Transformations

Both believed that patterns—often hidden or disguised—provide reassurance of meaning in the world. To explain how a cloak of invisibility can be penetrated, both access Gestalt figure and ground theory, applying it to explain perception and, more broadly, our understanding of ourselves, others, and reality. As Charissa Terranova explains, the Bauhaus practice of gestalt thinking is more than "an ossified totality and simple figure-ground measure of perception" (*Organism*, 2016, p. 37); it assumes ontological dimensions, affecting how we live, think, and move, and revealing components that are fluid and inter-influential. As is, few people assume a fresh and full situational perspective, but instead see only the obvious—whatever is hailed as culturally important. They miss elements recessed in the background, as well as the synesthetic play of various sensory elements together.

Recent atmospheric and sensory studies have made a serious study of the sensorium, building on what Kepes and McLuhan knew. In *The Sensory Studies Manifesto* (2022), David Howes presents the sensorium as understood differently across cultures, so that it is arbitrary to think of five senses, common in recent Western practice, and more accurate "to imagine the ever-shifting divisions and relations among the senses" (p. 69). Gernot Boehme (2017) explores how the condition of unity involved in the operation of synesthesia suggests that sensual perceptions may "reach down to bodily feelings" which thus prompts consideration "that feeling something physically is an additional sense on top of the others"

(p. 72). Anticipating this updating, Kepes and McLuhan advocated for exploration of the powerful, multi-valent and untapped possibilities of the human sensorium.

Applying figure and ground theory can extend sensory awareness and cultivate an open aptitude to all that can be "understood"–"understanding" being the word McLuhan preferred for conveying the provisional and even subjectively-tinged nature of knowing. Figure and ground theory also explains the character of "pattern" at the heart of Kepes and McLuhan's systems of knowing. If human understanding is based on acknowledging some things and blocking others, what most are able to see is usually information or attributes that make up popular cultural understandings. In *City as Classroom* (1977), McLuhan admonished young people to grasp more perceptual information and make relational mosaic-style connections to imbue life with vital patterns: "Patterns and structures 'make sense' of things. Understanding structures enables us all to avoid feelings of helplessness and frustration that makes us want to shout, 'Stop the world—I want to get off!'" (p. 165).

For Kepes, figure-and-ground logic was germane to making sense of the abundance of new insights delivered by advances in scientific technologies, unveiling new figures. Breaking cultural habit, the West was emerging from a long period of looking at one thing at a time and attempting its discrete representation in image or word. This break occurred because new tools and visual information reveal nothing as singular and fixed but as many-sided and transforming; human viewers, taking in the flux, are themselves in a process of motion and change. Kepes argued that to accommodate "the notion of the world in movement" we need to accept that "we move and what is around us moves" (*New Landscape*, 1956, pp. 226–227). Technologies enable us to see "the translations, transmutations, condensations, distortions, exaggerations, simplifications and other aspects of transformation" (pp. 227–28), so that shapes are always reconfiguring as in a kaleidoscopic image— or, in Kepes's more technical image, like "the stroboscopic multiple exposure record of forms in motion" (p. 227). Artists make art objects, which viewers participate in making. As we move toward a square object, for example, the retina takes in " a fluid pattern of changing shapes, sizes and colors," yet rather than processing this constant shifting, we grant the object a sort of stability, assuming "there is a maintained identity, a persistent object; and thus we establish a connection between us and it" (p. 226). If we understand motion as part of vision, we can enrich visual experience and, relatedly, update individual and cultural attitudes.

Kepes often accompanied his discursive exploration of how technology permits new angles of vision and liberates new light effects with photographs and images, usually of unlike things constellated to provoke imaginative connections. Images of unrelated objects were tagged without extended explication, leaving viewers to ponder analogous qualities amidst more obvious contrastive features: artifacts from the far past appeared alongside those from the present, animate alongside inanimate objects, microscopic beside panoramic angles. Biographer John Blakinger dismisses such assemblages as "pseudomorphosis" (p. 216), as optical trickery that presents images "with a formal precision that hints at hidden meaning" (p. 103). Showing a four-slide grouping in *The New Landscape* (1956), Kepes put old and new world images in collision, harnessing together a Sumerian mosaic of "Stone and Mother of Pearl (3000 BC)", a tapestry from Peru ("ca. 700–900 A.D."), a Byzantine mosaic ("VI Century"), and a 1911 canvas by Mondrian (see *The New Landscape*, 1956, FIGS. 46–49, pp. 54–55). In Blakinger's view, "Byzantium and Mondrian have nothing to do with one another" and these "patently false comparisons" engage viewers in a baseless exercise of "making meaningful what is otherwise meaningless" (p. 105). In Blakinger's view, this approach, borrowed from ancient sources, leads to connections more fanciful than "factual": "similar to ritual acts of divination like counting stars, deciphering tea leaves, or gazing into a crystal ball (there are starry skies, leaf samples, and all manner of crystals in the book).... Studying his images is like reading entrails" (p. 105).

A recent study like Philip Ball's *Pattern in Nature* (2016) provides a more supportive way of reading Kepes's relatively early adoption of new visual media tools to capture recurrent pattern-based structures.[3] In Kepes's own words, he worked from a concept of unity "as a fundamental proposition: a model of basic relationship" (*New Landscape* 284). He linked Goethe's understanding of unity to Taoist philosophy, saying that unity "in nature was expressed with great imaginative force by the most perceptive minds of both East and West." Citing Taoistic understanding of the world as "complete, all embracing, and... whole," he described connectivity shooting through "[all] images, all feelings, all thoughts...[in] a common basic model, a fundamental analogue. These models are frames of reference by which we try to comprehend the life around us as a unity. We see feel and think only to the extent that our basic models allow it." Kepes was excited by technological imagining that expanded what we have seen and known. Yet if the tools and theory of science offer new ideas and explanations, his analogue theory and collaging method argue such revelations are not entirely novel, but precedented and connected. For Kepes, identifying likeness in difference, far from an exercise in visual chicanery, enabled seeing beneath surfaces: "The world of pattern gives us a new way to see ... Not only our vision changes but also our outlook" (*New Landscape*, p. 226).

In *Art as Organism* (2016), Terranova links Kepes's curatorial penchant for image juxtaposition to his integrative gestalt vision. When she says he displayed disparate images to show "circulation, change, and perverse and profound imagistic adjacencies," (p. 106), allowing viewers "perceptual shifts [that] are central in the making and overall experience, or completion of the work of art" (p. 105), one hears echoes of McLuhan's use of collage to provoke new connections and insights.

McLuhan and Kepes placed similar epistemic value on exercising pattern recognition. Combining image and text, providing minimal textual gloss, suggesting links from past and present, inviting audience involvement—there are resounding presentational similarities. Like Kepes, McLuhan often drew upon literary and arcane sources, rather than using scholarly citations. McLuhan's mosaic strategy corresponded most strongly with Kepes's approach in celebrating unexpected relationships. One of his four laws of media urges the principle of retrieval (along with change). Illustrations of these laws show how apparently unrelated things are interactive and even transformative across a range of fields or ecologies, so that, for example, the car does not simply replace horse and buggy as mode of transport but reintroduces (in updated forms) social gestures and values like courtesy and privacy (p. 148). Their shared use of figure/ ground theory informed their relational thinking and pattern-finding: figure and ground are interactive and alter each other. Kepes and McLuhan provide perceptual training opportunities that encourage audiences to find pattern in what appears, superficially, as mixed and chaotic and in so doing provide evidence of structural repetition countering fear of the present as formless and disjointed.

Imagining an Artist-led Commons

In "Toward Civic Art," Kepes observed that attuned artists perform cultural leadership. There are broad political implications in this. He imagined a political arrangement unlike any we know, led by artists who enjoy populist support, introducing "a new scale of opportunities to inter-thinking and inter-seeing; the condition of a truly embracing participatory democracy" (p. 90). He imagined leadership as a "collaborative enterprise in which artists, scientists, urban planners, and engineers are interdependent" (p. 91). Such leadership—to advance quality of life and mind—is sustained by and sustains a supportive commons. He did not say outright that the common realm he had in mind related to a new form of planetary governance, yet such is implied by his frequent references to a new sociality of relationality, unity, and holistic interactivity. McLuhan, too, imagined benign artist-led governance, defining artists broadly as those in "any field, scientific or humanistic," who are interested in bridging these fields to align what we think and do with new possibilities and options at hand (*Understanding Media*, 2003, p. 96). Artists at the helm would establish a humanistic focus creating conditions for engagement and responsivity. McLuhan was short on details, but implied global reach. By the same token, he gestured to responding to particular local needs, to adjusting media delivery and coverage, for example, in ways supporting community health: "By such orchestrated interplay of all media, whole cultures could now be programmed in order to improve and stabilize their emotional climate" (*Playboy*, 1969, p. 263).

Both Kepes and McLuhan are proposing a form of governance for which there is no extant model. To extend their speculative thinking, we might read Bruno Latour and Isabelle Stengers on the formation of participatory global governance—such as when Stengers defines a "Cosmopolitics" accommodating earth and "peoples of the earth" guided by leadership that decentres authority, distributed amongst "diplomats" and "experts" (*Another Science*, 2018, pp. 151, 153). If Latour's diplomat figure is a "designer" and Stengers' a "heretic," (Janicka, 2023, p. 24), these characterizations bring to mind McLuhan and Kepes's artist leader who is both a creative and an iconoclast—even a criminal in McLuhan's probe into the anti-authoritarianism of counter environments ("Invisible Environment," p. 165).

In *McLuhan's Techno-Sensorium City* (2021), I explore how both McLuhan and Kepes believed that the "era of individualism had come to an end" (pp. 103–107). McLuhan often framed collectivity in positive terms:

> The individualism of the mechanical culture and environment was paid for at the cost of much alienation from man and work, and society. It was also accompanied by an almost total denial of participation in the creative process on the part of the public. The mechanical culture and environment produced the spectator and the consumer instead of the participant and co-creator.... [Now the] art object is replaced by participation in the art process. This is the essential meaning of electric circuitry and responsive environments. ("Emperor's Old Clothes," pp. 94–95)

Kepes also presented the potential advantages of ever-increasing interdependence, positing a technologically supported collective and profound awakening to how everything is connected. Here is Kepes on interconnectivity fostered by technologies as a force of sensory stimulation and creativity:

> The more powerful the devices we develop through our scientific technology, the more we are interconnected with each other, with our machines, with our environment, and with our own inner capacities. The more sensitive and embracing our means of hearing, seeing and thinking become through radio, television and computer technology, the more we are compelled to sense the interaction of [humans and their. . .] environment. Our new tools of transportation, communication, and control have

brought a new scale of opportunities to inter-thinking and inter-seeing: the condition of truly embracing participatory democracy. ("Art and Ecological," 1972, pp. 7–8)

While both welcome an incoming state of hybridity and liaison, both also discouraged complete immersion. We might remember that part of the reason to exercise understanding is not just to welcome change, but also to identify time-worn practices worthy of salvage and reintegration. *Understanding Media* counsels understanding the risks of going too far into collective identity and the value of reserving some space for "human autonomy" (p. 76). Likewise, Kepes capped arguments for a vigorous commons by praising individuality and the personal; we live, he said, "on many levels" and must remember the "dynamic complementarity of the personal and the civic" so that even when "our experiences are amalgamated into unified understanding," we "feel the single climatic glow" ("Toward" p. 94). Both were concerned to balance the claims of the one and the many in ways that continue salient in political discussion—Richard Sennet, for example, entitling the conclusion to *Building and Dwelling* (2018) "One Amongst Many."

Part of Kepes's insistence on revealing the principle of connectivity was its implicit argument against the principle of divisiveness that governed Cold War logics—a powerful principle applied to separate "the righteous West from evil Others" and to sponsor combative competition and distrust as part of the "deformations caused by the Cold War" (Beck & Bishop, 2020, p. 19). Fred Turner (2013) sums the political goals Kepes sought to bring to life when he describes "the utopian impulses of the early Bauhaus" as expressed in the belief "that a change in perception could change the social order" (p. 98).

In McLuhan's view, because we are loosening our connection to external environments and relying on virtual connections and/or digital spaces—with media performing more of the duties formerly performed by bodies in place—we need to develop new ways of exercising our senses and new ways of relating to others to preserve (to salvage and reintegrate) humanity and community. In a 1961 letter to Claude Bissell, he wrote of the unifying and engaging influence provided by urban materialism and industrialism in modernity: "So long as the externalization of senses were rudimentary in the form of writing and architecture, the pressures for consensus could be met by urban order" (*Letters*, p. 279). He imagined us heading for an undifferentiated and dematerialized future state—one shorn of boundaries that provide a sense of individualism and independence. At the end of *War and Peace,* he dipped into evolutionary biology to play with the possibility of a future without species differentiation, imagining a single species working with a common mind. He quoted biologist Ernst Mayr's description of the disordered and disruptive outlook of a world without species differentiation, where there is "no possibility of a gradual improvement of genetic combinations" and we are without "a protective device against the breaking up of its well-integrated co-adapted system" (p. 188). While McLuhan did not believe in evolutionary progress, he did advocate for recognizing configural change and continuity. Imagining loss of all species differentiation (the human body melting, along with all other solids, from buildings, borders, nations, to language) is the dark flipside to his image of humanity free floating in a cosmic choir. For McLuhan, an optimal rather than a dismal outcome—radiant relationality rather than numbed coercion—rested on the success of education and participation.

"Interthinking" and "interseeing" are key Kepes concepts. Blakinger says Kepes evolved the term "interseeing" to suit his visual project: "Ideas and images might be read through and against each other, producing new ideas and new images. Such intellectual miscegenation would create new knowledge: to think between ideas, to see between images, might then advance human culture" (p. 181). This reading might imply Kepes believed in progressive evolution; he was, I think, closer to following McLuhan's model of change and retrieval. Both McLuhan and Kepes saw the end of celebrating individualism as potentially beneficial so long as there was benign oversight of this process. Both believed they lived in pivotal and charged times, with media inserted into the environment changing perceptual and cognitive abilities and creativity and communication in turn requiring an overhaul of social and political life. Living in the "atomic age" and walking the corridors of MIT where experiments were being visibly advanced, Kepes reckoned "the promises and menaces inherent in our potent technology" ("Civic Art," p. 73); McLuhan echoed this deep ambivalence, citing "grounds for both optimism and pessimism" (*Playboy*, p. 20).

For both Kepes and McLuhan, a coming age of collectivity required a revised political and economic framework. New collectivism meant redefining human identity, citizenship and leadership. Corporations would no longer have free reign to roll out endless new products; instead, products and technologies would be distributed to serve our needs as understood by those given the role of government oversight. While neither provided much economic theory, the form of state- controlled distribution they imagined runs counter to capitalistic supply and demand. Citizens give up individual free market choice to instead rely on a cadre of artists and scientists, who use our collective responses in a dynamic process of adjustments. Their texts argued for benign environmental management, for we need intentional design in everything to establish a state of equilibrium and promote values such as "beauty and sense of purpose" ("Civic Art," p. 94), "pleasure and comfort" (*Understanding Media*, p. 65). Without holistic systemic revision, we will continue helpless, barraged by inexplicable novelties and competing violently for resources, with time on our hands to watch technologies take over. The control tower image was a packed metaphor for large-scale interventions.

Summary: Art/Ontology/Politics

According to Fred Turner, imagining democracy as a sort of redesigned collectivism put McLuhan and Kepes in step with social movements of their day. In *The Democratic Surround* (2013), studying the period from World War II to the 60s in America, he narrates how public intellectuals were drawn to revitalizing democracy by projects aimed at using media to engage citizens. There was opposition to control mechanisms associated with fascism and objections to the powerful role of capitalism in democracy, debasing freedom to the mere matter of consumer product choices. Mead and Bateson led various groups to expand democratic freedoms and engage collective awareness,[4] and Turner says Kepes and McLuhan were influential players in these projects.

McLuhan frequently stated that artists create "counterenvironments" that expose current environments, and by so doing create possibilities for remaking the world. In "The Emperor's Old Clothes," he updated what Kepes had called "The New Landscape" in 1956 with his term "a new environment" (to encompass space as well as earth) (p. 90). Like Kepes, he means we have more data and tools that "change our habits of perception" with this technology, we have power to "program the planet itself by understanding the actions under and above its mantle" (p. 92). In such a regime, the real leaders charged with oversight would be the artists and scientists, yet their choices would be linked to public input and feedback. Leaving modernity for digital times meant exchanging individual identity for entry into an active "mass" of creative people "deeply involved in one another" (p. 102). Politically, building life in a connected global city meant dissolving old pacts and decentralizing city functions, with citizens becoming active participants in global theatrics: rather than following historic agreements or written constitutions, we are (and will be) interactively making something new together.

The new subjectivity and planetary formation they saw building was both like and unlike the collectivism of past oral cultures. According to Kepes, preliterate culture was buoyant with sensorial complexity and fully relational identity, with "no break in the spectrum of life [that was] everywhere in men, beasts, plants, stones and water"; so that "the pearly iridescence of seashells, the sparkling of a crystal, the phosphorescent glow of the sea at night, and the sunlight caught in droplets above the waterfall are all signs of an embracing, living thing … Everything is permeated by life. Everything seems in contact, interacting, interliving" ("Civics,"

p. 72). The possibility of recapturing even some of this good energy allowed for some optimism in the face of incoming change. There are striking similarities between his description and a more recent depiction of the beauties of sensorial sensitivity explained as part of [mostly] lost indigenous cultural ways:

> "Shimmer" is a gift, too, of the Yolngu people of Australia ... the seasonal kiss of mutually thrilling encounters among flying foxes and flowering eucalyptus trees, flying fox people, rain, and rainbows ... *Bir'yun* [a shimmering not brilliance'] attends to temporal patterns that emerge from more-than-human shimmerings and dreamings—pulses of ancestral power, of life riding a wave that is always coming: "*bir'yun*' shows that the world is not composed of gears and cogs but of multifaceted, multispecies relations and pulses." (*Arts of Living on a Damaged Planet*, 2017, p. 11)

Compared to this recent description of localized sensorial acuity, McLuhan and Kepes's version of its role in pre-literate life is more universalized. Intersensorial experience is a human legacy all can draw on. It is potentially attainable and essential to regaining balance and new unity—not a way of being out of general reach and belonging only to a specific group of humans.

Reading Kepes and McLuhan together conveys the high seriousness of their goal: saving humanity and planet from the growing tangle of human- made artifice, accelerant from many directions, changing worthwhile forms of doing, having, and being. Against chaos and noise, each believed in unlocking the power of the unseen and forging connections across fields of knowledge—so that as McLuhan wrote, "modern physics and painting and poetry speak a common language at once in order that our world may possess consciously the coherence that it really has in latency" ("Culture Without Literacy," p. 136). Along with uniting current forms of knowledge, they also provided evidence of recurrent patterns or forms in a time binding arc connecting now to then—and now into the future. Kepes captured this in saying we need "a new way of thinking ie seeing that takes into account qualities of change, interpenetration and simultaneity" ("Introduction," *New Landscape*, p. 20). Their deeply relational thinking was keyed to creating a world principled by unity.

Both made high-flying utopian professions of faith in the future, rewarding human growth and unity. McLuhan's expressed hope that "the new [human] linked in a cosmic harmony that transcends time and place, will sensuously caress and mold and pattern every facet of the terrestrial artifact as if it were a work of art" (*Playboy*, p. 268). Kepes also imagines us as shaping and caressing the stuff of our world, building on intimations of such genius already apparent in "peak achievements in shaping, caressing, invigorating and enriching urban forms" (*Arts of the Environment*, 1972, p. 170). Yet both feared we might crash. Threats arise from inserting media into the environment, augmenting some of our abilities, yet limiting some other creative and communicative capacities. They do not seek or offer firm blueprints, but imagine a process that, as McLuhan wrote to Kepes (and as cited in the chapter title) "we are already living in a new form of world city."

There is no better salvo than their rallying call to publics to cultivate sustainable relations with others and the world, and to wake up to the drum of technology—to enjoy its benefits and its regulation. Today various books echo a similar response to crisis. James Crary (2022), for example, puts an alarmist spin on it, warning that by living digitally we are losing "the ability or even the interest in engaging the gaze or voice of another" (p. 111) and "curiosity about otherness or about the wondrous plenitude of non-human life" (p. 123); we need to cultivate egalitarian values and solidarity to avoid "barbarism" (p. 124). Placing more emphasis on brokering a deal with technologies that make the world go round, James Bridle (2018) judges that "technologies that so inform and shape our present perceptions of reality are not going to go away, and in many cases we should not wish them to"; it is "entirely within our capabilities" to understand these systems and take control of "the conscious choices we make in their design" (p. 252). Shoshanna Zuboff also rallies publics to shake off the dangerous quietude McLuhan referred to as "motivated somnambulism," (*Culture*, p. 4). In her words, we need "to break the spell of enthrallment, helplessness, resignation, and numbing" and instead "use our knowledge, to regain our bearings, to stir others to do the same, and to found a new beginning" (*Surveillance*, 2019, p. 524). Although she identifies George Orwell as inspirational, this chapter has explored how McLuhan and Kepes demonstrated similar motivational creativity and courage.

Notes

1. In "Toward Civic Art," (1971) Kepes wrote: "Some artists were like distant early warning systems of the human condition today … We were not unwarned about the lethal consequences of the wholesale devastation of the natural landscape" (p. 70). Shifting to warning of incoming social change, McLuhan wrote of "the role of arts and sciences" as "a Dew Line or Distant Early Warning System" ("Emperor's New Clothes," 1968, p. 144).
2. See, for example, *Understanding Media* (p. 96), where McLuhan described the artist as moving "from the ivory tower to the control tower." He also used this phrase in his article for Kepes, "The Emperor's Old Clothes," (1966): "The art object is replaced by participation in the art process. … The artist leaves the Ivory Tower for the Control Tower" (pp. 104–5).
3. Phillip Ball reports massing evidence drawn from science to support Kepes's approach to identifying recurrent patterns, finding symmetries that cross from biology to geology, to climatology; using photo montages reminiscent of those in Kepes's publications, he shows, for

example, fractal patterns that make "mountains like molehills" (p. 48) and replicated spiral formations in plants, mollusks, and hurricanes (pp. 97–101).

4   Turner reports that in 1942, Margaret Mead stated that she would likely feel out of step with free citizens in the sort of egalitarian community she and her colleagues worked to establish: "We who have dreamed it could not live in it" (p. 293). McLuhan expressed similar personal ambivalence, heralding a future "free of fragmentation and alienation" as one requiring "the dissolution" of a way of life meaningful to him: "No one could be less enthusiastic about these radical changes than myself" (*Playboy*, 1969, p. 267).

References

Ball, P. (2016). *Patterns in nature: Why the natural world looks the way it does*. University of Chicago Press.

Beck, J., & Bishop, R. (2020). *Technocrats of the imagination: Art, technology, and the military-industrial avant-garde*. Duke University Press.

Blakinger, J. R. (2019). György Kepes: *Undreaming the Bauhaus*. MIT Press.

Böhme, G. (2017). *The aesthetics of atmospheres* (J. P. Thibaud, Trans.). Routledge (Original work published 2016).

Botar, O. (2017). The biocentric Bauhaus. In C. N Terranova & M. Tromble (Eds.), *The Routledge companion to Biology in art and architecture* (pp. 17–51). Routledge.

Bridle, J. (2018). *New dark age: Technology and the end of the future*. Verso.

Crary, J. (2022). *Scorched earth: Beyond the digital age to a post-capitalist world*. Verso.

Genosko, G. (2025) *Harley Parker: The McLuhan of the Museum*. University of Calgary Press [pending]

Halpern, O. (2014). *Beautiful data: A history of vision and reason since 1945*. Duke University Press.

Howes, D. (2022). *The sensory studies manifesto: Tracking the sensorial revolution in the arts and human sciences*. University of Toronto Press.

Janicka, I. (2023). Reinventing the diplomat: Isabelle Stengers, Bruno Latour, and Baptiste Morizot. *Theory, Culture & Society, 40*(3), 23–40. https://doi.org/10.1177/02632764221146717

Kepes, G. (1944). *Language of vision*. Paul Theobald.

Kepes, G. (1953). Art and science. *Explorations: Studies in Culture and Communications, 1*, 72–78.

Kepes, G. (1956). *The new landscape in art and science*. Paul Theobald.

Kepes, G. (1965). The visual arts and sciences: A proposal for collaboration. *Daedalus, 94*(1), 3–12.

Kepes, G. (Ed.). (1965). *The man-made object*. George Braziller.

Kepes, G. (1970/1972). *Toward civic art*. https://monoskop.org/File:Kepes_Gyorgy_1970_1972_Toward_Civic_Art.pdf

Kepes, G. (Ed.). (1972). *Arts of the environment* . George Braziller.

Kitnick, A. (2021). *Distant early warning: Marshall McLuhan and the transformation of the avant-garde*. University of Chicago Press.

McLeod Rogers, J. (2021). *McLuhan's techno-sensorium city: Coming to our senses in a programmed environment*. Lexington.

McLuhan, M. (1961). Inside the five-sense sensorium. *Canadian Architect, 6*(6), 49–54.

McLuhan, M. (1966). The emperor's old clothes. In G. Kepes (Ed.), *The man-made object* (pp. 90–95). George Braziller.

McLuhan, M. (1967). The invisible environment: The future of an erosion. *Perspecta, 11*, 161–167.

McLuhan, M. (1970). *Culture is our business*. McGraw-Hill.

McLuhan, M. (1977, June 27). *The medium is the message* [Lecture]. *ABC Radio National*, Monday Conference. https://www.youtube.com/watch?v=fFtspEielxI

McLuhan, M. (1987). *Letters of Marshall McLuhan* (M. Molinaro, C. McLuhan, & W. Toye, Eds.). Oxford University Press.

McLuhan, M. (1995). The Playboy interview. In E. McLuhan, & F. Zingrone (Eds.), *Essential McLuhan* (pp. 233–69). House of Anansi Press Inc. (Original work published 1969)

McLuhan, M. (1997). Culture without literacy. In M. Moos (Ed.), *Media research: Technology, art, and communication* (pp. 126–138). G+B Arts International. (Original work published 1953)

McLuhan, M. (1997). The electronic age—the age of implosion. In M. Moos (Ed.), *Media research: Technology, art, and communication* (pp. 16–38). G+B Arts International. (Original work published 1973)

McLuhan, M. (2003). *Understanding media: The extensions of man* (Critical ed.) (W. T. Gordon, Ed.). Gingko Press. (Original work published 1964)

McLuhan, M., & Fiore, Q., with J. Agel. (1967). *The medium is the massage: An inventory of effects*. Gingko Press.

McLuhan, M., & Fiore, Q., with J. Agel. (1968). *War and peace in the global village*. Bantam.

McLuhan, M., Hutchon, K., & McLuhan, E. (1977). *City as classroom: Understanding language and media*. Book Society of Canada.

McLuhan, M., & McLuhan, E. (1992). *Laws of media: The new science*. University of Toronto Press.

McLuhan, M., & Nevitt, B. (1972). *Take today: The executive as dropout*. Harcourt, Brace Jovanovich.

McLuhan, M., & Parker, H. (1968). The emperor's new clothes. In *Through the vanishing point* (pp. 237–261). Harper and Row.

Molinaro, M., McLuhan, C., & Toye, W. (1987). *Letters of Marshall McLuhan*. Oxford University Press.

Nagel, A. (2012). *Medieval modern: Art out of time*. Thames & Hudson.

Nevitt, B., & McLuhan, Maurice. (1996). *Who was Marshall McLuhan?* Stoddart.

Sennett, R. (2018). *Building and dwelling: Ethics for the city*. Yale University Press.

Stengers, I. (2018). *Another science is possible: A manifesto for slow science* (S. Muecke, Trans.). Polity. (Original work published 2013)

Strate, L. (2022). *Concerning communication: Epic quests and lyric excursions within the human lifeworld*. Institute of General Semantics.

Strate, L. (2017). The effects that give cause, and the patten that divides. Anton, C., Logan R. K., & Strate, L. (Eds.), *Taking up McLuhan's cause: Perspectives on media and formal causality* (pp. 93–119). Intellect.

Terranova, C. N. (2016). *Art as organism: Biology and the evolution of the digital image.* I.B. Taurus.

Tsing, A., Swanson, H., Gan, E., & Bubandt, N. (Eds.). (2017). [Introduction]. Haunted landscapes. *Arts of living on a damaged planet.* University of Minnesota Press.

Turner, F. (2013). *The democratic surround: Multimedia and American liberalism from World War II to the psychedelic sixties.* University of Chicago Press.

Zuboff, S. (2019). *The age of surveillance capitalism: The fight for the human future at the new frontier of power.* Public Affairs Hachette Book Group.

CHAPTER 5

Curating the Cybernetic: the Brief Collaboration of György Kepes and Marshall McLuhan

CHARISSA N. TERRANOVA

Introduction: Two Men, Two Words

This is an essay about two men and a word closely affiliated with the twentieth century: György Kepes, Marshall McLuhan, and the cybernetic. The other prominent word in the title—curating—is more tightly connected to our own moment in the twenty-first century. If today individuals carefully curate their lives on social media as a means of self-centered entrepreneurialism, mid last century Kepes curated hybrid, eclectic art-and-science exhibitions and anthologies in order to propagate a vision of transdisciplinary holism for the public. An essay by McLuhan appeared in one of Kepes's chimerical tomes thereby connecting the two men for posterity. I call Kepes's habit of collecting forms, images, and essays from various disciplines—art, physics, physiology, biology, art history, architecture, design, anthropology, the mass media, history, motorbike riding, engineering, mathematics, poetry and more—"curating the cybernetic." In this exercise, Kepes taught the world about the imaginative if not now prophetic idea that fields otherwise vastly disparate—art and science, very generally– could unite to solve major social and ecological problems. The message emanating from these projects, simply put, was the unity of art and science promises to change the world for the better, with the former giving a measure of warm life to the cold statistical tendencies of the latter.

Artist Kepes and writer McLuhan made their livelihoods as professors. Each man was affiliated with a large research university, the former MIT 1946–74 and the latter mostly the University of Toronto 1946–80. These institutions gave them much latitude for their creative research practices. A long leash allowed Kepes to transpose the ideas of the European avant-garde, in particular the German Bauhaus, for a postwar mid-century academic audience that was modern, international, and truly shaped by the first half of the twentieth century rather than the second. McLuhan became famous beyond the academy via film and television. Kepes, the lesser known of the two and primary focus of this essay, is a member of what I describe as the "diasporic Bauhaus," the postwar life of the avant-garde design school of Weimar Germany.[1] He was an acolyte and colleague of the proto new media artist László Moholy-Nagy who taught 1923–28 at the Bauhaus. Moholy-Nagy and Kepes were Hungarian émigrés ultimately living in the Anglophonic world, while McLuhan was Canadian.

Kepes and McLuhan were long distance colleagues with shared interests. Not exactly close friends, they were men of a shared moment seventy years ago, when the human sensorium was becoming ever more prosthetic, each sense a technologically enhanced extension of the body. Their work effloresced around a fusillade of technological disruption 1890–1970, and how these tools and distributed networks supplemented the haptic-sonic-optic human sense trifecta. From photography and x-ray to crystallography and the computer, these technological regimes were largely visual in nature, even while McLuhan aimed to retrain the human senses beyond ocularcentrism.[2] Given that the word "vision" appears in seven of his book titles, Kepes was comfortable with the dominance of vision, even motivated to hone its power. I explore how the cybernetic, its culture and technology, shaped these ideas. Let us begin by defining generally the cybernetic as the machine-human interface and mechanical-cum-digital feedback. The biological roots of cybernetic feedback, distinct from mechanical and electrical engineering, figure strongly in their work. For McLuhan, the human body is a central locus, from which technologies extend the senses. Distinct from this, Kepes forwarded an early twentieth-century template fusing biology, botany, anatomy, physiology, embryology, ethology, and vitalist philosophy, which Oliver Botar calls "biocentrism" into mid-century cybernetics.[3] This unique amalgam influenced certain historic avant-garde art practices of the early twentieth century, including art criticism, abstract photography, Constructivism, and the early functionalism of the Bauhaus. Biocentrism shaped complementary notions of holism and feedback in Kepes's work, giving rise to "biocentric cybernetics."

The work of both men was prescient. Nonetheless the life of McLuhan's has fared better than Kepes's. Postmodern skepticisms of authenticity and science make little room for Kepes's late modern idealism.[4] Postmodern doctrines of linguistic interpretation, cultural fragmentation, and irony marked a paradigm shift starting in the 1950s away from Kepes's earnest universalizing references to cybernetics. By the late 1960s, the Vietnam War and the student protest movement made any art-and-science movement appear complicit with the American war machine (Blakinger, 2019, pp. 291–356). Yet, given the numerous institutions of higher education that received funding from the American military in the postwar period and the more recent apotheosis of digital communication systems, these criticisms seem moot (Abrams, 1989). Postmodernism's trademark of relativism is now wielded by extremist rightwing groups in preposterous and deadly ways in the form of misinformation on the internet and via global white nationalisms. It is time for a renewal of sincerity and truth-telling. For this reason, among others, Kepes's work begs revisiting with fresh eyes from the perspective of the current moment. Kepes and McLuhan used insights from cybernetics for bridge-building between disparate intellectual worlds. This was constructive rather than destructive, providing paths to problem-solving today—in a world where the well-being of the planet and democracy are under grievous threat. The logic of cybernetic feedback, or the circular movement of information that affects both input and output, is a revolution in thinking.[5] It empirically sets in relief the role of nonlinear forces within everyday systems. Feedback's circular movement and nonlinear causality explain a wide array of phenomena, from ethology to consciousness, helping us get at, for example: why a flea perched atop a blade of grass drops when it senses the butyric acid emanating from the body of a nearby mammal; why poverty and racism are systemic; how organic life is like and unlike a machine; and how so-called mind and consciousness are emergent qualities. Yet we proceed cautiously since the very distributed network of electronic communication that the work of Kepes and McLuhan foretold is pharmakon here—both cause and cure, precipitator and salve of large systemic problems.

This essay explores Kepes's up-building curating of the cybernetic and McLuhan's place within it. After an introduction to cybernetics and its position in both figures' work, two sections on curating the cybernetic follow. The first begins with McLuhan's essay "The Emperor's Old Clothes" in *The Man-Made Object* (1966), edited by Kepes, looking to Kepes's distillation of the cybernetic as a textual endeavor in the creation of several image-rich anthologies. The next focuses on *The New Landscape* (1951) and *Explorations* (1970), two exhibitions curated by Kepes and his curatorial work as founder of the Center for Advanced Visual Studies (CAVS) at MIT starting in 1967.

Defining Cybernetics within the Practices of Kepes and McLuhan

The science of cybernetics percolated through the cultural and academic ether of the mid twentieth century often not identified by name. While neither Kepes nor McLuhan frequently used the word "cybernetics" or called themselves "cyberneticians," they used other words and phrases that were part of its vernacular, like "pattern recognition," "circularity," "non-linear," "gestalt," "input," "output," "self-regulation," and "equilibrium."[6] Add to this batch of terminology the word "feed-forward" coined by I. A. Richards, McLuhan's professor at the University of Cambridge. Rhetoricians Richards and acolyte McLuhan brought feedback and feedforward down to the ground of everyday human dialogue. For these writers, feedback was reactive, non-concrete, and constitutive of basic communication, while feedforward was proactive, contextual, and necessary for avoiding misunderstandings.

McLuhan wrote about the idea of feedforward for popular presses in the late 1960s in mellifluous, playful, and profound ways. He queried, "If a data feedback is possible through the computer, why not a feedforward of thought whereby a world consciousness links into a computer?" (Playboy, 1969). Similar to cybernetic artist Roy Ascott's "telematic embrace," feedforward augured global collective consciousness via the immaterial interconnection of electronic pulses: networks of networks facilitating the true altruistic utility of the mainframe. Computers were "not [made] to expedite marketing or solve technical problems," McLuhan contended, "but to speed the process of discovery and orchestrate terrestrial—and eventually galactic—environments and energies."[7] Artists would use feedforward for prophetic research, McLuhan thought, thereby erasing the individual ego-self for a clearing in which a calm ecstasy of Zen emerged. "Poets and artists live on frontiers," McLuhan wrote. "They have no feedback, only feedforward. They have no identities. They are probes" (McLuhan & Watson, 1970, p. 44). Kepes similarly believed artists messianically portended a better world.

Academics working across fields fluidly used the lingo of cybernetics, even while the inclusive science was itself an emergent entity. Scholars from vastly different areas of expertise, like anthropologists Margaret Mead and Gregory Bateson, mathematician and radar expert Norbert Wiener, physiologist and cardiologist Arturo Rosenblueth, electrical engineer Julian Bigelow, literary critic Ivor Richards, and psychologist and computer scientist Joseph Licklider, among others, met in the series of meetings sponsored by the Josiah H. Macy Foundation in New York City 1946–53 that defined cybernetics as a field.[8] In fact, I.A. Richards, who also contributed an essay to one of Kepes's anthologies, introduced the concept of "feedforward" in 1951 at the 8th Macy Conference entitled *Cybernetics: Circular Causal and Feedback Mechanisms in Biological and Social Systems* in a talk titled, "Communication between Men: The Meaning of Language."[9] He was one of the few attendees of the Macy conferences, fount of modern cybernetics, trained in the humanities instead of hard sciences. Clearly, cybernetics was an interdisciplinary project, which appealed to Kepes and McLuhan. Yet, like the two men, most of these thinkers did not call themselves "cyberneticians." Nonetheless the collective work of this kaleidoscopic collection of thinkers was itself algorithmic and cybernetic in nature, with its mutational brain-trust collecting knowledge from various specialties and toggling between the creation and mimesis of what was just on the horizon: global computational automation.

Cybernetics further coalesced around two notable publications. The first was the essay "Behavior, Purpose, and Teleology" by physiologist Rosenblueth, mathematician Wiener, and engineer Bigelow. Published in 1943, before the Macy conferences, the article established the idea that "behavior" was a valid lens through which to measure the activities of organic and inorganic systems, biological life and robots. It also rejuvenated the concept of teleology, a term that scientists scorned, deeming it irrelevant since Charles Darwin's publication of *On the Origin of Species* in 1859 because of its association with Creationism and intelligent design. The word "teleology" signifies in general the movement toward a state of perfection or a goal. Rosenblueth, Wiener, and Bigelow redefine teleology for the postwar science of cybernetics as goal-seeking behavior. Behavior is a pliable term, useful for describing the actions of organic and inorganic systems thus making it useful for the burgeoning field. The coupling of teleology and behavior gives shape to circular feedback, insomuch as "teleological behavior [is] synonymous with behavior controlled by negative feed-back [sic]," or signals from the goal of given action that return to the system—organic or mechanical—to correct its course.[10] By the end of the 1940s, Wiener published *Cybernetics: Or Control and Communication in the Animal and Machine*, a pithy volume that explained the new universal science of cybernetics in 168 pages and the second groundbreaking publication for the field. The book expands the work the three scientists began for a general audience, relinquishing none of its moorings in hard science as the text contains many examples of modeling via mathematical equations.

In *Cybernetics* (1948) Wiener generalizes the mechanisms of a radar-based calculating device called the antiaircraft [AA] predictor, which he and Bigelow had developed during the War. The AA predictor is an automated antiaircraft gunner that functions as a servomechanism, which is based on a human pilot-as-servomechanism (Galison, 1994, p. 264). A servomechanism, which literally means "slave machine," is an automatic device that corrects the performance of a system by negative or corrective feedback (Galison, p. 236). Note the biological and corporeal lineage here. In addition to the metaphorical referencing of slave labor within the word "servomechanism," Wiener and Bigelow developed the radio-wave technology of the AA predictor by looking to a mammalian nervous system, through studying carefully the behavior of a human pilot mid-flight. Wetware literally bodies forth the newly codified union of hardware and software, setting in relief how the process of robotic technological development comes from mirroring natural systems.

Cybernetic technology was not new. In 1788, James Watt invented the steam engine fly-ball governor, which manages speed. In 1868, James Clerk Maxwell wrote a theoretical account of it which spurred Wiener to coin the term "cybernetic" in 1948, or so he thought.[11] Wiener was unaware of physicist André-Marie Ampère's use of the word "cybernétique" to identify the science of government in 1834.[12] In the Introduction to the first edition of Wiener's book, he explains how the interdisciplinarity of the new field, that it emerged at its core from a combination of biology and engineering—wet-, soft-, and hardware—made it difficult to name. In fact, it was mathematician Wiener *and* cardiologist Rosenblueth (to whom Wiener dedicated the book) who together rediscovered word. "Cybernetics," as Wiener put it, is an "artificial neo-Greek expression [we intended] to fill the gap."(Wiener, 1961, pp. 11–12) They took the word "cybernetics" from the same Greek root of "governor," *kybernetes* [κῠβερνήτης], which means "steersman" to identify the communication of control- or guide-information that occurs through negative feedback in animals and machines. The idea of "control" central to cybernetics does not mean control of another but oneself. It is autopoietic in nature, referring to "self-propelling," "self-steering," or "self-guidance," as in the Greek *kubernáō*, which means "to steer." Cybernetics spreads selfhood and teleological agency beyond the human realm to nonhuman animals, machines, objects, and the environment. Cybernetics bears the sheer logic of automation, which Wiener later warned could have terrible repercussions in the form of "learning machines," an earlier version of AI, for overall employment and the human brain itself (Weiner, 1960, pp. 1355–1358).

Wiener and Kepes became colleagues and friends at MIT, where Wiener had been a professor in the Mathematics Department since 1919 and Kepes joined the School of Architecture and Planning as professor of visual design in 1946, right in the flux of the cybernetic imagination.[13] While they shared ideas on the daily bus ride to and from MIT and an occasional dinner, true collaboration is documented in print in at least one instance with Kepes publishing Wiener's essay, "Pure Patterns in a Natural World," in *The New Landscape in Art and Science*

(1956), the catalogue-cum-anthology connected to Kepes's exhibition *The New Landscape* (1951) discussed below.[14] Kepes did not attend any of the Macy conferences. He was nonetheless a wide-ranging interdisciplinary intellectual like those who did, including Wiener.[15] Yet, Kepes's cybernetic curatorial efforts leaned more toward the natural sciences than engineering in terms of scientific influence. As Kepes scholar John Blakinger states, "Kepes was more naturalist than technologist" (2019, p. 20). Kepes's naturalism, Gestalt-orientation, biocentric-cybernetics should be emphasized in this context, for this perspective sets in relief how Kepes harnessed his connections to scientists at MIT for the sake of bigger, more holistic causes: engaging science for the new 1950s cybernetic complexity, connecting the historic avant-garde, notably *not* the postwar neo-avant-garde, to information science just as mechanical computation was giving way to digital. In the late 1960s, Kepes integrated art and ecology for the remediation of environmental problems using these energies. In short, Kepes brought the biocentrism of the historic avant-garde to the postwar era as he practiced biocentric cybernetics.

Kepes's biocentric cybernetic practice is part of an older German tradition of *Naturromantik*, German Romantic biology, dating back to the late eighteenth-century writings of Immanuel Kant (see Richards, 2002). According to László Moholy-Nagy expert Oliver Botar, this strain of thinking makes its way into modern art as "biologisches Denken"—biological thinking—or "biocentric modernism." (Botar, 2016, p. 17) Kepes's ideas about light and interactive art—the notion that light is homologous to life and interactive art is one with the ecological fray—emerge from this tradition by way of Moholy-Nagy's Bauhaus-era proto-cybernetic approach to art and design. The two Hungarian artists, Moholy-Nagy and Kepes, are part of a chain of extraordinary scientist-philosophers that includes, among others, the Baltic-German biologist Jakob von Uexküll, Austro-Hungarian botanist Raoul Francé, and German embryologist Hans Driesch. This sets in relief a baseline intellectual mosaic for cybernetics that is deeply biological and ecological in orientation and, moreover, divergent from the inchoate military industrial complex of WW II that many argue is its twentieth-century origin.

Unlike Kepes, McLuhan had little personal or direct intellectual relation to Wiener. Yet, like Wiener's *Cybernetics: Or Control and Communication in the Animal and the Machine*, McLuhan sought to prepare people with books for a new world of accelerated mediatized circular communication. The circular feedback logic of hot and cold media within his most famous work, *Understanding Media: The Extensions of Man* (1964), define the culture of cybernetics and was first articulated by Wiener. Even so, McLuhan rejected Wiener's mathematical theories of cybernetics, showing not simply his dedication to the irreducible poetics of writing, but to the possibility that this irreducibility would inhere in cybernetics as well, a zone where feedback and complexity reign. Korean-American intermedia artist Nam June Paik found the work of the two thinkers intimately compatible for this very reason: the challenging complexity and irreducibility of cybernetics. For Paik, the coupling of electronics and physiology constituted an important "parallel between the two thinkers," giving a John Cagean Fluxus-style indeterminism to art practices (1967, p. 7). "Indeterminism, a core in the thought of the twentieth century from Heisenberg via Satre [sic] to Cage," Paik argued, "was reflected also in Wiener and McLuhan. For Wiener indeterminism was entropy, a classical terminology of statistics, and for McLuhan indeterminism was the 'cool media with low definition'" (p. 8). While arguably present throughout his published work and public lectures, the most obvious and literal invocation of cybernetics was in the two-page Foreword McLuhan wrote for British-Canadian engineer Arthur Porter's *Cybernetics Simplified* (1969). There he wrote lyrically about pattern recognition, the new information environment, and "Nature," with a capital "N." McLuhan found the new "Nature" to be inorganic and algorithmic in ways the old nature was not, a carrier of new epistemologies of creativity itself, just as Ada Lovelace predicted in the 1840s.[16] McLuhan wrote, "'Nature' is now content, as it were in a man-made environment. One of the unexpected effects of the new feelings toward Nature has been the programming of invention itself" (McLuhan, 1969, p. vi). While Kepes's ideas about nature are more a matter of literal natural ecology, he thought, like McLuhan, art could be precisely that—a programmable intervention in nature.

Curation 1: György Kepes's Books

McLuhan's essay "The Emperor's Old Clothes" appeared in *The Man-Made Object* (1966), a volume in the *Vision and Value Series* (1965–66; 1972) [V&V] edited by Kepes (pp. 90–95). Seven volumes, six from 1965–66 and one from 1972, make up the V&V, which were the result of several inter- and transdisciplinary seminars at MIT organized by Kepes. Kepes invited a diverse roster of figures from art, design, and science for the meetings to discuss abstract themes applicable across fields, including "the nature and art of motion," "sign, image, symbol," "structure in art and in science," "education of vision," "module, proportion, symmetry, rhythm," and "arts of the environment." The book form was perfect for his project. In McLuhan-esque fashion, it was medium and mediation: a unique art form unto itself to be exploited in speculative fashion and a transducer of information (Blakinger, 2019, p. 91). Because of the innumerable images of all type, the books read like a lesson in pattern recognition (Blakinger, pp. 79–216). In turn, pattern recognition is central to cybernetics, as reading patterns is an essential learning process for any system with goal-seeking or teleological behavior, mechanical or biological.[17]

Upon request from Kepes, Wiener wrote an essay about patterns for *The New Landscape in Art and Science* (1956), which was, like the later V&V books, encyclopedic in nature. The images on its book jacket cybernetic symbols: an x-ray photograph of a fresh rose with computer punch tape atop. In "Pure Patterns in a Natural World," Wiener explained to his reader how the short essay came into being. Kepes sent Wiener a packet "comprise[d of] several interesting patterns which occur under the microscope, or in the examination of physical processes, and which are rich in the evocation of emotional experience, when they are inspected not merely with the intellect but the eye" (Wiener, 1956, pp. 274–276). There were seven images, all monochromatic and abstract, taken from the exhibition discussed below. Given the nature of the photographs, that they are abstract, and that the book was published in 1956, the images read *prima facie* like they are related, for Kepes a painter himself, to the current painting movement Abstract Expressionism. They are not. When coupled with the short essay by Wiener, they read differently. Wiener describes the figures as follows: a cross-section of a plant, a photograph of a poly-crystalline aggregate, a dialectric in the process of breakdown, a Schlierendiagramm of the flow of a liquid, an image related to the spiral motion of a charged particle in an electromagnetic field, a reading from "some sort of spectroscope." These are images about "the new landscape of art and science" notably made possible by the technological extension of vision. They show minute natural qualities otherwise invisible to the naked eye made by wondrous new visual technologies intended for use by scientists. Kepes brought these visualizations into the world of art recasting them as hybrid works of art-and-science.

A similar type of visionary art-and-science heterogeneity characterizes *The Man-Made Object*, the V&V book containing McLuhan's essay. His piece shared space with essays by the English writer and founder of the London Institute for Contemporary Arts Herbert Read, Bauhaus figure and modern architect Marcel Breuer, modern painter Jean Hélion, art critic Dore Ashton, historian of modern architecture Françoise Choay, architect and proto postmodern urban theorist Christopher Alexander, and Texas-born Harvard PhD student Henry S. Stone Jr. who wrote the essay "Youths and Motorcycles." With the exception of Alexander and Stone, the group is part of the modernist legacy. Unique from the other V&V books, there are no essays by scientists, but as with all its volumes, it contains many images, including: photographs of a railroad station coal stove, two-oven electric range, shaman's copper rattle, portable TV set, pueblo pottery, the Katsura palace, Tugendhat chair and couch designed by Mies van der Rohe, paintings by Hélion, chairs designed by Bertoia, young men on motorcycles, and works of art by Duchamp, Hausmann, Oppenheim, Ernst, Kaprow, Dubuffet, Appel, Rauschenberg, Chamberlain, Burri, Tinguely, and Nevelson. The eclecticism of Kepes's books provides an infinite puzzle. Are they a throwback to Aby Warburg's Mnemosyne Atlas (1927) or Le Corbusier's Mundaneum (1929)? An adjacent articulation of André Malraux's *Musée imaginaire de la sculpture mondiale* (Museum without Walls, 1952–54)? An analogue precursor of the internet? I argue they are part of the long history of modern biocentrism in their materialization of biocentric cybernetics. Here biocentrism manifests in holism. *The Man-Made Object* is holistic in its comprehensiveness, as it offers insights from varied practitioners and an array of. Collectively, the books in the V&V series constitute a collaboration of artists and scientists led by Kepes. This constitutes another holism. The most important sense of holism at work here is that which denies vulgar reductionism, for holism by definition refers to the whole being more than the sum of its parts. In all of their complexity, Kepes's books deny easy interpretation. Understanding them is like reading runes; they are unique works of art.

McLuhan's catholic approach to knowledge fits well here. His essay is short, rich, and inclusive, a little over five-page meandering excursus on art, technology, the artist, and the environment. Mirroring the intermixture of Kepes's work, he cites a variety of figures and sources: a book about legal history, Alan P. Herbert's *Uncommon Law*, another about the philosophy of science, Milic Capek's *The Philosophical Impact of Contemporary Physics*, another about perception from an airplane, E.A. Gutkind's *Our World from the Air*, Aristotle's *Poetics*, James Joyce's *Finnegan's Wake*, modern painters Picasso, Seurat, and Rouault, James Bond, Humphrey Bogart, Rimbaud, Hemingway, and Nielsen ratings. Books and people alike navigate space as though on equal ground. Cybernetic technology renders all things equal, turning specific objects into streams of information, so many 0's and 1's of binary code. Feedback is central to the essay's logic. Old technology circles into new, transforming itself into art through its movement into desuetude and reuse. He writes, "Old environments are the nutriment of the new ones. As they are assimilated by the new energy system, the older systems are transformed into art forms" (p. 91) Similar to natural evolution and the diversification of species, the circular movement of feedback is generative of varied forms and ideas. He argues that poets learn from cinema and photography how to move beyond ocularcentrism, as they make "all the senses participate at once" (p. 91). Technology flows to and from biology as biology flows to and from technology: "Electric circuitry is an organic thing, an extension of our nervous system" (p. 92). The space capsule and satellite have left behind earth, turning it into a work of art—an anti-environment. Art as an anti-environment reflexively reveals otherwise invisible qualities—truths and realities that tell of regular, more basic though imperceptible infrastructural environments, such as radio waves and satellites. Anti-environments set in relief what is camouflaged, namely concatenations of different technologies within media ecologies. "The planet has become an anti-environment, an art form, an extension of consciousness, yielding new perception of the new man-made environment," which is collectively formed by technological tools, the mass media, and manifold cybernetic networks (p. 93). Art simply *is* an anti-environment for McLuhan: like classical Marxist ideology, art pulls back a veil of invisibility to reveal a truth, to show a reality underneath.[18] Individual and shared consciousness coevolve and become one with technological artifice: "The next phase of this extension will naturally concern the action of making consciousness technologically" (p. 93).

McLuhan was skeptical about the convention of the hallowed art-object, contending that it was imminently to give way to information. Informatics promised its deliquescence into action and information flows: "Art as a classified activity dissolves with the advent of electric circuitry. The art object is replaced by participation in the art process" (1966, p. 94). Here McLuhan voiced an anti-tradition and anti-art market position similar to other art critics circa 1968. McLuhan's essay resonated with "Systems Esthetics," artist-critic Jack Burnham's article arguing that a new wave of art—conceptualism—caused the tradition of the handmade object to wither away, disappearing into systems (1968, pp. 30–35). McLuhan predicted the transformation of the artist from maker to programmer, from crafter to information organizer. Burnham made the same argument when he wrote systems aesthetics give rise to *homo arbiter formae*, man as maker of esthetic decisions, a shift from classical *homo faber*, or man as maker (Burnham, p. 35). Also in 1968, John Chandler and Lucy Lippard described the dematerialization of art, the emergence of a new ultra-conceptual art in which objects were secondary to concept and performative intention (pp. 31–36). In his concluding remarks, McLuhan writes, "The artist leaves the Ivory Tower for the Control Tower, and abandons the shaping of art objects in order to program the environment itself as a work of art" (1966, p. 94). Similar to Kepes, the artist for McLuhan is akin to a shamanist guide, someone who helps others contend with new technology. This is precisely how Kepes envisions the exhibitions discussed below; they are intended to teach viewers about new technologies and modes of scientific visualization. Both men cast a vision of the artist as problem-solving leader. According to Blakinger, McLuhan had Kepes in mind when he identified the artist in the Control Tower. Yet, unfortunately Blakinger frames this negatively, arguing that Kepes played an "oddly antiquated role," the "artist" reborn as "technocrat" (2019, p. 11). This misreading of Kepes is regrettable but conceivable given the challenge posed by the multifarious V&V.

The curating of the cybernetic by Kepes is eccentric and confusing, appearing rearguard while it was in fact future-oriented. It shot the biocentric aesthetics of the early twentieth century historic avant-garde through the prism of mid-century publishing and cybernetic culture precisely during the ascendence of a new avant-garde, of which he was not a part. A younger generation of artists with new ideas had arrived. For the most part, they did not epistemologically prescribe to the holistic vision of an art-science-technology unity, even while at times deploying science and technology in imaginative ways. Kepes's unity, its universalism and aspiring polymathy, was simply not their cause. The shift in the fine arts beginning at mid-century, materializing in pop art, minimalism, conceptualism, performance art, feminist and queer art came to be known as the neo-avant-garde.[19] The neo-avant-garde marked a turn away from modernism and the full-throttle entrance of postmodernism. It has been unclear how to position Kepes's work because of its liminal status, that it embodies neither historic nor neo-avant-garde, but something in between—a late modernism, second modernism, or non-stop modernism, but not postmodernism.[20] Postmodernism in our current moment is normative while fusty: outworn yet all too present in the monstrous relativisms borne of global white nationalism and its presence on the internet. Because of this, Kepes's work is newly relevant. Understanding its place within biocentric cybernetics, as it carries forth an organicist, anti-reductionist, holistic mode of complexity-thinking, one sees it in an altogether different light, refulgent in its sober, creative, and open-ended pragmatism.

Curation 2: György Kepes's Exhibitions and C.A.V.S.

In 1951, five years prior to the publication of Wiener's essay in *The New Landscape of Art and Science*, Kepes installed the exhibition *The New Landscape*, from which the book's name was derived. The space, the Hayden Gallery at MIT, was clean and new, the university's first contemporary visual arts center opened in 1950.[21] From current perspectives, *The New Landscape* seems more like installation art than an exhibition, a form of embryonic conceptualism without any of its characteristic irony.[22] The exhibition did not focus on the art of Kepes's contemporaries. Rather it consisted of several scientific images that Kepes had amassed from researchers. He then enlarged and mounted them on board and hung them on the covered curtain glass wall and within a grid of thin metal scaffolding. A group of sculptural objects suggestive of mathematics and measuring lay on the floor in one section of the framework. Together, pictures and objects read as an hygienic take on Albrecht Dürer's engraving, "Melancholia" (1514), the studio of a renaissance man for the

Mad Men era. Though not x-ray images, that they appear to float makes them similar, unencumbered by cultural reference or social context, shorn of subjectivity, and readied for scientific reading. Rather than deracinated, they are intentionally austere, a protracted engagement with the design strategies of Bauhaus "functionalism" and biocentrism.

Hung without frames and within the barest armature, the images communicate transparency and functionalism. They are simple figurations brought into being by technologies of scientific visualization. They are a testament to truths of the "new landscape of art and science." This research is based on Botar, 2010. Their fact-bearing presence is reminiscent of the New Objectivity [*Neue Sachlichkeit*] in painting, design, and architecture of the Weimar Republic. Above all, the New Objectivity sought to make reality transparent. The paintings were figural, while the architecture was bare-bones modern. Paintings by Otto Dix, George Grosz, and Max Beckman were purposefully raucous and ugly. Bloated bourgeoisie, rail-thin aging prostitutes, and automata military generals exposed social, economic, and government corruption. Transparency in architecture manifested in the free façade of the curtain glass wall and unencumbered flow of the open plan, design elements made possible by the technological breakthroughs of the nineteenth century. Founding Bauhaus director Walter Gropius designed the flagship structure of the Bauhaus in Dessau, Germany 1925–26. Transgressing age-old ideas about propriety in architecture, it is more like a factory than an art school, with its student workshop a rectangular glass box that, like the images in Kepes's exhibition, seems to float because of a grid of white concrete columns visible from outside. Gropius's vision combined art, design, and the labor politics of socialism. The furniture of the New Objectivity was similarly clever and elemental. Marcel Breuer designed the Wassily Chair (named for the painter Wassily Kandinsky who taught at the Bauhaus) 1925–26 using a few strips of leather and basic tubular steel the idea of which he took from his bicycle handlebars.

In calling scientific imagery in the exhibition "a new landscape," Kepes describes a world of scientific visualization in abstract light-images. Landscape is not literal but suggestive of a new way of thinking about abstract art through scientific visualization, images such as "the inner structure of microscopic mineral [and] the outer reaches of the solar system" (Blakinger, 2019, p. 79). An image of the gallery shows photographs of cellular form foregrounding a remarkable image of a bright, ecstatic blast of energy, a "Lichtenberg figure," named for the eighteenth-century physicist and satirist Georg Christoph Lichtenberg who experimented with electricity. [Images 1–2] As though in feedback, the pictures point back to their media ecology: their facticity, the scientific information that is figured in abstract form, points to what is unseen, the technology and context of its making. In the phrase "media ecology," I locate the logic of Kepes's exhibition within the cybernetic *topos*, to use Botar's term, in which McLuhan sees media as a matter of prosthetic technology working on behalf of obscure networks of software and hardware.[23]

Another common topos for Kepes is the early twentieth biocentrism of art critic Ernö Kállai and Bauhaus teacher and designer László Moholy-Nagy, both of whom were working in Berlin in the late 1920s and early 1930s. Kepes left Hungary during this time to work for Moholy-Nagy in his Berlin design office, before the two men, accompanied by Gropius, departed for London in 1935. In his practice, Moholy-Nagy used a panoply of sources—scientific and otherwise—finding abstraction to be a matter of form and technology alike. He used scientific images that were atypical to art conventions, those which are the result of scientific "self-imaging," such as microscopy, telescopes and x-ray photography and film. They became part of a robust and intentional comingling of art and science, or biocentrism (Botar, 1998, pp. 126–127). Building on a welcoming of abstract figuration from science, what Botar identifies as the "naturamorphic analogy," artists developed a full-fledged aesthetics of the scientific image in the 1920s. The facticity of scientific visualization brings a jolt of awe and wonder and, in turn, scientific knowledge becomes aesthetic information for the artist. Moholy-Nagy integrated scientific photography in the 1925 publication of *Painting, Photography, Film* [*Malerei, Photographie, Film*] that was part of the Bauhaus book series and the 1929 exhibition FIFO [Film und Foto] of the Deutsche Werkbund [the German Labor League of artists, designers, and craftsmen] in Berlin. This research is based on Botar, 2010. Moholy-Nagy notably installed the images of FIFO in the cool fashion of the New Objectivity, with images seeming to float mid-air attached to an industrial grid like Kepes's *The New Landscape*. Book and exhibition placed adjacent scientific imagery and abstract photography to show their shared aesthetic qualities while also turning them into cybernetic information, 1s and 0s, having them play on equal ground. This blunt information sends viewers into a whorl of materialist scientific wonder, such as with the Lichtenberg figure in *The New Landscape*.

In the decade after *The New Landscape*, Kepes focused curatorial energies primarily on publications, the V&V published primarily 1965–66. Kepes resumed curating in space, first through his "research lab" for the "visual arts and sciences," the Center for Advanced Visual Studies [CAVS] at MIT launched in 1967, then the exhibition *Explorations* at MIT's Hayden Gallery in 1970 (Blakinger, 2019, p. 312). *Explorations* showed the work of several CAVS inaugural fellows Jack Burnham, Ted Kraynik, Otto Piene, Harold Tovish, Wen-Ying Tsai, Stan VanDerBeek, and Takis Vassilakis. In addition, Charles Frazier, John Goodyear, Newton Harrison, Les Levine, and Lila Katzen had work in the exhibition. In the 19 years between the two shows at the Hayden Gallery, Kepes's biocentric thinking about cybernetics evolved away from the historic avant-garde into the realm of postwar systems, kinetic, and interactive art. The art in *Explorations* was whimsical and experiential, creating engagements that involved the entire body rather than just looking. Such immersive art—spatial, installation-oriented, and mechanical—approximated life in its biological repletion, giving shape to biocentric art as Moholy-Nagy imagined in the multimedia "Score for a Mechanized Eccentric" (1924–25) and large-scale quasi-architectural "Kinetic Constructive System: Structure with Movement Tracks for Play and Conveyance" (1928). Kepes included a piece he made in collaboration with William Wainwright, titled "Photoelastic Walk," a temporary architectural space, a walkway made of plastic sheets and polarizing screens that created optical illusions as people walked through it. Another work of temporary architecture, Lila Katzen's "Liquid Environment" was a thirty-five-foot tunnel made of vinyl filled with fluorescent fluid and lit by ultraviolet light. Wen-Ying Tsai's "Cybernetic Sculpture System" was also in the exhibition. A work of abstract automated art, the work is made of industrial materials and has moving and responsive parts—an electric motor, stroboscopic light, and an electronic audio feedback control system.[24] Its feedback- controlled oscillator varied the rate of the strobe light that responded to ambient noise by vibrating when viewers passed nearby (Blakinger, 2019, footnote 80, p. 312).

Kepes shot the socialism of the original Bauhaus through the language of cybernetics.[25] 312). Curating the cybernetic was here a matter of ecology in the plural, an environmental and community endeavor. Unlike McLuhan's ideas about ecology, which were fundamentally bound up with technology and artificial networks, Kepes used "environment" and "ecology" to reference actual nature. His essay, "Toward Civic Art," that was part of the exhibition catalogue for *Explorations*, is replete with the language of cybernetics. Referencing autopoiesis, Kepes argued, "Individually and collectively men are self-regulating systems" (1970, p. 87). He claimed that humans and artworks interact via feedback loops, using teleology or "goals" to guide behavior: "In order to achieve our goals we must learn to proportion our efforts to the flow or return of information … Central to the self-regulating system is the notion of feedback, or to express it more generally, interdependence" (p. 88) Kepes equated cybernetic feedback with interdependence, thereby casting a decidedly socio-ecological take on the science of cybernetics. He identified paths to repair environmental degradation by way of urban transdisciplinary art. He included in the essay a black-and-white photograph of dead fish amid garbage on the shoreline. Kepes told readers, "Contemporary anthropology, psychology, and applied science all bring us converging messages that the evolutionary key to the resolution of major disturbances in our individual and common lives rests in achieving a harmoniously functioning human ecology" (p. 91). Kepes used neologisms like "interseeing," "interthinking," and "interliving" to build on "interdependent," "interwoven," "interconnecting," and "interacting" underscoring cybernetic feedback loops create the energy of society, fueling and binding it together.

In the years leading up to his retirement from MIT in 1974, Kepes continued to see the amelioration of ecological problems through the lens of cybernetics. Using its language in "The Artist's Role in Environmental Self-Regulation," Kepes's contribution to the last volume of the V&V titled *Arts of the Environment* (1972), Kepes wrote with hope that the "reckless industrialization and urbanization of an earlier day" came to a close because of "broad ecological feedback machines that sense our danger and work toward resolving the problem of man's relation s with his surroundings" (p. 167). While the machines to which he refers are uncertain, he clearly believed civil engineering and civic art played a shared role in rehabilitating the environment: "engineers ... may collaborate with artists whose minds are geared to an environmental scale of objectives toward the development of imposing features that may serve as symbolic forms of man's attempt at self-regulation" (p. 171). He cites many examples of this kind of work in his essay, none of which were realized. These include James Taggart's "Small-scale model of a Sound Oasis" in the city, his own "Simulated Light Architecture for Boston Harbor," made from light sources floating on cables programmed to create the transformation of space, Ted Kraynik's "Synergetic Light Buoys," and Juan Navarro-Baldweg's "Proposals for Citizen Feedback on a Civic Scale." In Kraynik's work, "synergic light buoys ... respond to the activity of individual facets of city life ... becoming[ing] a symbolic throbbing heart describing the life processes of the urban landscape" (p. 186). Navarro-Baldweg's "Citizen Feedback," combines information and architecture with "display towers in the city ... scan[ning] and transmit[ting] information about the urban dynamics in 'real time.' The visual language is embodied in laser beam configurations. These possibilities suggest an encephalography of the social organism" (p. 187).

Conclusion

The connection between Kepes and McLuhan was itself cybernetic, a matter of circular interaction about electronic networks of communication. Neither man fetishized cybernetics, but used its language as a means to explain the rising ubiquity of networks and the cultural transformations they wrought. As discussed in the Introduction, they did not wear badges of cybernetics, calling themselves "cyberneticians." Rather, they took its language and ideas of feedback and systems to use imaginatively and pragmatically. Following their lead, I use the word similarly in the essay to identify how Wiener's thinking influenced theirs and, in turn, how their practices, Kepes's most obviously, shows a strain of cybernetics with strong biological—biocentric—rather than ballistic origins. I also used the word as it means holistic, transdisciplinary collaboration, as well as the workable gatherings of knowledge and imagery that such inclusion bears. At the same time, a common lens of cybernetics also reveals differences that unfold around each man's ideas about art, nature, the environment, and ecology. For Kepes, the language of feedback explained new ways to ameliorate polluted natural environments and create tightly connected and economically just communities. Cybernetics offered tools for literal action upon natural ecologies that, in turn, promised stronger human bonds within social ecologies. For McLuhan, the language of cybernetics did not provide tools of amelioration, but set in relief how technology completely reconfigures ideas and things. Feedback's motion fundamentally redefines art. No longer a "thing," it is a system in process. Art appears with the desuetude of a given technology. Such dead technology in turn makes evident an environment, that is, a collection of groundline technologies that were otherwise invisible.

To what do we attribute these significant differences in the application of cybernetics? Was it a matter of generation, that Kepes was born five years earlier than McLuhan in 1906? Or, was it their disciplinary distinctions, that Kepes was a painter and McLuhan a writer? Was it a matter of their origins, that Kepes was Hungarian and McLuhan Canadian? Let us contemplate similarities over differences for it bodes construction instead of destruction, coming together rather than pushing apart. Kepes and McLuhan made works of art pointing to their cybernetic future that is our present. Their precedents, behavioral and otherwise, are guidebooks to our present and future.

Notes

1 *Diasporic Bauhaus: Functionalisms, Geographies, and Holisms beyond Germany*, Chair, Charissa N. Terranova, Speakers included Marton Orosz, Charissa N. Terranova, Oliver A. I. Botar, John Blakinger, Discussant Eva Forgacs College Art Association Panel, 107th Annual Meeting of College Art Association, New York City, February 13–16, 2019.
2 Such tools include but are not limited to photography, cinema, crystallography, the conventional and electron microscope, and x-ray, and networks include those made by telephone, film, radio, television, and computer. See Marshall McLuhan lecture from 1966 at Fordham University, https://www.youtube.com/watch?v=M5tv5GE2gDo, Accessed 07/04/2022; and Jaqueline

McLeod Rogers, McLuhan's *Techno-Sensorium City: Coming to Our Sense s in a Programmed Environment* (Lexington Books, 2021).

3   László Moholy-Nagy expert Oliver Botar has pioneered the discourse on biocentric modernism among Austro-Hungarian and German artists and scientists in the first half of the twentieth century. See Oliver Botar, *Prolegomena to the Study of Biomorphic Modernism: Biocentrism, László Moholy-Nagy's "New Vision" and Ernő Kállai's Bioromantik* (UMI 1998) and Oliver Botar and Isabella Wunsch, eds., *Biocentrism and Modernism* (Routledge, 2017).

4   Another term for late modernism is "second modernism." I have also called it "nonstop modernism." See Caroline Jones, "Artist/System," in *A Second Modernism: MIT, Architecture, and the 'Technosocial' Moment*, eds. Arindum Dutta, et. al. (MIT Press, 2013), pp. 506–49; and Charissa N. Terranova, "Nonstop Modernism: Continuity in Jack Burnham's Systems, Structures, and Occultism," in *Perception and Agency in Shared Spaces of Contemporary Art*, eds. Cristina Albu and Dawna Schuld (Routledge, 2017), pp. 199–210.

5   For a discussion of how cybernetics opens new world-views within the arts see: Bruce Clarke, "Finding Cybernetics," *World Futures, (75)* 2019, pp. 17–28; Christina Iuli, "Information, Communication, Systems: Cybernetic Aesthetics in 1960s Culture," in *The Transatlantic Sixties: Europe and the United States in the Counterculture Decade*, eds. Grzegor Kosc, et. al. (DeGruyter, 2013), pp. 226–255; and Edward A. Shanken, "Cybernetics and Art: Cultural Convergences in the 1960s," in *From Energy to Information: Representation in Science and Technology, Art, and Literature*, eds. Bruce Clarke and Linda Dalrymple Henderson (Stanford University Press, 2002), pp. 155–77.

6   The word "cybernetic" appears nowhere in Kepes's published work. However, Kepes scholar Marton Orosz claims Kepes made comments about cybernetics in unpublished notebooks. Email dialogue between author and Orosz 06/28/2022. See Marshall McLuhan, Foreword, *Cybernetics Simplified* by Arthur Porter (Barnes & Noble, 1969) pp. v–vi.

7   McLuhan, *Playboy Magazine*, Interview (March 1969). See also Roy Ascott, *Telematic Embrace: Visionary Art, Technology, Consciousness* (Los Angeles: University of California Press, 2007).

8   Heims, Steve Joshua, *Constructing a Social Science for Postwar America* (MIT Press, 1991); and https://asc-cybernetics.org/foundations/history/MacySummary.htm. Accessed 07/03/2022.

9   Richards' "Structure and Communication" appeared in Kepes's *Structure in Art and Science* (1965), a volume of the *Vision and Values Series*. The essay provided a technical exploration of "structure" in linguistics, accompanied by a host of spartanly designed diagrams.

10 Rosenblueth, Arturo, Norbert Wiener, Julian Bigelow, "Behavior, Purpose, and Teleology," *Philosophy of Science*, 10*(1)* January, 1943, p. 19. In fact, the authors preferred to use the word "behavior" instead of "causality" since "causality implies a one-way, relatively irreversible functional relationship, whereas teleology is concerned with behavior, not with functional relationships"(24). Behavior and teleology *are* feedback, while causality itself is deterministic. I am using the phrase "circular causality" here for ease of access to the greater rubric of cybernetics.

11 Porter, Arthur, *Cybernetics Simplified* (Barnes & Noble, 1969), pp. 23–24. See also Nobert Wiener, *Cybernetics: Or Control and Communication in the Animal and the Machine*, Second Ed. (MIT Press, 1961); James Clerk Maxwell, "On Governors," *Proceedings of the Royal Society of London*, 1867/1868, 16, pp. 270–283; and Otto Mayr, "Maxwell and the Origins of Cybernetics," *Isis*, 62*(4)* Winter, 1971, pp. 424–444.

12 See André-Marie Ampère, "Essay sur la Philosophie des Sciences, Part 2," [Paris, 1843]; Otto Mayr, "The Origins of Feedback Control (MIT Press, 1970) p. 2; and Walter Daniel Hellman, *Norbert Wiener and the Growth of Negative Feedback in Scientific Explanation with a Proposed Research Program of "Cybernetic Analysis,"* Doctoral Dissertation, Oregon State University Library (December 16, 1981) p. 17.
13 Masani, P. R., *Norbert Wiener 1894–1964* (Basel: Birkhäuser Verlag, 1990), 181; Blakinger, xv; https://www.technologyreview.com/2011/06/21/193920/the-original-absent-minded-professor/. Accessed 07/04/2022.
14 Email dialogue between author and Kepes scholar Marton Orosz 06/28/2022.
15 Wiener attended the meetings until 1951. See Eric Peterson, *Finding Mind, Form, Organism, and Person in a Reductionist Age: The Challenge of Gregory Bateson and C.H. Waddington to Biological and Anthropological Orthodoxy, 1924–1980 Vol. 2*, p. 167, https://curate.nd.edu/show/jq085h75x7x. Accessed 04/05/2022.
16 McLuhan, Marshall, Foreword, Cybernetics Simplified by Arthur Porter (New York: Barnes & Noble, 1969) vi. See also John A. Maurer, "A Brief History of Algorithmic Composition," https://ccrma.stanford.edu/~blackrse/algorithm.html. Accessed 07/04/2022.
17 Nechansky, Helmut, "Elements of Cybernetic Epistemology: Pattern Recognition, Learning, and the Base of Individual Psychology," *Kybernetes*, 41(*3/4*), pp. 444–464. Light and computation artist Vladmir Bonacic (1938–1999) earned a PhD in the field of pattern recognition and hidden data structures at the University of Zagreb. His art engaged pattern recognition. See https://monoskop.org/Vladimir_Bona%C4%8Di%C4%87. Accessed 04/06/2022.
18 According to Larry D. Busbea, "The Emperor's Old Clothes" is one of several essays published in 1965–66 containing McLuhan's ideas about the environment. Another is "Art as Anti-Environment," *Art New Annual*, 32, 1966, pp. 55–57, which was dedicated to Harold Rosenberg. See Larry D. Busbea, "McLuhan's Environment: The End (and *The Beginnings*) of Architecture," http://we-aggregate.org/piece/mcluhans-environment. Accessed 07/05/2022.
19 Dezeuze Anna, "'Neo-Dada,' 'Junk Aesthetic,' and Spectator Participation" in David Hopkins and Anna Katharina Schaffner, *Neo-Avant-Garde* (Editions Rodopi BV, 2006) 49–73; Hubert van den Berg, "On the Historiographic Distinction between the Historical and Neo-Avant-Garde" in Dietrich Scheunemann, *Avant-Garde/Neo-Avant-Garde* (Editions Rodopi BV, 2005), pp. 63–76; and Peter Bürger. Theory of the Avant-garde, trans. Michael Shaw (University of Minnesota Press, 1984).
20 See Caroline Jones, "Artist/System," in *A Second Modernism: MIT, Architecture, and the 'Technosocial' Moment*, eds. Arindum Dutta, et. al. (MIT Press, 2013), pp. 506–49 and Charissa N. Terranova, "Nonstop Modernism: Continuity in Jack Burnham's Systems, Structures, and Occultism," in *Perception and Agency in Shared Spaces of Contemporary Art*, eds. Cristina Albu and Dawna Schuld (Routledge, 2017) pp. 199–210.
21 https://listart.mit.edu/about/history#:~:text=1950%20The%20Hayden%20Gallery%20opens,cornerstone%20of%20the%20Permanent%20Collection. Accessed 07/08/2022.
22 Kepes's exhibition is remarkably similar to an exhibition also in 1951 by British artist Richard Hamilton at the Institute for Contemporary Arts in London titled "Growth and Form." Like Kepes,'s Hamilton's exhibition was not a collection of work by his friends and colleagues in contemporary art, but his interpretation in moving and still photographic images mounted in an experimental gridded armature of Scottish zoologist D'Arcy Wentworth Thompson's unique scientific tome, *On Growth and Form* (1917). For a comparison of the two exhibitions, see

Charissa N. Terranova, "The Epigenetic Landscape of Art and Science c. 1950," in *The Routledge Companion to Biology in Art and Architecture*, eds. Terranova and Meredith Tromble (Routledge, 2016). See also Charissa N. Terranova, "Exhibition as Extended Organism: The Evolutionary Agency of Richard Hamilton's *Growth and Form*," in *D'Arcy Wentworth Thompson's Generative Influences in Art, Design, and Architecture: From Forces to Forms*, eds. Ellen Levy and Charissa N. Terranova (Bloomsbury Press, 2021).

23 Botar, Oliver, "György Kepes' New Landscape and the Aestheticization of Scientific Photography," in *The Pleasures of Light: György Kepes and Frank Malina* (Budapest: The Ludwig Museum, 2010), pp. 120–121.

24 A similar work titled "Cybernetic Sculpture System No. 1" by Tsai won second prize in a competition sponsored by the avant-garde artist-engineer group Experiments in Art and Technology [E.A.T.]. Curator Pontus Hulten then selected this work for the landmark art-science-technology exhibition at MoMA November 25, 1968–February 9, 1969, "The Machine as Seen at the End of the Mechanical Age." https://tsaifoundation.org/art, Accessed 07/10/2022.

25 Both were embodied in Gropius's call to get rid of "divisive class pretensions [between] artists and craftsmen" in the Bauhaus Manifesto of 1919, which were in turn echoed in the factory designs of its flagship building in Dessau. See Walter Gropius, "Programme of the Staatliches Bauhaus in Weimar," in *Programs and Manifestoes of 20th-c. Architecture*, ed. Ulrich Conrads (MIT Press, 1971), p. 49.

References

Abrams, R. M. (1989, March). The U.S. Military and higher education: A brief history. *Annals, Aaps, 502*, 15–28.

Blakinger, J. R. (2019). *Undreaming the Bauhaus*. MIT Press.

Botar, O. (1998). *Prolegomena to the study of bimorphic modernism: Biocentrism, László Moholy-Nagy's "New Vision" and Ernő Kállai's Bioromantik*. UMI.

Botar, O. (2010). György Kepes' new landscape and the aestheticization of scientific photography. In *The pleasures of light: György Kepes and Frank Malina* (pp. 120–121). Budapest: The Ludwig Museum.

Botar, O. (2016). The Biocentric Bauhaus. In Charissa N. Terranova & Meredith Tromble (Eds.), *Routledge companion to Biology in Art and Architecture* (pp. 17–51). Routledge.

Burnham, J. (1968, September). Systems esthetics. *ArtForum, 7*(1), 30–35.

Galison, P. (1994). The ontology of the enemy: Norbert Wiener and the Cybernetic vision. *Critical Inquiry, 21*(1, Autumn), 264.

Kepes, G. (1970). Toward civic art. *Explorations* [exhibition catalogue]. National collection of fine arts. Unpaginated.

Kepes, G. (1972). The artist's role in environmental self-regulation. In *Arts of the environment* (pp. 167–87). George Braziller.

Lippard, L., & Chandler, J. (1968, February). The dematerialization of art. *Art International, 12*(2), 31–36.

McLeod Rogers, J. (2021). *McLuhan's techno-sensorium city: Coming to our senses in a programmed environment*. Lexington.

McLuhan, M. (1966). The emperor's old clothes. In G. Kepes (Ed.), *The man-made object* (pp. 90–95). George Braziller.

McLuhan, M. (1969, March). *Playboy magazine*. Interview, 53–74+.

McLuhan, M. (1969). Foreword. In A. Porter (Ed.), *Cybernetics simplified* (pp. vi–x). Barnes and Noble.

McLuhan, M., & Watson, W. (1970). *From cliché to archetype*. Viking Press.

Paik, N. J. (1967, August–September). Norbert Weiner and Marshall McLuhan. *Institute of Contemporary Arts Bulletin, 172*(3), 7.

Richards, R. J. (2002). *The romantic conception of life: Science and philosophy in the age of Goethe*. University of Chicago Press.

Wiener, N. (1956). Pure patterns in a natural world. In G. Kepes (Ed.), *The new landscape in art and science* (pp. 274–76). Paul Theobold.

Wiener, N. (1961). *Cybernetics: Or control and communication in the animal and the machine* (2nd ed.). MIT Press.

Conclusion: Legacy for Emergency: World Ending and Making

"The world we are living in is not one I would have created on my own drawing board, but it's the one in which I must live, and in which the students I teach must live. If nothing else, I owe it to them to avoid the luxury of moral indignation or the troglodytic security of the ivory tower and to get down into the junk yard of environmental change and steam-shovel my way through to a comprehension of its contents and its lines of force ..."
—McLuhan, *Playboy* interview, 1969, p. 268

"We must plan by design and not simply by decree."
—Tyrwhitt, 1972, "The Pedestrian in Megalopolis: Tokyo," *Human Identity*, p. 603

"In becoming a collaborative enterprise in which artists scientists, urban planners and engineers are interdependent, art clearly enters a new phase of orientation in which its prime goal is the revitalization of the entire human environment..."
—Kepes, 1971, "Civic Art" 1971, p. 9

Our chapters have identified remarkable intersectional moments and matters amongst McLuhan, Kepes, and Tyrwhitt, three mid-century figures who pursued linked if not lockstep value-based programs infused with awareness of social and environmental crisis. In common, they believed in the value of art as humanistic expression, the value of melding art and science to humanize technology, and the value of engaging publics in art and social life. They all believed technology could be useful or, in rogue form, dangerous. With varying proximity, all lived through the destructive rage of World War II (whose finale was the detonation of atomic bombs); the implementation of social controls via government propaganda and mass communication (deeply felt during Cold War years); threats and outbreaks of military violence, with the presence of advanced weaponry; civic unrest and assassinations made into media events; noticeable environmental degradation; and vicious viral outbreaks. While details differ, similar traumas continue in our time.

Alike, the three figures examined here—McLuhan, Tyrwhitt, and Kepes— understood they were living in a world of power abuse and imbalance. Each contributed to projects (not always aligned) committed to securing public involvement and promoting freedom—and opposed to the tyrannies of authority and its outcome of thoughtless, even dangerous, conformity.

Although the term "Anthropocene" was coined in 1980 and not popularized until our century,[1] these three demonstrate that concern about the human impact on land, water, organisms and the atmosphere (rippling across ecologies) entered scholarly conversation before the term itself. McLuhan, Tyrwhitt, and Kepes each proposed strategies for adjusting the relationship between humans and earth to promote survival and cooperative interdependence. This is the basis for the claim this text makes that those before us were not unwitting pawns and practitioners of exploitation and expropriation, nor were they unduly optimistic about human nature and futures. None imagined technocratic rebuilding to recapture a new normal. Understanding them in this way as intellectual forebears and allies may be generative of finding places to extend work they started, calibrating it to the challenges really facing us.

Similarities aside, some readers may feel acceleration puts a wedge between the level of crises then and now—the severity and the salves. Yet, following McLuhan and Kepes in particular, another way of thinking about history and change is as configural (reassembling figure and ground components) rather than linear and directional. Rather than viewing our present as an extreme stand-alone moment, this text recommends seeing how crisis now is both like and unlike what has come before. Making such connection may enable informed response and discourages helpless witnessing of the sort now being advocated in climate trauma literature.[2]

McLuhan and Kepes thought we were facing accelerant change, unprecedented for being provoked by human-made innovations and already deeply embedded in the environment. They wanted to prevent technologies from tumbling forward without strategic interventions (orchestrated by art and science). Yet while they identified the crisis formation as new, they also recognized it as reconfigured from times past: they did not that think theirs the first generation to face devastating change. If some eco-critics currently cite scientific records of prior extinctions to contextualize what's ahead, McLuhan went to history to cite more devastating change events than those in his day, events that had shattered human and, by extension, non-human relations and conditions (caught in an associative net). For example, he proposed that the transition from orality to literacy in past times was more violent than the shift from literacy to new aurality occurring in his day:

> Literacy creates very much simpler kinds of people than those that develop in the complex web of ordinary tribal and oral societies ... The oral man's inner world is a tangle of complex emotions and feelings that the Western practical man has long ago eroded or suppressed within himself in the interest of efficiency and practicality.
>
> The immediate prospect for literate fragmented Western man encountering the electric implosion within his own culture is his steady and rapid transformation into a complex and depth-structured person emotionally aware of his total interdependence of human society. (*Understanding Media*, 2003/1964, p. 75).

The above passage underscores McLuhan's detachment from the idea of linear progress often assumed to be part of modernist thinking. Neither was he romanticizing the loss of orality so much as admiring its relational and affective complexity which he predicted was reassembling as part of new aurality. This passage provides evidence he was no apologist for modernism and did not esteem Western "civilization" as superior to other formations.[3] Orality nurtured complexity which literacy in modernity reduced to practicality; he hoped new aurality might usher in complexity and emotional awareness of "total interdependence."

Connections to Our Time

McLuhan, Tyrwhitt, and Kepes are easily aligned with current forms of posthumanism, sharing a deeply relational ontology that put webs of connection ahead of human exceptionalism. While they gravitated to addressing human claims and concerns before others, they recognized other claims in as much as they recognized principles of dynamic exchange and vulnerability, wherein we impact other life forms and inorganic things, and they impact us. Theirs could be called an ecological perspective, defined by Lance Strate as recognizing limitless ways "the interdependency of systems" sparks both "intended and unintended effects" (2017, pp. 172–73). Tools, machinery, and electricity have interrupted and damaged this ecology, and McLuhan, Tyrwhitt, and Kepes all proposed strategies for rebalancing vital connections amongst humans and the world of others and objects.

Alike, they charged the human species, responsible for planetary degradation, with responsibility for restorative healing. They held that humans need to cultivate innate capacities to know the world in multiple ways, anticipating a range of characteristics that Arola and Rickert associate with Indigenous knowing that are that are "practical, emotional, intellectual, technical, embodied, esthetic, spiritual and more"; seeing the self inter-related to the environment presupposes understanding matter as vital and agency "as coproduced by, through and with all relations (humans, nonhumans, time, space and the unknowable)"(2022, p. 190). Viewed this way, earth is not commodity but co-habitant and the duty of care extends to both human and non-human realms. When McLuhan wrote "we are all crew on spaceship earth," the new collective role he was imagining was not only a fanciful image of freedom and flight but encompassed the labour of sentient involvement ("At the Moment," 1974, p. 49).

Neither were they fully globalist or universalist in envisioning one shared future, for in varying registers they recognized regional differences and local character. They avoided generic one-size fits all proposals, whether, on the respectful note struck by Tyrwhitt, to maintain vernacular cachet or, more instrumentally in McLuhan and Kepes, to adjust technological support to respond to demonstrated place-based irregularities. They were aware histories differ and that communities and cultures are formed by emplaced doing, not "by decree" to borrow from Tyrwhitt's statement reproduced in the epigraph. On the related matter of individuality within collectivity, they wrestled with balancing the claims of the one and the many.[4] They sought unified arrangements accommodating—rather than flattening—difference and dynamism.

Arguably, the scale of climate and planetary crisis was somewhat smaller mid-century, lessoning existential threat and the need for "pre-emptively apocalyptic thinking" (Taussig, 2009, p. 14). Yet, certainly McLuhan, never a rear-view mirror thinker, faced the possibility of apocalypse as a dark yet avoidable outcome of "a totally new situation" (*Medium*, 1967, p. 74). With effort, things could go right; without, things would be dire. He warned we could face the entire "unraveling" of society, "[c]ataclysmic environmental change" and possible apocalypse (*Playboy*, p. 22), "the end of nature" and loss of species (*War and Peace*, 1968, p. 190). The recent *Dark Mountain Manifesto* tells us to abandon narratives of progress and accept the unfolding of "*Uncivilization*"(2017, 2009). Elements of this argument seeded McLuhan's support for Buckminster Fuller's proposals for "unsettlement," an idea which conveyed the need to come up with new ways of living rather than repeating how things have been done. They floated the idea of "unsettlement" at a 1972 international symposium on world development. Of the three mid-century figures, McLuhan showed the least interest in ameliorative programs meant to improve current conditions, calling these rear-view mirror concerns based on looking "backwards into the future" (*Medium*, p. 75).

He attending dangers and gave voice to the dangers of impending crisis as well as the shielding effects of environmental programming, recommending the protective capacity of computers to modulate cultural conditions. He went so far as to recommend programming whole cultures "to keep their emotional climate stable" (*Understanding Media*, p. 45). As I explored in *McLuhan's Techno-Sensorium City* (2021), he imagined humans at the helm, programming environments to be "responsive to human sensory needs" (p. 11). Thus, he was not proposing technological interventions as stand-alone solutions, but always advocating a model of computer/human interaction. His humanism made him more anti- than pro-cyberneticist, for he spoke of human involvement and intervention and against becoming dependent on a mechanistic, self-correcting system. His view was close to what Katherine Hayles describes as third wave cybernetics, which sees the human/nonhuman dynamic operating as a "cognitive assemblage," as "collectivities, not exclusively human, not exclusively organic, through which information, interpretations, and meanings circulate" (2024, p. 95).

If McLuhan spoke of apocalypse and human/machine interventions more fervently than Kepes and Tyrwhitt, they were more direct than McLuhan in expressing bio-protective eco-consciousness. Typically less future-directed, they took aim at eco-problems already apparent. Tyrwhitt, trained under renowned landscape architect and theorist Patrick Geddes, was a lifelong proponent of ecological landscaping and left as a legacy a garden in Greece designed to protect and add to "the vitality of the local ecosystem" (Shoshkes, 2016, p. 227). Kepes was outspoken about environmental protections, using DEWLINE imagery he shared with McLuhan to say that artists can perform "as distant early warning systems" to sound warnings "about the lethal consequences of the wholesale devastation of the natural landscape" (*Toward*, 1972, p. 70). They recognized the immanence of what climate-crisis theorist Michael Richardson now characterizes as "This Mess We're In" (*Nonhuman Witnessing*, p. 11), and, like him, viewed change as intersectional and accelerant, calling for an ethics of care and balance, for activated and educated sentience and cognition.

From amongst the common themes these figures pursued, two are particularly germane to current theoretical efforts to meet and quell multi-crisis. First is the role of art to engage and educate. Chapter 4 explores McLuhan's and Kepes's urgent advocacy of art as gateway to human and planetary survival. Second, involving all three figures, is the recognition of the need to merge art and science to graft ethics onto science and to secure public understanding of science principles. Merging the two knowledges strikes a blow at binary thinking and promotes what Latour calls post-critical monism, involving rapprochement between the "two cultures" of sciences and humanities. His call for a more unified approach to solving multiverse problems and to modify "the relation between scientists and the world with which they are trying to enter into resonance" (*Facing Gaia*, 2017, p. 29) sounds a timely extension of the mid-century call to merge art and science and to involve publics in blocking dangerous accelerant innovation.

Calling on art for enlightenment and calling for knowledge sharing across fields may sound like tame and even ineffectual advice in facing multi-layered crises—not much of a stay against the world ablaze, with temperature, winds and waters rising, AI and data platforms spreading, and economic disparity, exploitation, and violent conflicts deepening. Yet both initiatives signal a turning away from modernist habits that have caused so much harm and toward a philosophical reorientation keyed to recognizing relationships and valuing unity.

Producing Engagement: New Alliances and Feelings in Theatre, Visual, and Atmospheric Art

Giving a recent keynote address, urbanist and sociologist Richard Sennett described witnessing antagonistic public exchanges between supporters of the Left and Right at an international climate summit ("Ruling by Acting," 2023). He noted finding fierce antagonists to be calm and conversational outside marches and apart from their tribes. As a possible bridge-building strategy, he suggested repurposing Brechtian theatre to encourage solidarity amongst citizenry, who might set aside differences to align with its anti-authoritarian stance. A long-time advocate of "disorder by design," he was arguing not only for planners and architects to avoid replicating structural rigidities (Sendra and Sennett, Designing Disorder, 2022), but also for populist engagement in struggles to redefine cultural and social issues as those in which they have shared stakes–to break through people being absorbed into troupes and conformed to scripts.

In another keynote at the same Media Ecology event, communications theorist Douglas Rushkoff (2023) recommended a different form of theatre play to promote understanding, civility, and hope. He suggested local theatre groups might explore issues germane to them, and then share these widely online via Zoom to achieve unbounded interactive engagements ("I Will Not be Auto-Tuned," 2023). Local theatre group exchanges update the Habermasian public sphere on several fronts: placing an emphasis on locality, on speculative or open-ended treatments, and on collective presentation rather than more individualized self-expression. Creating liminal spaces of assembly—connecting local places in virtual space—allows for another modelling of the many and the one that respects commonality and subjectivity.

Presented as forms of theatre, these projects models tech-assisted ways to produce more engaged citizenry. Sennett's Brechtian theatre pushes against what McLuhan (via Ellul) denounced as environmental propaganda ("Invisible Environment", 1967, p. 164). Rushkoff (2019), celebrates dialogue and encounter (Team Human, 2019), aims to reveal human strength and capabilities by loosening the stranglehold of technologies and propaganda: this reminiscent of McLuhan's "breakdown as breakthrough" aphorism (*Culture is our Business*, 1970, p. 27). By linking pluriverse dramas online, he suggests harnessing technology to produces spaces for sharing and connecting.

Apart from seeing theatre as improving subjectivity and sociality—opening opportunities for connection, expression, and resistance—visual arts and artists have also performed some of the bridging work anticipated by McLuhan and Kepes.[5] What stands out here are multi-media or intermedial projects that treat audiences as participants rather than viewers and stimulate multi-sensory responses, exploring science as a metaphysics that open horizons. Dawna Schuld, who researches intersections between perception and light and space art, observes that McLuhan's foundational work using technology to expand perception and alter habitual social arrangements erupted in 1980's installation art. It continued in later productions, like Erwin Redl's *Matrix II* (2005),[6] which presents McLuhan's "semi-mystical" image of consciousness extended into the environment. Redl's work combines "scientific and artistic epistemes" to posit "that the culturally constructed strategies and technologies embedded in our environment and through which we share knowledge are in turn embodied by us and extended back into the social matrix" ("Mind Matrix," 2017, p. 297).

In the area of atmospheric studies, Chris Salter explores the increasing uses of media to elicit sensorial responses that entangle body and media, with participants "discovering (or recovering) felt experience, situated context and sensory affect that cannot be reduced to text, code, or photons aimlessly floating on the screen" (*Entangled*, 2010, p. xxi). Salter's recent work with David Howes—known for hailing McLuhan's influence on sensory studies[7]—develops unbounded "performative sensory environments," where "art is dematerialized in the sense that it comes off the wall, off the pedestal etc., and instead suffuses the space of the installation with a symphony of sensations by engaging multiple modalities via diverse media, whence its intermediality" (Howes, 2022, p. 181). Howes provides a nuanced history linking sometime-McLuhan affiliate R. Murray Schafer to current performative sensory environment projects. Bringing technologies and artifacts together, Schafer's multisensory project *The Theatre of the Senses* (presented in 2005) was reminiscent of "a 1960s Happening"; it was "a truly collaborative project, in which all the senses, like all the arts, conspired and were transmuted into each other, just as the conventional line separating actors from audience was effaced, liberating us from our respective roles, and permitting us to experience each other's presence in surprising new ways" (Howes, p. 185). Particular content is less important in this kind of art than formal capacity to reveal connections and provoke feeling. Howes uses McLuhanesque terms to describe the performative sensory environments in current productions, replacing "medium" with "intermediality" to convey the synesthetic focus: "'intermediality is the message,' and with intermediality comes intersensoriality, and with intersensoriality. . . comes the possibility of enhanced intercultural empathy and communication" (p. 204). The performative sensory environment Howes describes sounds much like the global environmental conditions McLuhan and Kepes called for, enabling citizes/participants to feel connected to everything other and to open up to provisionally balancing an ever-shifting "ecology of the senses" (p. 204).

Making Worlds: Art, Science, and Storytelling

Christine Nystrom, a founding figure of Media Ecology, articulated the need for art as narrative that captures some of what McLuhan and Kepes had in mind when they spoke of artists warning of dangers and prescribing safety routes. According to editors of her recently published writings, her cosmology "placed symbolic activity at the core, within an ecological perspective informed by insights from particle physics, systems theory and evolutionary biology" (Wiebe & Maushart, 2020, p. xiii). Like her colleague Neil Postman, she offered as twin truths that no species can survive "with inadequate information about its world" or "with too much information about its world" ("The Crisis," 1989, p. 181). We were, she thought, endangered by the latter situation, awash in complex information without narrative frame or filter, standing "at a point where the literate, digitalizing mind presents us with knowledge of the universe that our senses cannot fathom" (qtd. in Wiebe & Maushart, 2020, p. xiii). Her statement mirrors Kepes's observation that the new instruments of science have furnished/burdened people with a wealth of information

> The extended world revealed by science exhibited unfamiliar vistas of phenomena and concepts: things too big to be seen, too small, too hidden; ideas too evasive to grasp—subnuclear particles, the indeterminacy principle, computers and transistors, lasers, pulsars, DNA, and inorganic crystals that could change into organic viruses and back again. Few of these were accessible to ordinary human senses or were capable

of being related to human bodies that [humans] use to find their bearings. ("Toward Civic Art", 1970, p. 85)

Like Nystrom, he believed the information, overwhelming in raw form, needed public dissemination via art. McLuhan and Kepes often spoke of innovative implements (telescopes, telephones, computers, and the like) as threatening our sense of scale and equilibrium by providing new in need of being organized and circulated via art to expand learning.

Whereas Kepes gravitated to art in the form of visual narratives and encounters, Nystrom focused on the need for discursive narratives. In this, she was in concert with McLuhan, whose mind and values Lamberti characterizes as "literary" before all else in looking to "language, or—even better—*storytelling* ... as the unifying agent" (*Mosaic*, 2012, p. 37). McLuhan wrote: "Words are complex systems of metaphors and symbols that translate experience into our uttered and outered senses" (*Understanding Media*, p. 85). Nystrom, too, saw language as key to making sense of sensory experiences, "a way of creating new distinctions and re-combinations, of generating new ideas in mind and then introducing them into the physical and social world to enlarge and transform it ("The Crisis," 1989, p. 181). Unique as "creatures of the word," we have the capacity to code, store, and pass on information essential to surviving our increasingly complex environment—an environment now amplified into impenetrable entanglements recently characterized by designer Tony Fry as "the complexity of the complexity" (Online seminar).

Against chaos, Nystrom argued for narrative as "a kind of information sieve" (p. 182) to make experience manageable and meaningful. We have, she noted, survived "for some 70,000 years since language, at conservative estimate, began" (p. 182) by sharing stories that give meaning and purpose: "From the dawn of speech itself, no family, group, or nation, no human alone or in tribes, has survived without integrating experience into a coherent and life sustaining tale. Without an adequate narrative to guide and direct us, we humans cannot survive" (p. 180). Science discoveries have undermined shared stories about spiritual origins and endings that had connected humans to others and the earth and bestowed a sense of purpose. The dilemma of our time is having no framework to make sense of the mounting storm of information, no guidance about what to attend to or ignore. Describing collective despair, Nystrom used the word "catatonia" to invoke active self-harm and loss through suicide, drugs, and alcohol, whereas McLuhan favoured images of collective somnambulance and sleepwalking, .

In calling for sense-making narratives, she is calling for what McLuhan referred to as counterenvironments of art, narrative that goes beyond "here and now" and "sings of the future":

> Somewhere, our age must find a truer larger tale, a narrative sweeping enough, and hopeful enough, to restore dignity and purpose to all human life. We need a tale that goes beyond chanting of here and now and tribal triumphs and despairs, a tale that sings of the future of our species and ennobles the long and painful journey from the savannas of our past. ... [S]uch a song [is] a species song... (p. 184)

In presenting our need to feel, imagine, believe, and reason—with humans timelessly bound to elemental powers in a relationship we no longer acknowledge or comprehend—she anticipated Latour's thesis on "the intrusion of Gaia," an eruptive eternal force exceeding human compass that we must face and that "might bring us closer to all the gods" (*Gaia*, 2017, p. 288).[8] Her hope for a species song also echoes—and helps make sense of—McLuhan's "deep and abiding belief" in the human potential "to plumb the depths of ... being and to learn the secret songs that orchestrate the universe" (*Playboy*, p. 23).

Humanities and Applied Science: Ethics and Programming

Much as the Mariner's survival depended on observing the whirlpool to adjust to its rough ride, our survival, McLuhan and Kepes argued, requires recognizing the pressures of technologies while learning how to rely on, play with, and control them. In Kepes, this view is encapsulated in his inclusion of a century-old passage from William Morris, where the British artisan and socialist who advocated for a return to hand crafting called for industrialists to invest in mechanisms designed to clean up their waste. Morris puzzled that only a few had begun to think about remedies for "the defacements of our big towns by all that commerce brings"; he wondered why there were no machinic advances so that Manchester could "consume its own smoke" or Leeds get rid of its "superfluous black dye without turning it into the river," design problems more worthy of attention than "the production of the heaviest of heavy black silks or the biggest of useless guns" (qtd. in "Toward Civic Art," p. 86).[9] Along these lines, but less focussed on environmental protection, McLuhan explored the position that we are responsible for the world we have altered—that we need to attend to and craft the artificial environment surrounding us, still in the making, and—always in process or flux—requiring design and crafting interventions.

Calling on technology to clean up human-made technology-based problems comes, of course, with danger flags and is easily misread as naïve if not shameless techno-utopianism. Yet neither McLuhan nor Kepes favored market-driven clean-up-as-you-go tactics. A central aim of their new form of artist-led governance and participatory civics was to interactive channels. Drawing on a passage from *Understanding Media*, this is how I state his position in *McLuhan's Techno-Sensorium City*: "Computers and technology can play a support role in establishing 'a new equilibrium among all the senses and faculties' to help 'shape and rearrange the patterns of human association and community'" (*Understanding*, pp. 171, 173; in *Sensorium*, 2021, p. 12). In McLuhan's view, programming is not about finding openings for more technology but making adjustments to support a balanced environment and sensory opportunities. We find a position like this in Joi Ito's *Against Reduction: A Manifesto* (2017), where he counsels humans to take a relational outlook on working "with" machines—to direct innovation in a way that supports life.

There are also arguments for working with technology in Holly Jean Buck's *After Geoengineering* (2019), where she explores the potential of technology (such as cloud seeding and marine cultivation) to control CO_2-fuelled climate change—doing so in a way that takes full stock of human and planetary impacts, losses and risks with gains. In what sounds like a reframing of arguments made by McLuhan and Kepes, she exhorts us to avoid dealing with earth climate as siloed hard science, as if human content and emotions could be separated out. Rather, we need everyone involved in work that is "cultural, empathetic and relational" and includes "creating new stories about retreat and ending and change" (*Ending*, 2021, p. 180). She does not call on technology to fix all that we have broken, but calls for using everything we have to scale down fossil-fuel dependence and warming emissions, webbed and wicked problems not soon or simply "solved": "If we develop the special, cultural, and political capacities to phase things down, we can apply that capacity to degrow certain things that we decide are not socially valuable" (*Ending*, p. 48). There are echoes of McLuhan and Kepes in her injunction to get everyone involved—not just "technocrats and the policy elites" (*Ending*, p. 180). She spins McLuhan's call for controlling technology in asserting that "managed decline, managed retreat, managed rejection" is not negative but about "taking control of our own destiny" (*Ending*, p. 22).

It may seem Tyrwhitt has fallen out of this summary discussion. While Kepes and McLuhan addressed monitoring and redressing adverse effects of sweeping computer-based technologies that effect information—what counts and flows—Tyrwhitt's concerns turned to social and practical questions about equitable housing and access to services and to urban infrastructure matters, like controlling traffic flow, crowding, and lighting. That she grasped futuristic metaphysics but preferred addressing present and pressing issues—"staying with the [visible] trouble" to adjust Haraway's catchphrase—was evident when she wrote to McLuhan that "of course you are right" about there being elements of space other than the visual, but that "the only space architects can handle is physical space, which is, basically, visual space" (see Chapter 2 here; and qtd. in Darroch (2008), p. 166). Yet it is inaccurate to paint Tyrwhitt as solutions-oriented or practical in *opposition to* McLuhan and Kepes as dreamers of newly configured futures. Their intellectual relationships indicated a strong exchange and interweaving of ideas and values, important for symmetries and differences that, read together, provide a richer script. Examining a range of perspectives for interplay is a process that Isabelle Stengers says leads to understanding complexity and avoiding unnecessary divisions as part of participating in "struggles aimed at the creation of a future worth living" (*Another Science*, p. 127).

Hope in a Dark Place

Fred Turner's story of the 60's depicts a polarized public, with violence and a "self-centred search for satisfaction" (2013, p. 293) on one side, and a more idealized search for fellowship and social justice on the other. Media images from this time show scenes of fear, anger and revolt which Turner confirms provide "windows on the historical moments in which they were produced" (2013, p. 10). Alternately, he reminds us of trends that were the legacy of the 40's and 50's when intellectuals like Margaret Mead and Gregory Bateson headed influential movements to promote ethical decision making and community service and thus to secure "the future of the nation and, in a nuclear world… the future of the globe" (p. 179). Turner tells us Mead conceded as early as 1942 that she was bound to feel out-of-step with something like the hippy movement that eventuated in the 60's, for she predicted a changed world would change people and values: "Were the world we dream of attained, members of that new world would be so different from ourselves that they would no longer value it in the same terms" so that "we who have dreamed it could not live in it" (qtd.in Turner, p. 293). McLuhan's project, unfolding several decades later, imagined media supporting radical unity on global scale. As the epigraph to this "Conclusion" (taken from his 1969 *Playboy* interview) conveys, he felt, much as Mead did, dislocated from the world he hoped for which was "not one I would have created on my own drawing board." There is is charged ambivalence in their stepping away from futures of their own devising.

Bruno Latour's philosophy—especially his later work on Gaia as a complex of earth forces—updates and extends many of the mid-century arguments we have visited about crisis, loss, and hope. As McLuhan, Tyrwhitt, and Kepes did, he addresses the need for science and art to merge so that citizens might re-form relationships amongst themselves and with the non-human. His description of the "intrusion of Gaia" resonates with McLuhan's announcement of "the death of nature," although Latour may be less bold than McLuhan in observing that "gradual artificialization is making the notion of 'nature' as obsolete as that of 'wilderness'" (*Facing Gaia*, 2017, p. 121). Yet Latour encounters a more advanced stage of decay and artifice than was evident mid-century, and contends that "Gaia" is now an "eruptive" force in high relief—that we are not threatened as of old by others, but by "an ecological other" (Latour, 2017). Gaia, left in the background, ignored and exploited, has now flipped to become figure, and the work ahead is to reconfigure and repair our relationship to the Gaia principle, a prospect that requires humility and involves "uncertainty" (*Gaia*, p. 219). Without surety, there is still the prospect of survival and adjustment. Latour tells Anna Tsing that more than living in the ruins—more than learning "arts of living on a damaged planet," to pick up the title of her 2017 collection—there may still be "many opportunities in these ruins" ("Anthropologists," 2018, p. 594). This echoes McLuhan's rather grim encouragement to "get down into the junk yard of environmental change" to find ways to adjust and survive. Shades cooler than optimism, both retain hope that a relational principle may undo cross-ecological divisions and permit new alignments.

McLuhan and Kepes used dramatic language, as in McLuhan's reference in the chapter epigraph to inhabiting a "junk yard of environmental change" or in Kepes's multiple references to "exploded" and "explosive" times ("Toward Civic Art," 1971, p. 84). Tyrwhitt took a more even tone, but she too advised of the webbed threat of population and urban growth and pollutants affecting "the climatic balance of the world itself," and cited Waddington's admonition to create designs "resistant to change and catastrophe" (Bell & Tyrwhitt, 1972, p. 48). Recently asserting a similar claim that "resistance is possible" (Another Science, 2018, p. 133), Isabelle Stengers says we can consent or evade "the possibility that we are able to make worthy additions to the weaving of situations that will enable resistance against the coming barbarism" (*Another Science*, p. 129). Donna Haraway (often cited by both Latour and Stengers) also uses the image of weaving in her description of amassing story strands in a cat's cradle assemblage, in a process she refers to as "Story Telling for Earthly Survival" (1994). In *Staying with the Trouble* (2017), she argues we need inclusivity that does not privilege one species story over another, in a process of sharing, listening, and making relations. The weaving and cat's cradle image gives us a deepening—perhaps softening—of McLuhan's mosaic imagery. Alike, these images recommend the creative force of collecting and displaying knowledge and wisdom in ways that solicit engagement and interpretive input—forming a provisional and dynamic sort of unity or universalism that brings together elements of diversity.[10]

We are facing crisis on many fronts. Some current analysts attempt to offer easy solutions. Political journalist Ian Bremmer, for example, tells us in *The Power of Crisis: How Three Threats—and Our Response—Will Change the World* (2022) that survival rests on facing three problems (AI, pandemics, and climate) and that his advice sets us up to beat them. This is not "staying with the trouble" in the purposeful and empathic way Haraway had in mind when she recommended acknowledging entanglement and taking responsibility for evolving respectful relations. Nor is defining a solution what Stengers has in mind when she points out "devastation and reparation or regeneration are not symmetrical" and regeneration, when it happens, is "about creating or reactivating, step by step, relationships that are always tentacular, always partial, always to be cultivated" (*Making Sense*, 2023, p. 179). Consulting our mid-century figures contributes to present-day renunciations of simplistic and solution-oriented approaches—approaches attempting to regain what has been lost, establishing "a new normal" rather than pushing for transformations and reconfigurations that address new conditions and challenges.

The legacy of these three figures shared here is not as comprehensive and detailed as I expected it would be. Originally, drawn to their commitment to facing nascent presentations of current problems, I expected to uncover a variety of strategies for acting now. I expected clearer expressions of optimism and hope. Instead, the three are more toughminded. As we have seen, their hope was tempered with the darker realization of dangers ahead if we fail to prepare for incoming environmental change by stepping up some activities and curtailing others. Moreover, seeing them as figures of hope is a bit misdirected since, as their inheritors, we have not moved in directions that inspired their optimism. Yet there may still be time to enact key suggestions: to cultivate the principle of relationality as world-changing worldview and to seek balance and unity, an arm of which involves controlling technology so that it supports sustainable and regenerative arrangements.

Taking into account how McLuhan, Kepes, and Tyrwhitt characterized incoming challenges and how many of these characterizations still apply conveys that crises now are not singular or simple—not to be answered or solved but requiring attention and understanding. We need to continue the energy of Tyrwhitt's commitment to addressing tangible problems affecting quality of life and the condition of the earth, fostering international dialogue and standards. We also need to theorize with McLuhan and Kepes about meeting less visible effects of change, still in the process of forming addressing established problems, remembering that McLuhan spoke of being ready for total change. Their expansive figure/ground thinking signals the human potential to know and do more and other than current restrictive practices allow—if we explore untapped senses and collectively seek an environment designed to coax intersensorial experience. Another promise of their relational thinking was artist-led governance and participatory civics. had positive world-making power. Whether this form of oversight and cooperation can gentle technologies and address both local and planetary needs still awaits testing.

Notes

1 In "Extinction Events and Entangled Humanism" (2018), Michael Connolly summarizes the debates that have swirled around the term, which he uses for provisional purposes. See pp. 23–24. ftn 13.
2 There is growing advocacy in climate crisis literature for accepting crisis as leading to human extinction and, from this, for humans to practice forms of witnessing (see Savransky, M. (2021). After progress: Notes for an ecology of perhaps. *Ephemra: Theory & Politics in Political Organization*, 21(1), pp. 267–81; and Richardson, M. (2024). *Non-Human witnessing: War data and ecology after the end of the world*. Duke University Press.
3 As noted in Chapter 1, McLuhan admits his personal attachment to literacy and modernism (in *Playboy* interview), but the point made here is that he does not confuse preference with actual value.
4 See, for example, the last chapter in Richard Sennett's *Building and Dwelling* (Yale UP, 2018), called "One Among Many."
5 Several recent studies have tracked the influence of McLuhan on art projects that challenge conventions. Adam Lauder takes up dematerializing tactics and sensory effects in pre-internet projects in *Out of School* (2022) and Alexander Kitnick, in *Distant Early Warning* (2021), examines "the divergent paths" of Avant Garde artists who, if they did not change the future, "forecast" it (pp. 141, 144).
6 See Redl's *Matrix II* and later installations in the series: http://www.paramedia.net/installations2.php.
7 See acknowledgement of McLuhan's influence in *Ways of Sensing: Understanding the Senses in Society*, David Howes and Constance Classen (Routledge 2013) and in *Ritual, Performance and the Senses*, eds. Michael Bull and Jon P. Mitchell (London: Bloomsbury, 2015).
8 Such hope for a universal narrative does not deny local and community claims. As discussed in the "Introduction" to this book, McLuhan, Tyrwhitt, and Kepes wrote of the need for a shared human mission, yet not one so strict as to impose uniformity. They held that humanity needs to partake in a shared process of understanding but can pursue collective ends using different crafts.
9 See *The Collected Works of William Morris*, vol. xxii, (New York: Russell and Russell, [1877] 1966), pp. 24–25.
10 Perhaps more rigid mosaic imagery can be found in Whitehead's use of the term "welding," a metallurgic operation described by Stengers as an effective metaphor for how ideas gathered in assemblage appear with tangible joints attaching them. Putting contrast ideas together does not erase difference but creates new contexts and possibilities, so that dominant ideas are no longer accepted as "normalized," as they are situated alongside "nonconforming propositions" in a way that helps us to recognize or remember "our abstractions as living" rather than hegemonic and intractable (*Making Sense in Common*, 2023, University of Minnesota Press, p. 145).

References

Arola, K., & Rickert, T. (2022). The ancestors we claim: Conversations toward a future new materialism across boundaries. *Rhetoric Society Quarterly, 52*(2), 190–198. https://doi.org/10.1080/02773945.2022.2032815

Bell, G., & Tyrwhitt, J. (Eds.). (1972). *Human identity in the urban environment*. Penguin Books.

Buck, H. J. (2019) *After geoengineering: Climate tragedy, repair, and restoration*. Verso.

Buck, H. J. (2021). *Ending fossil fuels: Why net zero is not enough*. Verso.

Bremmer, I. (2022). *The power of crisis: How three threats—and our response—will change the world*. Simon & Schuster.

Darroch, M. (2008). Bridging urban and media studies: Jaqueline Tyrwhitt and the explorations group, 1951–1957. *Canadian Journal of Communications, 33*(2), 147–169.

Fry, T. (2021, March 15). *Tony Fry and Arturo Escobar on a new political imagination & the Terracide* [Seminar]. https://www.youtube.com/watch?v=c-HSO3p8hQE

Haraway, D. (1994). A game of Cat's Cradle: Science studies, feminist theory, cultural studies. *Configurations, 2*(1), 59–71. https://doi.org/10.1353/con.1994.0009

Haraway, D. (2017). *Staying with the trouble: Making kin in the Chthulucene*. Duke University Press.

Hayles, N. K. (2024). Detoxifying Cybernetics: From homeostasis to autopoiesis and beyond. In *Cybernetics for the 21st century* (pp. 85–100). Hanart Press.

Howes, D. (2022). *The sensory studies manifesto: Tracking the sensorial revolution in the arts and human sciences*. University of Toronto Press.

Ito, J. (2017). *Resisting reduction: A manifesto*. MIT Press. https://jods.mitpress.mit.edu/pub/resisting-reduction/release/19

Kepes, G. (1971). *Toward civic art* [slightly edited version of introduction to catalogue of Explorations exhibit], 84–94. https://monoskop.org/images/f/f8/Kepes_Gyorgy_1971_Toward_Civic_Art.pdf.

Lamberti, E. (2012). *Marshall McLuhan's mosaic*. University of Toronto Press.

Latour, B. (2017). *Facing Gaia: Eight lectures on the new climate regime* (C. Porter, Trans.) Polity Press. (Original work published 2015)

Latour, B. (2018). *Down to Earth: Politics in the new climate regime* (C. Porter, Trans.). Polity Press. (Original work published 2017)

Latour, B., Stengers, I., Tsing, A., & Bubandt, N. Anthropologists are talking—about capitalism, ecology, and apocalypse. *Ethnos: Journal of Anthropology, 83*(3), 587–606.

McLuhan, M. (1967). The invisible environment: The future of an erosion. *Perspecta, 11*, 161–167.

McLuhan, M. (1970). *Culture is our business*. McGraw-Hill.

McLuhan, M. (1974). At the Moment of Sputnik the planet became a global theatre in which there are no spectators but only actors. *Journal of Communication, 24*(1), 48–58.

McLuhan, M. (1997). The Playboy interview. In E. McLuhan & F. Zingrone (Eds.), *Essential McLuhan* (pp. 233–269). Routledge. (Original published 1969)

McLuhan, M. (2003). Art as survival in the electric age. In S. McLuhan & D. Staines (Eds.), *Understanding me: Lectures and interviews* (pp. 206–224). McClelland & Stewart. (Original work published 1973)

McLuhan, M. (2003). *Understanding media: The extensions of man* (Critical ed.), (W. T. Gordon, Ed.). Gingko Press. (Original work published 1964)

McLuhan, M., & Fiore, Q., with Agel, J. (1967). *The medium is the massage: An inventory of effects.* Gingko Press.

McLuhan M., & Nevitt, B. (1972). *Take today: The executive as dropout.* Harcourt Brace Jovanovich.

Nystrom, C. (2020). The crisis of narrative. In C. Wiebe & S. Maushart (Eds.), *Genes of culture: Towards a theory of symbols, meaning, and media* (vol. 1, pp. 180–184). Peter Lang. (Original work published 1989)

Rushkoff, D. (2019). *Team human.* W.W. Norton.

Rushkoff, D. (2023, June 24). *I Will Not Be Auto-tuned: Art as Soul in the Digital Media Environment* [Keynote Address]. Media Ecology Association 24th Annual Convention. Arts/ Symbol/Context/Meanings. Fordham University, NYC, USA.

Salter, C. (2010). *Technology and the transformation of performance.* MIT Press.

Schuld, D. (2016). Mind matrix: Situating cognition in the sculptural grid. In C. N. Terranova & M. Tromble (Eds.), *The Routledge companion to biology in art and architecture* (pp. 285–302). Routledge.

Sendra, P., & Sennett, R. (2022). *Designing disorder: Experiments and disruptions in the city.* Verso.

Sennett, R. (2023, June 24). *Ruling by acting* [Keynote Address]. Media Ecology Association 24th Annual Convention. *Arts/ Symbol/Context/Meanings.* Fordham University, NYC, USA.

Stengers, I. (2018). *Another science is possible: A manifesto for slow science* (S. Muecke, Trans.). Polity Press. (Original work published 2013)

Stengers, I. (2023). *Making sense in common: A reading of Whitehead in times of collapse.* (T. Lamarre, Trans.). University of Minnesota Press. (Original work published 2020)

Strate, L. (2017). *Media ecology: An approach to understanding the human condition.* Peter Lang.

Taussig, M. (2009). *What color is the sacred?* The University of Chicago Press.

Tsing, A. L., Swanson, H. A., Gan, E., & Bubandt, N. (Eds.). (2017). *Arts of living on a damaged planet.* University of Minnesota Press.

Turner, F. (2013). *The democratic surround: Multimedia and American liberalism from World War II to the psychedelic sixties.* The University of Chicago Pres.

Tyrwhitt, J. (1972). The Pedestrian in Megalopolis: Tokyo. In G. Bell & J. Tyrwhitt (Eds.), *Human identity in the urban environment* (pp. 595–603). Penguin Books.

Wiebe, C. & Maushart, S. (Eds.). (2020). *The genes of culture: Towards a theory of symbols, meaning, and media. [vol. 1]. Christine L. Nystrom.* Peter Lang.

Index

A

acceleration[ism] and speed up 3, 29, 61, 100, 127
    accelerant technologized conditions 107, 144, 147–148
acoustic environment 49, 57–67
    acoustic space 38–39, 58, 86
    See also aural, aurality, new aurality
activism 63–64
AI (artificial intelligence) 41, 45, 65, 148
anthropocene 2, 5, 97, 144
apocalypse and apocalyptic 4, 11, 146–147
architect, architecture 50–52, 57–58, 76, 154
Architectural Association school (AA) 72–73, 76
art 41–43, 100–102, 104–106
    role of 106, 132, 147–148
    Avant garde 122, 132
    immersive 135
    multimedia/intermedial 149–150
    representational 27, 54, 100–101
    urban transdisciplinary 135
art and science (humanities and science) 1, 2, 8–11, 25, 28, 34, 42, 45, 75, 104–108, 121, 129, 143–145, 148
    scientific and humanistic and scientific humanism 9, 74, 81 147–148, 153
    and civics 97, 105–107, 111–115, 136, 148, 157
    and environment 121
        and ecological and social 127, 133, 136
    and technology 6, 8, 81, 144–145
    artist[s] 76, 97, 100–102, 111–115, 122, 124
artists and collaborative governance (commons) 28, 64, 102, 111–115, 157
auditory space 86 *see also acoustic space*
aural, aurality, and new aurality 5, 16, 38–39, 57, 145
aural culture (see also acoustic environment) 23, 40, 57–63
autopoietic 126

awareness 42, 56, 59, 73, 101, 105, 108–109, 143, 145

B

balance 63, 65
   and imbalance 65, 101 *see also equilibrium*
Bauhaus 7, 13, 53, 103, 108, 113, 122
   New Bauhaus 7, 73, 78, 103
   Black Mountain 104
beauty 36, 52, 54, 87, 115–11
bifurcation, refusal of 35–36
bio-aesthetic 8
biocentric and biocentrism 103–104, 130, 133–137
bioregional planning 71, 73
   bioregionalism 75, 77–79
biotechnic society 71, 73
bomb, atomic 1, 2, 8, 15, 144
breakdown as breakthrough 17, 149
   and loss, erosion 25–26

C

Cambridge University 72, 73, 124
capitalism 18, 37, 72, 115
cataclysmic 3, 51, 146
catastrophe, catastrophic 3, 5, 50, 155
   and disaster 2, 65
   and chaos 116, 151
CAVS (Centre for Advanced Visual Studies) 7, 104, 123, 132, 134
Christian 11, 36
   Catholic 11, 35, 44, 73, 74
   See also God
CIAM (International Congresses of Modern Architecture) 7, 59, 60, 67, 73, 74, 76, 77, 81–84, 88, 90
circularity *See non-linearity*
city, cities 6, 16, 26, 52–53, 56, 58–59, 65, 79, 81–83, 86–88, 97, 115, 117, 136
   see also urban environment

civics 97, 105
   participatory civics 153, 157
climate crisis 14, 65, 102, 144, 146–148, 153, 156
Cold War 8, 15, 81, 107, 113, 144
collaborative, collaboration 3, 12–13, 37, 80
collectivism 13, 42, 54
colonial, colonizing 3, 37
commons 37, 41, 102, 107, 111–113
community 51, 56, 61
complexity 12, 29, 54, 66, 88, 99, 101, 115, 127–128, 132, 145, 151, 153–54
computer[s] 25, 32, 42, 50, 58, 65, 124, 147, 153
   and global computational automation 125
configuration 12, 105
   and reconfiguration 104, 156
conformity (habit) vs. play 98
   vs. freedom 144
   art as (iconoclastic) challenge 100–101, 106
   cliché 50, 54
consciousness, expanded 55, 62, 65, 98, 106–108, 116
   and relational consciousness 98–99; perception, cognition and consciousness 106
continuity and change 98–99, 114
control 11, 108, 144, 152
   controlling technology 154
   self regulation 136
control tower 105, 115, 131
core (of the city) 59, 81, 82, 86
cosmic harmony 11, 26, 45, 101, 116
counterculture and hippie movement 3, 154
counter environment[s] (also counterenvironments) 26, 27, 65, 101, 106, 112, 115, 130–131, 151
crisis, crises 1, 3, 5, 16, 117, 143–144, 146, 148, 155
   as climate and planetary 4, 146
   as communication crisis 102
   as social and environmental 101, 143

INDEX

Culture and Communications seminar 72, 79, 81, 86
curate, curating [the cybernetic] 121–128, 132, 135
Cybernetic[s] 16, 15, 72, 81, 102, 121–129, 131, 135–137, 147
    key terms and defined 124–126
    biocentric cybernetics 122, 128, 132
    second order 102

D

Delos symposia 7, 57, 65, 72, 79, 86, 89–92, 97, 103, 105
democratic, democracy 3, 76, 107, 111, 115
design, designer[s] 1, 37, 50–52, 55, 58, 76, 97, 112, 148
Dewline (Distant Early Warning System) 57, 101, 147
diffractive reading, diffraction 1, 13–15

E

East vs./and West 6, 43–44, 52–56, 107–109, 110
eco-consciousness 147
eco-criticism 4, 145
ecology, ecological 2, 4, 72, 73, 97, 145, 147, 152–153
ecological tragedies 102
education (public education) 41, 45, 73, 74, 101, 104–105, 111, 128, 147
effects of media 5, 26, 58, 64, 90
Ekistics 7, 57, 59, 66, 87, 91, 92, 97, 103
Ekistics 7, 77, 88, 92–93
electric, electricity 10–11, 58, 61, 73
electronic media and networks 57, 60
engagement (citizen and populist) 1, 3, 115, 147–148
    See also involvement (citizen)
England 7, 73, 74, 75, 77, 78

entangled, entanglement(s) 3, 14, 151
environment[s] and environmental 1, 5, 41, 73, 87, 91–92, 112, 128, 135, 137
    and change 81
    artificial (and human-made) 10, 100–101, 105, 114–115, 117, 128, 131
    sensory 86, 149–150
        environmental programming 29, 51, 64, 105, 124, 128, 147
environmental crisis 135, 143–144
    environnmental protection 147, 152–153
equilibrium 99, 153
    and balance 104
        rebalancing 145
    and equipoise 63, 65, 80
ethics, ethical 65–66, 148
Europe[an] 4, 7, 59, 74
evolution (progress) 85, 103 114
evolutionary humanism 77
exceptionalism 39, 145
exoticizing 44
Explorations group 87
Explorations 9, 49, 52, 63, 81, 85, 103
extensions 10, 13, 17, 30, 60, 102, 131
    amputations 56
    prosthetic[s] 103, 122
extinction 4, 145

F

Fatehpur Sikri 52–53, 86–88
feedback 123, 135
circular and non-linear 123, 127
    closed vs. open 102
    feed-forward 124
figure and ground 5, 12, 25, 27, 30, 34, 41, 50, 99, 106, 108–109, 111, 144, 156–157
Ford Foundation 67
formal cause 12, 30–31, 45, 100
futures, futurism 5–6, 28–29, 45, 66, 75, 101, 137
    speculative futurism 28, 45. 66

G

General Semantics 32, 99
    time-binding 32, 99, 117
Gestalt 50, 108, 110, 124
global 2, 6, 15, 17, 28, 35, 40, 43, 57, 61–62, 65–66, 77, 91–92, 97, 103, 112, 125, 150, 154
global consciousness 8
global governance 15, 29, 111–112, 115
global village 75, 89, 91, 93
    and world city 115, 117
God 10–11, 34–36
governance 15–16, 43, 113–115
    and politics 29
    artist–led 153, 157
    See also art and civics
Gutenberg culture 38–39
    See also literacy

H

haptic 11–12, 13, 122
Harvard University 7, 72, 78, 88, 89, 90
    Graduate School of Design 78, 88
history 3, 71
    and anonymous 13, 86
    and change 51, 144–145
holism, holistic 98, 121, 130 (defined), 137
    wholeness 39 *See also* unity
    See also relationality
hope 4–6, 9, 16, 17, 25, 30, 32, 33, 43, 45, 65, 93, 101–102, 116, 136, 148, 152, 154–156
human/non-human 3, 4, 12, 43, 45, 66, 102, 116–117, 146–147, 154–155
human activity/impact 2, 66
    See also Anthropocene
humanism, humanist, humanistic 29, 36, 72, 73, 75–76, 79, 83, 143

I

imagination, imaginative 31, 38, 101, 109, 121
indeterminism 128, 150
industry and industrialized 2, 59, 72, 103
information 90, 100, 105, 107, 109, 123, 126–128, 130–131, 134–136, 147, 150–151, 153
inner and outer 6, 10, 51, 56, 62
    inside and out 12
innovation[s], media and technology 4, 29, 40, 45, 52, 58, 97, 144, 151
    and effects 2, 4, 29–30, 34, 40, 101, 153
    See also control
"inter" (as neologism) 100, 111, 136
interaction 102, 103–104
    interconnectivity 7, 31, 37, 98, 111–115
intermixture 130
international 6, 25
intersectional 2, 65, 143
interdisciplinary 1, 7, 63, 75, 83, 125, 128
    cross-disciplinary, multidisciplinary, transdisciplinary, and inter-faculty 74, 80, 85, 87, 121, 137
invisible 52, 56, 60, 102, 105, 108
involvement, citizen (public) 98, 115, 144, 146–147 (and intervention), 153
    and participatory civics 155–156

K

Knowledge, indeterminate. uncertain 11, 17, 155
    and relational 116

L

language 26, 31, 59, 61, 84, 86, 100, 150–151
laws of media 5, 12–13, 99, 111

tetrad 2
linear[ity] 52–3, 87
    non-linear[ity] and circularity 11, 51–52, 123–125, 127, 144–145
literacy and print literacy 38–39, 56, 60–61, 145
literary and literature 9–10, 151
locality and local culture 37, 146, 149
London 72, 74, 76
loss 27–28, 40–41, 100, 146, 155

M

magic, and spirit and faith 34–35, 39, 41
make and making (world) 41–43, 100, 103, 107, 109–110, 115–116, 143, 150–151, 156–157
    and making and process 100, 109–110, 137
Mariner 16, 33–38, 104, 152
MARS (Modern Architectural Research) 73, 76, 77, 81
mediation and mediated world 40, 58, 84
    virtual 58
    discarnate being 60
Media Ecology 5, 133–134, 145, 147
mid-century 5, 8, 143, 147–148
MIT (Massachusetts Institute of Technology) 7, 76, 78, 79, 80, 82, 87, 88, 89, 92, 104, 122–123, 132
Modernist, modernity, modernism 29, 38, 54, 73, 74, 75, 145
    and leaving modernity 115–116
    and postmodern 123, 126, 132
monism 62–63, 104, 148
    against binary thinking 27–28
mosaic 11–13, 109–110, 156
multisensorial *See* senses

N

Narcissus 28–29, 100–101

narrative and story 31–32, 38, 150–152
nature 10, 71, 87, 116, 126, 128, 135
    and landscape 43, 51–52, 147
    and end of nature —39–41, 100, 128, 146, 155
    and new and old nature 128
networks 57–58
    webs of connection 45
    communication network 75
North America[n] 7, 59, 76

O

occularcentrism and eye dependence 38, 52–56, 100, 122
oral, orality, oral culture/tradition (pre-literate culture) 59, 64, 98, 115–116, 145
organic 79, 97
    and inorganic (natural and technological) 126
outered, outering 40, 64

P

pattern and pattern recognition 34, 99, 102, 106–11, 124, 128
    and latent coherence 104, 116
    and epistemic value 111, 128–129
    See also education (public education)
perception 26–27, 49, 53, 86, 98, 101
    and cognition (and expanded consciousness) 99, 106
perspective 50, 53, 85
pharmakon 5, 123
planet, planetary 66
    planetary degradation 146
    planning, urban 6, 16, 49, 54–56, 58, 64, 66, 71, 86, 88–89
    regional 74
    and town 6, 73, 74, 76, 83, 85
planning and art /aesthetics 76–77
planning and civic responsibility 78–79

166 | INDEX

political and economic theory 29, 43–4, 114
Political and Economic Planning (PEP) theory 72
probes 6, 10, 124
progress 2, 4
   and anti-progress 2, 5, 145–146
   see also configuration and reconfiguration
propaganda 26, 49, 143
   dogma 27, 29

Q

quantum [physics] 9–10, 107

R

rear-view mirror thinking 6, 28, 51, 59, 147
reconstruction of Britain 72, 74, 77
relational 34, 98
   and intersectional 13, 98
relationality principle 5, 13, 39, 98, 116, 146 156
relational ontology 17, 97–99, 116, 145, 157
   humans defined as relational creatures 116

S

sameness and difference 99, 110
scale 7, 75, 82, 90, 104, 107
   metropolitan scale 82
science and art
   See art and science
senses, sensory life, sensorial 11, 16, 40–41, 45, 49–56, 63, 64, 98–99, 104–107, 116, 149–150
   intersensorial 98, 108, 116, 157
   multisensory 9, 11, 100–101, 150
   sensory attunement 101
   sensory overload 99

sensorium, human sensorium 26, 39, 41–43, 98, 108–109, 122
servomechanism 125–126
settlement and housing 62, 65, 77, 97
somnambulant and sleepwalking 52, 117, 151
sonic experience 12, 122
sound[s], soundscapes 9, 59, 61
space-time 74
   eliminating time and space 10
   ahistoricity 11–12
   simultaneity 5, 116
speculative thinking
   See also futurism
spirit[ual] 25, 34–36, 92, 151–152
Sputnik 100
   and satellite 39, 120, 130
St. Louis 74–75
suburban 51, 59
survival and safety 31, 35–38, 150, 152, 155–156
   human and planetary 147
synesthesia, synesthetic 108, 131
   See also senses
systems theory 72, 150

T

Tao and Zen 110, 124
technology 32, 52, 56–57
technological environnement 64, 107
   See also [hu]man-made environment and artificial environment
technocrat[ic], technocracy (limits of) 30, 101, 131, 144
theatre 40, 148–149
time transfer 31—32,
   and time binding 98–99, 116
total change 3, 29, 38, 98, 146 156–157
totally new situation, total interdependence 3, 6, 145, 153, 157
   and total organism 98

Toronto 50, 52, 63, 80, 83–84, 88, 90, 103, 122
transform, transformation, transformative 10, 26, 37, 58, 98–99, 101, 109 (defined), 151, 156
  and faith 35, 37–38
  and perceptual habits and relational awareness 105, 156
transnational 72, 78
trauma 2, 144
  climate trauma 144
  technological trauma 105
Two Cultures 9
  See also art and science

##

UN (United Nations) 72, 77, 78, 81, 84, 86, 90, 91, 92
UNESCO (UN Educational, Scientific and Cultural Organization) 77, 78, 86, 92
unity 98, 101, 104–107, 110, 112, 116, 121, 154–156
universalism 37, 146, 155
urban constellation 82–83, 90

urban design 51–56, 77, 87
urban environment 50, 90
  urbanism, urban life 59
  See also cities
utopian 71, 116, 144
  anti-utopian 73, 116

##

vanishing point 52
Vietnam War 2, 15, 105, 123
vision, visible 50, 86
vision and motion 109
  and the technological extension of vision 128–129
visual [and literate] culture 16, 26, 38, 62

W

wicked problems 65, 153
without walls 8, 19, 58, 130
World War II 4, 15, 40, 72, 74, 103, 107, 115, 144
Wychwood 51–52, 53, 64

Index of Names

A

Aalto, Alvar 79
Abrams, Charles 78
Albers, Josep 104
Alexander, Christopher 129
Ampere, Andre-Marie 126
Appel Karel 130
Arola, Kristin 44
Ashton, Dore 129
Atwood, Margaret 59

B

Ball, Philip 110
Barad, Karen 1, 14
Bates, Stewart 87
Bateson, Gregory 32, 102, 107, 115, 124, 154
Bauer (Wurster), Catherine 78
Beckman, Max 133
Bell, Gwen 49, 62
Bigelow, Julian 124, 126
Bissell, Claude 113
Blake, William 33
Blakinger, John 8, 102, 104, 110, 131
Boehme, Gernot 108
Bohr, Nils 10, 14
Botar, Oliver 103–104, 122, 134
Bratton, Benjamin 37, 67
Brecht, Bertolt 148
Breuer, Marcel 8, 129, 133
Bridle, James 117
Buck, Holly Jean 153–154
Bullock, Nicholas 80
Burchard, John 76, 79, 80
Burnham, Jack 131, 134
Buxton, William 19, 67

C

Carey, James 65

Carpenter, Edmund [Ted] 7, 49, 84, 86
Carver, Humphrey 76, 83, 85, 87
Capek, Milac 130
Cavell, Richard 60
Chandler, John 131
Chermayeff, Serge 76
Chesterton, G.K. 73
Choay, Francoise 129
Coleridge, Samuel Taylor 33
Crary, James 117

D

Darroch, Michael 7, 55, 61, 63
Darwin, Charles 125
Davis, Bill [William] 63–64
Dean, Jodi 43
Diamond, Jared 37
Dix, Otto 133
Doxiadis, Constantinos 7, 57–60, 72, 76, 86, 87, 89–91, 103
Driesch, Hans 127
Dubos, Rene 91
Dubuffet, Jean 130
Duchamp, Henri 130
Durer, Albrecht 132
Durham Peters, John 4, 32, 44

E

Easterbrook, Tom 7, 49, 83
Ellul, Jacques 149
Elmhirst, Leonard and Dorothy 72–73
Ernst, Max 130
Escobar, Arturo 37

F

Fisher, Mark 28–29
France, Raoul 127
Fry, Max 78

Fuller, Buckminster 12, 57, 78, 146

G

Geddes, Patrick 71, 73–82, 85, 87, 147
Genosko, Gary 9, 104
Giedion, Sigfried 7, 12, 49, 60–63, 71, 72, 74, 75–87
Goethe, Johann Wolfgang von 110
Gropius, Walter 7, 125, 133–134
Groswiler, Paul 10
Grosz, George 133
Grusin, Richard 4
Gutkind, E.A. 130

H

Habermas, Jurgen 148
Haraway, Donna 3, 14, 154
Hausmann, Baron 130
Hayles, N. Katherine 3, 27, 147
Helion, Jean 129
Herbert, Alan P. 130
Holzman, Harry 81
Howes, David 27, 108, 149–150
Huxley, Julian 72, 72, 77, 92
Huxley Thomas 73

I

Illich, Ivan 41
Innis, Harold 27, 75, 79, 81
Ito, Joichi 45, 153

J

Jacobs, Jane 44, 63–64
James, Martin 81, 83
Joyce, James 12, 55, 57–59, 86, 130
Kallai, Erno 134

Kandinsky, Wassily 133
Kant, Emmanuel 34, 127
Kaprow, Allan 130
Katzen, Lila 135
Kitnick, Alexander 12, 26, 104
Klein, Naomi 5
Korzybski, Alfred 32, 99
Kraynik, Ted 134, 136
Kuhn, Thomas 33

L

Lamberti, Elena 11
Langer, Susanne 67
Latour, Bruno 3, 35–36, 37, 44, 112, 147, 152, 155
Lear, Jonathan 4
Le Corbusier 130
Lee, Dorothy 86, 89
Lichtenberg, Georg Christopher 133
Licklider, Joseph 124
Linan, Laura Trujillo 30
Lippard, Lucy 131
Logan, Robert 9
Lovelace, Ada 128
Lowenstein, Otto 41
Lusseyran, Jacques 40
Lynch, Kevin 87, 88

M

Mailer, Norman 2
Malraux, Andre 58, 130
Marchand, Philip 41, 75, 89
Marchessault, Janine 63
Maxwell, James Clerk 126
Mayr, Ernst 40, 112
Mbembe, Achille 14
McLuhan, Eric 10, 35
McLuhan, Maurice 10
Mead, Margaret 57, 86, 92, 107, 115, 124, 154–155

Moholy-Nagy, Lazlo 7, 53, 73, 76, 103, 104, 122, 134
Mondrian, Piet 110
Moos, Michel A. 2, 26
Morris, William 152–153
Mumford, Lewis 7, 75, 77, 78, 85

N

Nagel, Alexander 11, 104
Navarro-Baldweg, Juan 136
Nef Jr., John 75
Nevelson, Loiuse 130
Nevitt, Barrington 10
Nystrom, Christine 38, 150–152

O

O'Gorman, Marcel 5
Ong, Walter 27
Oppenheim, Dennis 130
Orwell, George 117

P

Paik, Nam Juin 128
Parker, Harley 9, 53, 104
Penrose, Roland 89
Piene, Otto 134
Pierce, Charles Sanders 100
Poe, Edgar Allen 16, 25, 31–38
Porter, Arthur 128
Postman, Neil 5, 150

R

Rauschenberg, Robert 130
Read, Herbert 129
Redl, Erwin 149
Richards, I.A. 124

Richardson, Michael 147
Rickert, Thomas 44
Rosenblueth, Arturo 124–126
Rowse, E.A.A. 73
Rushkoff, Douglas 148–159

S

Salter, Chris 149
Schafer, R. Murray 150
Schuld, Dawna 149
Schlesinger, Arthur 81
Sennett, Richard 65, 113, 148–149
Sert, Jose Luis 7, 81, 83, 84, 86, 88, 89
Sharma, Sarah 44
Smith, Sydney 83, 84, 85
Snow, C.P. 9
Sontag, Susan 2
Stimson, Blake and Gregory Sholette 13
Stengers, Isabelle 3, 34, 37–38, 154
Stone, Henry S. 129
Strate, Lance 30, 32, 99, 102, 145

T

Taggart, James 136
Taylor, Charles 4
Tingley, Jean 130
Tsai, Wen-Ying 1341, 135
Tsing, Anna 155
Turner, Fred 3, 81, 115, 154–155

V

Vallye, Anna 76
Van der Rohe, Mies 129
VanDerBeek, Stan 134
van der Tuin, Iris 14–15
Vassilakis, Takis 134
Volk, Tyler 102
Von Uexkull, Jaakob 127

W

Wainwright, William 135
Warburg, Aby 130
Ward, Barbara 29, 57, 91
Weschler, Judith 80
Weissmann, Ernest 84
Wiener, Norbert 8, 80, 84, 124, 126–129, 132
Wigley, Mark 12, 58
Whitehead, Alfred North 9, 17–18, 26, 34, 35–36
Williams, D. Carl 7, 49, 55, 84, 87
Wordsworth, William 34
Wurster, William 76, 78, 79

Y

Young, Liam 66

Z

Zuboff, Shoshanna 117

Lance Strate
General Editor

This series is devoted to scholarship relating to media ecology, a field of inquiry defined as the study of media as environments. Within this field, the term "medium" can be defined broadly to refer to any human technology or technique, code or symbol system, invention or innovation, system or environment. Media ecology scholarship typically focuses on how technology, media, and symbolic form relate to communication, consciousness, and culture, past, present and future. This series is looking to publish research that furthers the formal development of media ecology as a field; that brings a media ecology approach to bear on specific topics of interest, including research and theoretical or philosophical investigations concerning the nature and effects of media or a specific medium; that includes studies of new and emerging technologies and the contemporary media environment as well as historical studies of media, technology, and modes and codes of communication; scholarship regarding technique and the technological society; scholarship on specific types of media and culture (e.g., oral and literate cultures, image, etc.), or of specific aspects of culture such as religion, politics, education, journalism, etc.; critical analyses of art and popular culture; and studies of how physical and symbolic environments function as media.

For additional information about this series or for the submission of manuscripts, please contact:
    Lance Strate, Series Editor | strate@fordham.edu

To order other books in this series, please contact our Customer Service Department:
    peterlang@presswarehouse.com (within the U.S.)
    orders@peterlang.com (outside the U.S.)

Or browse online by series:
    www.peterlang.com

www.ingramcontent.com/pod-product-compliance
Lightning Source LLC
Chambersburg PA
CBHW061716300426
44115CB00014B/2712